The Sea Survival Manual

for cruising and professional yachtsmen

FRANCES AND MICHAEL HOWORTH

D1596141

SHERIDAN HOUSE

Credits and Acknowledgements

Without the help and assistance from a cast of hundreds, this book would never have been written. Of those, the following deserve our special thanks:

Steven Huxley MRCC Falmouth
Flight Lieutenant John Williamson former manager at RAF Kinloss
Commander Dee Norton of the US Coastguard
Surgeon Commander Geraldine Salmon P&O Princess Cruises
The firms of Ocean Safety Ltd, McMurdo Ltd, Inmarsat and Navtec

Permission to use the wonderfully amusing cartoons was given to us by the ever-helpful offices of the RNLI, to whom we say thank you, and it is to the gallant crews of those lifeboats that we dedicate this book.

The illustration on page 54 is reproduced from *Admiralty List of Radio Signals Volume 5 GMDSS (NP285)/Ocean Passages for the World (NP136)* by permission of the Controller of Her Majesty's Stationery Office and the UK Hydrographic Office.

This edition published 2005
by Sheridan House, Inc.
145 Palisade Street
Dobbs Ferry, NY 10522
www.sheridanhouse.com

Library of Congress Cataloging-in-Publication Data

Howorth, Frances.
  The sea survival manual for cruising and professional yachtsmen / Frances and Michael Howorth.
      p. cm.
  Includes bibliographical references and index.
  ISBN-13: 978-1-57409-216-5 (pbk. : alk. paper)
  1. Boats and boating—Safety measures—Handbooks, manuals, etc. 2. Yachting—Safety measures—Handbooks, manuals, etc. I. Howorth, Michael. II.
Title.
  GV777.55.H69 2005
  797.1'028'9—dc22

                              2005010109

ISBN 1 57409 216 2

Printed in Great Britain

Contents

Foreword

Authorities who write and speak about sea survival usually focus on the issues concerning the loss of a vessel. What do you do when your boat suffers such a catastrophe that there is no choice but for it to join Davy Jones? How do you create a new life within a life raft or lifeboat? That view, though, as these pages will reveal, is rather limited. Survival at sea begins from the time you step aboard and doesn't end until the time you disembark. What mariners must learn to accept is that survival at sea depends on a whole range of knowledge, training, and skills that regularly come into play even if the mother craft never springs a leak.

No sailor can deny there is a certain truth to the notion that anybody who'd go to sea for pleasure would go to hell for a pastime. Anyone who has ever spent any real time afloat knows that much of the waterborne life is spent trying to fix things that are constantly broken as the vessel bobs about on the world's biggest corrosive and storm-tossed soup. Murphy loves the sea. But mariners know that they simply cannot capture the incomparable pleasures and fulfillment of boating without accepting the risks, which are many, and figuring out ways to deal with them.

Still, nobody really wants to concentrate on all the things that might go wrong aboard. Some boating magazine publishers get nearly apoplectic if a photo appears on their covers that features a vessel battling a storm, or even out on a wild romp. They do not want the public to get the idea that boating involves the discomfort of getting splashed, not to mention possibly killed. Yet the reality of life afloat is that many, many things can go wrong that can result in injury or worse, and very often the sailor is left on his own to face the music.

Those who embrace the reality rather than the fantasy remain much more functional in a real emergency over which they might have some control than those who live in a state of denial. It is essential for any survivor to transcend a state of denial into a state of acceptance. There often are many crises within an overall catastrophe, requiring many steps to reach a successful conclusion, but by accepting the reality on the waves and attacking problems in achievable bits, you can keep putting one foot above the other until you reach the top.

Acceptance sounds easier than it actually is, though. Studies of oil-rig fires, plane crashes, office-building fires (including the World Trade Towers on 9/11) indicate that as much as 70 percent of an average population will wander about as if stunned when facing a disaster. They may go back to their desks to tidy up rather than fleeing the burning building, for example. The more catastrophic the crisis, the more it will wipe out any continuity, and therefore security, provided by 'normal life', and people will do whatever they can to reestablish some contact with something that is familiar, makes sense, and is under their control. The sense of time also becomes highly distorted. Too often, most people waste precious minutes or hours. Many become consumed by the crisis from which they might have fled.

An additional 15 percent or so will likely be in complete panic or a state of virtually catatonia, totally unable to save themselves and possibly endangering others. I've seen footage of a fisherman dragged to the bottom because he could not let go of his overturned boat's rudder to swim just a few meters to a waiting rescue boat. That leaves about 15 percent who can quickly assess alternative actions and their implied risks, form a plan and execute it in achievable steps. These are the people who are most likely to escape a disaster. Not surprisingly, policemen, firemen, airline pilots, doctors, sailors, and others who deal with various levels of crisis on a regular basis tend to make up this more highly functional 15 percent. And it is they upon whom the two thirds back cleaning their desks depend to get everyone moving in the right direction.

Studies have shown that the survival behavior of cleaners and perhaps even those in panic can be vastly improved if they become familiar with the two key ingredients that foster the positive approaches to disaster evidenced by folks like policemen, firemen, pilots et al: Preparation through the gaining of information and training, and experience in real life.

No book can give you experience in real life or training. What a book can do, though, is to inform you. With an added bit of training, you'll have a much better idea of what to do when something happens in real life, and you can with greater confidence attack the less critical problems of the seafaring life and gain experience in the process. It sounds too simple, a cliché. It is nonetheless true: Those who are prepared tend to live.

The Sea Survival Manual is not like other survival manuals. Its holistic approach covers vast areas, from international safety standards to flow charts of functional actions when facing a variety of onboard crises, from fire and crew overboard to damage control and life raft procedures. It recognizes that, accept or deny it, going boating is pretty much a constant state of survival, and it shows you what you really should know before one part of the boating experience blows up in your face, which it inevitably will should you do it long enough. It reminds us that the ocean wilderness is a sometime hostile place where we would be wise to hone our self-reliance and skills, and it gives us tools to keep the boat and the crew safe so they don't have to get into a life raft in the first place. Although it covers life rafts as well, the primary content is best consumed prior to leaving the dock and concentrates on the many challenges that may arise without leaving the deck.

That responsible boating requires us to face such realities and learn how to survive them is not really a depressing awakening. All the long-time mariners I've known have not only accepted the inevitable challenges of the sea but also actively seek new frontiers that then help them prepare for crises, should they come. Do we not push ourselves to explore new waters, expand our racing envelope, discover the sudden wonder of life emerging from the depths, all with unknown and possibly dangerous possibilities? Do not we love to spin our war stories over a brew once we get to a snug port? Are not the tales of how we jury rigged our mast, saved a crew fallen overboard, or contained a fire, more lasting and fulfilling than the story of how we won that race? Sailors love a challenge. Just like firemen and pilots and doctors. Maybe we're hard wired to embrace a certain level of risk, so are predetermined to accept the preparation required to face it.

Even so, few sailors would want to shipwreck themselves in order to be better prepared next time around. Real survival at sea may be a bit more challenging than anyone would really like. Even hands-on survival training at sea or in pools, may not be your idea of a vacation. But if there is anything we know about survival, it is that almost everyone can learn to become a better survivor. Not by jumping into flames or scuttling your boat in mid-ocean, but by experiencing the regular survival scenarios that are the sailor's life. Provided you are ready. Provided you are prepared.

There's a lot to consider, as indicated by the following pages. That's the start. Without information, even survival training can become overwhelming, but with information, you know at least intellectually what to expect and what you should do theoretically, and that gives you a certain freedom. Survival preparation need not be all doom and gloom. Even when the theoretical becomes impossible, with the knowledge of principles, you are more able to improvise and adapt, which can become surprisingly joyous. In the survival programs in which I've participated or have taught, I've shared a good deal of fun with trainees. Without urging, one group made a game of re-righting their capsized raft without having to get out of it! Should they ever have to step into a life raft for real, they'll not only know how the thing works but also how it might not work, and what it feels and smells like. Getting capsized will not inspire panic that might kill them. And whatever happens aboard, they are a lot less likely to waste time cleaning.

Adaptability is what it is all about, really. Aboard a boat, one must adapt constantly. But before we can play the adaptability game, we need instruction. Then we're free to enjoy, or at least accept the challenges before us. Be not afraid. As these pages also urge, when you're through filling your head with facts, figures, and procedures, if you haven't already, jump into a pool and play with a life raft, or at least put on your own life jacket and swim around in it a bit. I think you'll find the game a lot more instructive and fun than you might have imagined. And get whoever is back there polishing the stainless to dive in, too.

Steve Callahan
May 2005

Notes

This book is written especially for those who sail aboard pleasure vessels of any size, whether sail, motor or both. In the UK, a 'pleasure vessel' is defined as:

a) a vessel which at the time it is being used is
  (i) • in the case of a vessel wholly owned by an individual or individuals used only for the sport or pleasure of the owner or the immediate family or friends of the owner; or
      • in the case of a vessel owned by a body corporate used only for sport or pleasure and on which the persons are employees or officers of the body corporate, or their immediate family or friends; and
  (ii) on a voyage or excursion which is one for which the owner does not receive money for or in connection with operating the vessel or carrying any person, other than as a contribution to the direct expenses of the operation of the vessel incurred during the voyage or excursion;
b) • any vessel wholly owned by or on behalf of a members' club formed for the purpose of sport or pleasure which, at the time it is being used, is used only for the sport or pleasure of members of that club or their immediate family; and for the use of which any charges levied are paid into club funds and applied for the general use of the club; and
   • in the case of any vessel referred to in the paragraphs above no other payments are made by or on behalf of users of the vessel, other than by the owner.

A pleasure vessel of 13.7m (45ft) or more in length is classified as a Class XII vessel in the UK. A 'pleasure vessel' that carries more than 12 passengers ceases to be a UK Class XII vessel, while any size of yacht that is used commercially, for sport and leisure, such as charter boats, ceases to be a 'pleasure vessel'. Yachts that cease to be 'pleasure vessels' and/or Class XII vessels are subject to different legal requirements and Codes of Practice. Those regulations are not taken into account in this book and must be reviewed before any safety equipment is purchased.

This book complies with the International Maritime Organisation (IMO) resolution A.657(16).

Throughout this book the word 'Skipper' is used to describe the captain or master of a yacht. The Skipper is not necessarily the owner of the vessel, though he may be. Likewise, the use of the masculine and feminine pronoun is arbitrary. It does not indicate that one gender or another is preferred or desired for any particular job or function.

1 Being Prepared

This book is about survival at sea – not just under way, but at all times aboard the yacht. Knowing what to do in an emergency, having the right equipment and knowing how to use it, are all equally important in ensuring a happy outcome should some disaster occur. This book covers selecting safety and survival equipment for the crew and the yacht and dealing with the most common accidents or emergencies that can happen afloat, including one of the worst scenarios: the sinking of the yacht. The book is about being a *survivor* – not a victim or a fatality.

Preparation is vital; it involves training and planning and includes minimising risks, especially those that can result from the cost-cutting measures that everyone is too guilty of when purchasing safety equipment. The Cruising Association has produced a Code of Practice for cruising yachtsmen so that all who share the sea may do so in safety and without being a nuisance or danger to others or the environment. It makes an excellent offshore checklist, and with the kind permission of the Cruising Association it has been reproduced in Appendix 1.

When a disaster happens it is too late to discover that the fire extinguisher is empty, there is no liferaft aboard, that the EPIRB is registered in the name of another yacht, and that the flares are out of date. Good seamanship is the result of knowledge and common sense and helps to ensure safety at sea. With planning and forethought many disasters can be prevented, but sadly not all. The training needed by the crew, together with the equipment chosen for the yacht, depends to a large extent on the areas in which she sails or plans to sail, the weather conditions likely to be encountered and, to a much lesser extent, upon the size of the craft. A yacht planning to cross an ocean is likely to face greater hazards than another similar boat daysailing, in July, in an estuary. The most important factors influencing the choice of equipment are how likely the vessel is to be caught out in rough weather and how close she will be to the shore. A large yacht may need more of, or a larger size of, some equipment than her smaller sister, but most of the items will be identical if they are sailing in the same areas.

Training Courses

'*When in danger or in doubt
Run in circles, scream and shout*'   *Laurence J Peter*

An emergency can happen anywhere, at any time, through no one's fault, and research and experience have shown that at the moment when disaster strikes, most people will be stunned and bewildered. However, those who have been trained to expect and to cope with such possibilities show infinitely greater survival rates than those who have not. People caught in a crisis or emergency frequently respond by falling back on well-learned patterns of behaviour. For those who are untrained, other – often *inappropriate* – patterns of behaviour may emerge. While this may be expressed as panic, it is mostly

displayed as denial or disbelief. In contrast, calmness is contagious, and leadership, training and knowledge can contain – and therefore stop – the spread of panic and ensure that everyone works together.

In the UK, training courses are available nationwide for anyone planning to go sailing – from novices wanting to learn to sail a dinghy, to potential captains of ocean-going vessels. The RYA (Royal Yachting Association) courses are offered by over a thousand teaching establishments and are well known and highly regarded worldwide. Simply type the words 'sailing course' into any good internet search engine and it will spit out an endless list of possible training establishments. Teaching includes both practical and theoretical studies, evening classes, weekend courses and holidays, and some subjects can be studied as correspondence courses. There are also many other specialist courses that do not offer a widely recognised certificate, but provide valuable information on a specific subject – such as sailing around the world.

The RYA, though, now faces competition from a commercial training organisation based in Fort Lauderdale in the USA. International Yachtmaster Training (IYT) now has 25 licensed schools in 12 different countries, with the qualifications now accepted by 24 governments worldwide.

Training courses are available all over the USA both in the form of home study and administrator-led classes. Boating safety courses are required by many states, and classroom training is offered by state and local marine patrols, USCG auxiliaries, and US Power Squadron chapters. Online courses such as that offered by the Boat US Foundation are approved to meet the basic boater education requirements in certain states. The United States Sailing Association, like the RYA, encourages participation and promotes excellence in sailing and racing in the USA, and the online boating courses on its website are designed to present basic and advanced information about sailboats, powerboats and boat handling in US waters. A full spectrum of boating certification courses with certified instructors is available nationwide for sail and motorboats.

The Australian Yachting Federation (AYF) is the main body for all forms of yachting, both power and sail, throughout Australia. It has National Training and Certificate Programs for windsurfing, small boat and yacht sailing, and powerboating. Its website includes a list of those organisations across Australia that have received AYF approval as 'Recognised Teaching Establishments'.

Topics covered in personal survival courses

The 1998 Sydney–Hobart Yacht Race has drawn the attention of the yachting world to the tragic consequences of a lack of training in safety and sea survival. One result of the inquest that followed the race is that the International Sailing Federation (ISAF) has adopted a number of the recommendations of the coroner. For example, since July 2002, 30 per cent of racing crew taking part in Category 0 and 1 offshore races must have taken a personal survival training course, and all crew members in all racing categories are recommended to have the training.

The topics to be covered in the courses are a model for any Skipper and crew who are planning to sail outside sheltered waters. They include theoretical sessions in:

- care and maintenance of safety equipment;
- storm sails;
- damage control and repair;
- heavy weather – crew routines, boat handling, drogues;
- man overboard prevention and recovery;
- giving assistance to other craft;
- hypothermia;

- SAR organisations and methods;
- weather forecasting.

Practical sessions include:
- liferafts and lifejackets;
- fire precautions and use of fire extinguishers;
- CPR and first aid;
- communications equipment – VHF, GMDSS, Satcoms, etc;
- pyrotechnics and EPIRBs.

Regulations

Until the middle of the nineteenth century, all ships were free to move about the world's oceans without the hindrance of any rules or regulations. Only when a vessel came into port was it subject to the requirements of a nation or government, but the shore authorities saw this mainly as an opportunity to extract money.

While most ships safely travelled the oceans of the world, many did not. With no means of communication, those that foundered far out to sea were generally simply never heard from again. As maritime nations began to realise that some accidents at sea were preventable by adherence to rules for the building and operation of ships, a body of regulations began to develop in various countries to be enforced for their citizens and those using their controlled waters. With so many nations involved, this created a great diversity of rules and many problems resulted.

COLREGs

The first international maritime agreement was in 1863 between Britain and France and concerned regulations to prevent collisions at sea. These were originally based on British rules formulated in 1862 and finally made internationally effective after a conference in Washington, DC in 1889. Over the years, various amendments were made to these collision regulations.

When the Second World War ended there was a general determination that war on this scale must never happen again, and the United Nations (UN) was created to help to achieve this. The UN system involved the creation of various specialised agencies to deal with specific subjects, and in 1948 a body was formed to deal with shipping: the Inter-Governmental Maritime Consultative Organisation, as it was then known, later renamed the International Maritime Organisation (IMO). It took a further ten years for the IMO convention to receive enough votes to come into force, as governments feared it would interfere with commercial shipping activities to the detriment of the interests of their own vessels. At last, in 1959, there was a permanent international body capable for the first time of adopting legislation on all matters related to maritime safety, prevention of pollution, and liability and compensation following accidents.

Of the 193 countries of the world, some 163 – with over 98 per cent of the world's merchant shipping tonnage – are IMO member states. Individual countries are responsible for ensuring that ships flying their flag comply with the IMO's requirements. Each signatory to the convention has a duty to inspect the ships of other signature countries if there is strong reason to believe that the vessel or her equipment does not substantially comply with the requirements of the convention. This procedure is known as 'port state control'.

The Convention on the International Regulations for Preventing Collisions at Sea was adopted by an IMO conference in 1972, and is still in force today with amendments dating from November 1995. The International Regulations for Preventing Collisions at Sea (COLREGs) are fundamental to safety at sea, and they have since been adopted by nearly all the world's maritime states. The rules specify in great detail how ships must navigate in respect of one another, what lights must be shown, and what signals must be given in all conditions. Any infringement of this international code of conduct is accepted in all maritime courts of law as prima facie evidence of liability in any case of collision.

SOLAS

Out of disaster often comes some good, and so it has been in the maritime world. The loss of the *Titanic* shortly before midnight on 15 April 1912 had a huge impact, greater than any previous maritime disaster. This was partly because over 1,500 people died, and partly because so many of them were rich and famous. There was an outcry on both sides of the Atlantic and questions were raised about the wisdom of allowing individual countries to set standards of safety with the inherent risk that commercial considerations would take precedence. As a direct result of this disaster, the first International Convention for Safety of Life at Sea (known as SOLAS) was convened in London in November 1913. For probably the first time in shipping history, the protection of life was stated as a priority over property and the first SOLAS convention came into force in 1915.

Other accidents in the commercial world that will long be remembered for the tragedies they caused and the loss of life include the *Lakonia* in 1963, *Torrey Canyon* in 1967, the *Amoco Cadiz* in 1978, the *Herald of Free Enterprise* in 1987, the *Exxon Valdez* in 1989, a spate of bulk carrier accidents in the early 1990s, and the *Estonia* in 1994. These same ships, though, are probably indirectly responsible for saving the lives of countless other people and preventing environmental damage, because they caused new regulations to be brought into force worldwide via new SOLAS conventions.

The fifth SOLAS convention in 1974, administered by the International Maritime Organisation (IMO), provided for ongoing revisions of the convention as necessary. SOLAS 1974 is very much a living document, with numerous amendments to ensure that it stays current. The main objective of the SOLAS convention is to specify minimum standards for the construction, equipment and operation of ships, compatible with their safety.

Worldwide safety regulations for pleasure yachts

Small privately owned pleasure yachts used solely for cruising are exempt from many maritime regulations. However, there are some regulations that affect all vessels throughout the world, even if not all vessels are obliged by law to abide by them.

The COLREGs apply to every boat, no matter how small, as Rule 1a states: 'These Rules shall apply to *all vessels* upon the high seas and in all waters connected therewith navigable by seagoing vessels.' Every Skipper and watchkeeper must have a sound working knowledge of the COLREGs, such that they can be applied almost instinctively. It cannot be over-emphasised how important they are with regard to safety at sea and the prevention of disaster. Understanding and being able to interpret the rules correctly are vitally important for every watchkeeper, not only for the benefit of the boat, but also for the safety of other vessels sailing in the same waters. Common sense, forethought and courtesy must be used, in particular when a small sailing yacht meets a large commercial vessel. Power might have to give way to sail, but a laden ship is not nearly as manoeuvrable as a small boat. It is also important to remember that small boats are hard to see from high up on the bridge of a large ship, especially when the bridge is aft.

The United Nations Convention on the Law of the Sea requires all craft entering foreign territorial waters to fly their state flag and carry proof of that entitlement. Thus yachts that plan to visit other countries must be registered in their own country to comply with this law.

UK safety regulations for pleasure yachts

The internationally agreed rules and regulations drawn up by the IMO to ensure that vessels are run in a safe and seamanlike manner are made law in the individual signatory countries. These flag states all have their own organisations to issue directives and make certain they are adhered to.

In the UK, the Department of Environment and the Regions (DETR) is responsible for all transport – including that on the seas – and issues statutory instruments detailing the maritime law. The Maritime and Coastguard Agency (MCA) is an executive agency for the DETR. It sets, monitors and enforces standards of safety and pollution prevention on all UK vessels and enforces international standards on foreign ships in UK territorial waters. The MCA superintendents based at marine offices cover crew matters and documentation. Inspectors and surveyors are employed to ensure that vessels are complying with current regulations and issue certificates accordingly; also, a Marine Accident Investigation Branch (MAIB), not part of the MCA, investigates and issues formal reports, if deemed necessary, following any accident aboard or involving a UK vessel or in UK waters.

The MCA issues directives and advice on safety and other matters to those connected to the sea, including private and commercial vessels, owners, crew, Skippers, shipbuilders, etc, and this information is conveyed by Merchant Shipping Notices (M Notices), Marine Guidance Notes and Marine Information Notes.

The regulations that pleasure craft owned by British nationals must comply with include:

◎ COLREGs
◎ SOLAS V
◎ MARPOL pollution regulations
◎ EU Recreational Craft Directive (RCD)
◎ UK Merchant Shipping Regulations for lifesaving appliances and fire protection if the vessel is 13.7m (45ft) or longer (see chapter 2)
◎ Merchant Shipping (Accident Reporting and Investigation) Regulations 1999 if the vessel is 13.7m (45ft) or longer
◎ Harbour authority bye-laws and regulations
◎ Boat safety standards on UK inland waterways
◎ Crew agreements (where professional crew are carried)
◎ Health and safety at work (where professional crew are carried)

The COLREGs and pleasure craft

With respect to navigation and collision avoidance, any vessel that proceeds to sea, irrespective of size, must comply with the Merchant Shipping (Distress Signals and Prevention of Collisions) regulations 1996. These regulations emphasise the paramount importance of the COLREGs and set out the penalties for non-compliance; these can include fines of up to £50,000. Vessels over 13.7m (45ft) in length must report accidents to the Marine Accident Prevention Branch as soon as possible after the incident. Vessels less than 13.7m need not, by law, report accidents but are advised to do so in the event of a serious incident.

SOLAS V and pleasure craft

Most of the SOLAS convention only applies to larger vessels, but parts of Chapter V apply to small private pleasure craft too. In the UK, these rules came into force on 1 July 2002, in the Merchant Shipping (Safety of Navigation) Regulations. The regulations that particularly apply to small craft are 19, 29, 31, 32, 33, 34 and 35, and these deal with: ✧ radar reflectors ✧ lifesaving signals ✧ danger messages ✧ distress messages ✧ safe navigation and avoidance of dangerous situations ✧ misuse of distress signals.

Radar reflectors (Regulation V/19) This regulation requires that all small vessels fit a radar reflector if practicable, and a yacht longer than 15m (49ft) in length should be able to fit a radar reflector that meets IMO requirements of $10m^2$ (108 sq ft). Smaller yachts should fit the largest radar reflector that they can. As most large ships rely on radar for navigation and sighting other vessels around them, it is good sense to ensure that a small yacht is as visible as possible to radar. (Choosing a radar reflector is discussed in chapter 2.)

Lifesaving signals (Regulation V/29) This regulation requires that an illustrated copy of the recognised lifesaving signals is kept aboard every vessel, and is readily accessible by the watchkeeper for use in an emergency. These signals are for communication between search and rescue units and any person, aircraft or ship in distress. The signals are printed on pages 8 and 9.

Danger messages (Regulations V/31 and V/32) These regulations require all Skippers to pass on to the Coastguard and other vessels in the vicinity, by any means available, detailed information about navigation dangers encountered if this has not already been reported. These hazards would include, for example, a dangerous obstruction, tropical storms and winds of Force 10 or more for which no warning was received.

Distress messages (Regulation V/33) This regulation reinforces the duty of all Skippers to respond to any distress signal that is seen or heard and to help anyone or any boat in distress.

Safe navigation and avoidance of dangerous situations (Regulation V/34) This regulation makes passage planning for all vessels that go to sea, regardless of their size, a *legal* requirement instead of simply good practice. The various considerations involved are detailed in the following sections about passage preparation. The regulation emphasises the need to protect and prevent damage to the environment. It also states that the Master is the final authority aboard the vessel in regard to safe navigation and protection of the environment.

Misuse of distress signals (Regulation V/35) This regulation concerns the proper use of distress signals. It prohibits their use except for indicating that someone, not just a vessel, is in distress and prohibits the use of any signal that might be confused with a distress signal.

MARPOL pollution regulations
The Merchant Shipping (Prevention of Pollution by Garbage) Regulations 1998 applies to all vessels and details what garbage can be thrown over the side and where. MSN 1720 requires all vessels over 12m (39ft) to display placards giving details of the MARPOL regulations on board. Under a new EU directive, waste must be put ashore in appropriate receptacles before leaving port.

EU Recreational Craft Directive (RCD)
This regulation concerns the importation of recreational craft between 2.5m (8ft) and 24m (79ft) in length and the sale of home-built craft less than five years old.

Accident reporting and investigation
The Marine Accident Investigation Branch (MAIB) is responsible for investigating accidents involving, and aboard, UK vessels anywhere in the world and any vessel inside UK territorial waters. The captain of any vessel, including private yachts over 13.7m (45ft) in length, must report all accidents, including those that involve major and serious injury, to the MAIB. The main purpose of the accident investigation is not to apportion liability or blame, but to learn from it, and also to improve safety at sea. The MAIB is not an enforcement or prosecuting agency. (More information about accident reporting, including when and how, is included in chapter 8.)

Harbour authority bye-laws and regulations
Many harbours have regulations that must be obeyed by all vessels in their waters. These often include speed limits, and notices will be posted within the harbour area and information contained in almanacs and pilot books.

Boat safety standards on UK inland waterways
The Boat Safety Scheme (BSS) was jointly established in 1997 by the Environment Agency and British Waterways to promote safety on inland waterways in respect of boats, their installations and components; and meeting these safety standards in order to obtain a navigation licence became a requirement at the same time. An excellent booklet is available online or by post to guide the boatowner through these standards and this offers valuable advice.

Crew agreements
Any pleasure yacht of any size with five or more paid crew, undertaking non-coastal voyages, will require crew agreements and crew lists. Further information is contained in MSN 149 and MGN 111.

Health and safety at work
Where a paid crew is employed, then occupational health and safety regulation provisions apply. Further information is given in SI 1997 No 2962 and MGN 20. Medical stores requirements are covered in SI 1995 No 1802 and MSN 1726 (M&F).

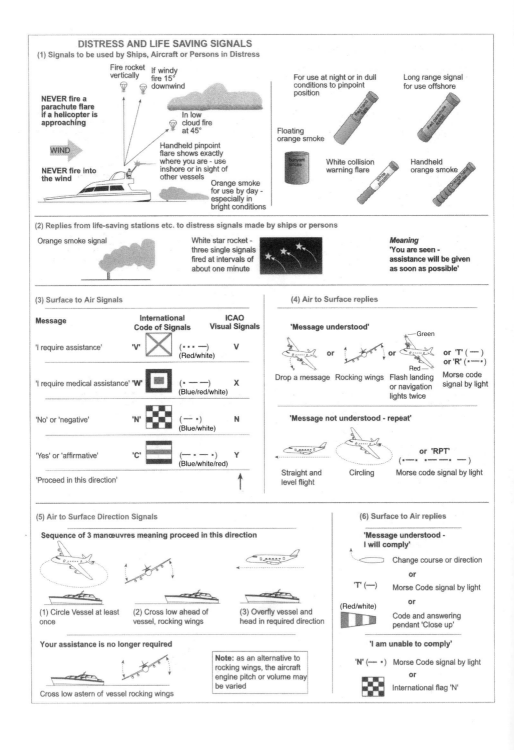

DISTRESS AND LIFE SAVING SIGNALS

(1) Signals to be used by Ships, Aircraft or Persons in Distress

Fire rocket vertically

If windy fire 15° downwind

NEVER fire a parachute flare if a helicopter is approaching

In low cloud fire at 45°

WIND

NEVER fire into the wind

Handheld pinpoint flare shows exactly where you are - use inshore or in sight of other vessels

Orange smoke for use by day - especially in bright conditions

For use at night or in dull conditions to pinpoint position

Long range signal for use offshore

Floating orange smoke

White collision warning flare

Handheld orange smoke

(2) Replies from life-saving stations etc. to distress signals made by ships or persons

Orange smoke signal

White star rocket - three single signals fired at intervals of about one minute

Meaning
'You are seen - assistance will be given as soon as possible'

(3) Surface to Air Signals

Message	International Code of Signals		ICAO Visual Signals
'I require assistance'	'V'	(· · · —) (Red/white)	V
'I require medical assistance'	'W'	(· — —) (Blue/red/white)	X
'No' or 'negative'	'N'	(— ·) (Blue/white)	N
'Yes' or 'affirmative'	'C'	(— · — ·) (Blue/white/red)	Y
'Proceed in this direction'			↑

(4) Air to Surface replies

'Message understood'

Drop a message — or — Rocking wings — or — Flash landing or navigation lights twice

Green

Red

or 'T' (—)
or 'R' (· — ·)
Morse code signal by light

'Message not understood - repeat'

Straight and level flight

Circling

or 'RPT'
(· — · · — · · — · —)
Morse code signal by light

(5) Air to Surface Direction Signals

Sequence of 3 manœuvres meaning proceed in this direction

(1) Circle Vessel at least once

(2) Cross low ahead of vessel, rocking wings

(3) Overfly vessel and head in required direction

Your assistance is no longer required

Cross low astern of vessel rocking wings

Note: as an alternative to rocking wings, the aircraft engine pitch or volume may be varied

(6) Surface to Air replies

'Message understood - I will comply'

Change course or direction

or

'T' (—) Morse Code signal by light

(Red/white)

or

Code and answering pendant 'Close up'

'I am unable to comply'

'N' (— ·) Morse Code signal by light

or

International flag 'N'

DISTRESS AND LIFE SAVING SIGNALS (continued)

(7) Landing signals for the guidance of small boats with crews or persons in distress. By night white lights or flares are used instead of white flags.

	Other signals	Meaning
Vertical motion of a white flag) or of the arms	International Code letter **'K'** (— · —) by light or sound	**'This is the best place to land'** (An indication of direction may be given by a steady white light or flare at a lower level)
 **Horizontal** motion of a white flag or of the arms extended horizontally	International Code letter **'S'** (· · ·) by light or sound	**'Landing here is highly dangerous'**
 **Horizontal** motion of a white flag followed by **2.** placing the white flag in the ground and **3.** by carrying another white flag in the direction to be indicated.	1. Signalling the code letter **'S'** (· · ·), followed by the code letter **'R'** (· — ·) if the better landing place is more to the right in the direction of the approach, or **2**, by the code letter **'L'** (· — · ·) if the better landing place is more to the left in the direction of approach	**'Landing here is highly dangerous. A more favourable location for landing is in the direction indicated'**

(8) Signals to be made in connection with the use of shore apparatus for life-saving

Signal	Meaning	**Signal**	Meaning
Vertical motion of a white flag (or white light or flare by night) or of the arms	**In general:** 'affirmative' Specifically: 'rocket line is held - tail block is made fast - hawser is made fast - man is in the breeches buoy - haul away'	**Horizontal** motion of a white flag (or white light or flare by night) or of the arms	**In general:** negative. Specifically : slack away - stop hauling

(9) Signals to be used to warn a ship which is standing into danger

International Code flag **'U'** (Red/white)

or **'NF'** (Red/white)

International Code signal **'U'** by light or sound · · —

(10) Signals used by Sub-Aqua divers

 'I am OK'

 'I need assistance'

Passage preparation

Even a short coastal hop requires planning and organisation, with safety being the prime consideration, to ensure a successful and happy experience. The amount of planning required will, to some extent, depend upon the length of the passage and can be divided into: ✧ advanced preparations ✧ specific preparations ✧ final preparations.

Advance preparations

Advance preparations are concerned with generalities rather than the specifics of planning the actual passage. They can and should be made some time in advance as they may highlight things that need to be rectified before the voyage can be undertaken safely. There are four areas to think about well in advance of any voyage: the Skipper; the crew; the yacht; the safety equipment on board (this subject is covered in chapters 2 to 6).

The Skipper

Call him the 'captain', 'master' or 'Skipper', it matters not, but in this book we have chosen the word 'Skipper'. On each and every vessel there can only be one Skipper, and no matter how small or large his craft, he is always responsible and accountable, both legally and morally, for the safety of the vessel and crew. This is still true when the Skipper is not on watch, and even when he is asleep. This is a 24 hours a day, 7 days a week job that only ends when the Skipper is replaced by another person who formally takes over the job. Among a Skipper's many skills, he must:

◎ Be able to handle the boat in all conditions.
◎ Be familiar with the boat and its equipment.
◎ Be trained and ready to deal with all possible emergencies.
◎ Fully understand and comply with applicable regulations.
◎ Be able to navigate safely using all available equipment.
◎ Be able to forecast weather or obtain weather information.
◎ Be able to provide crew training where necessary.
◎ Be tolerant of other people's foibles as long as they do not jeopardise safety.

Perhaps most important of all, the Skipper must be a good leader, able to:

◎ Promote group cohesion.
◎ Ensure he is never too rigid.
◎ Listen to other views, but make the final decision.
◎ Delegate.
◎ Supervise unobtrusively.
◎ Be seen to distribute popular and unpopular tasks fairly.

Safety at sea is the result of experience, training, organisation, and forethought. A Skipper must always ensure that his vessel and crew are in the best possible condition, properly equipped, and sailing in suitable conditions. Cold, tiredness and seasickness will dramatically affect anyone's performance and should be avoided if at all possible.

The Skipper must practise risk assessment, and be aware of and prepared for every possible danger, bearing in mind any likely hazards, and the preventative measures that can reduce the risks. He needs to be fully aware of possible resolutions to all likely problems, and to ensure that he has the necessary equipment on board to facilitate those solutions.

Standing orders The Skipper must ensure that his crew, particularly all watchkeepers, are never in any doubt about what he wants them to do, when and how. The simplest method to prevent any confusion is to have written 'standing orders', supplemented with special written instructions for any particular day or night.

Standing orders may be as simple as a typed list permanently attached inside the deck log book, or they may involve a longer booklet for each member of crew dealing with more than just watchkeeping issues. What sort of information is appropriate will depend on the size of the yacht and the number of crew, but must include: ✧ when safety harnesses and/or lifejackets must be worn ✧ watchkeeping instructions ✧ when to call the Skipper.

Standing orders aboard a large yacht will include guidance on: ✧ individual duties ✧ watch and emergency procedures ✧ security ✧ training ✧ procedures for getting under way ✧ logs and inventories ✧ crew policy and guidelines ✧ meals and provisions ✧ use of yacht equipment ✧ environmental and personal safety ✧ general practice.

Using a Daily or Night Order Book on a long passage, as an addendum to the Standing Orders, can help prevent confusion and ensure that the Skipper is summoned in plenty of time if conditions change. In the Order Book, the Skipper should write a few sentences each day telling the watchkeeper what he wants done during each watch, particularly taking into account the condition of the yacht, the present and future position of the vessel, and the weather – including the forecast. These notes might include:

◎ An instruction to call the Skipper when:
  – a particular light or landfall is sighted;
  – a particular light or landfall is *not* sighted;
  – the yacht enters soundings;
  – wind speed exceeds a certain speed;
  – the next weather forecast is due.
◎ Notes about expected shipping, especially unlit fishing vessels.
◎ A weather forecast synopsis.

Training requirements for Skippers

Voluntary training for recreational sailing, rather than any legal requirement, is common in many countries and there is good evidence to suggest that this encourages higher standards than is possible from a compulsory system, which will be a test of the *lowest* acceptable level of proficiency. At present in the UK there are no licence requirements to skipper a pleasure vessel of less than 80 GRT for sport or recreation, but there is still the necessity to comply with certain international regulations. It is, however, illegal to operate a radio without a Ship's Radio Licence, and anyone using the radio must have a Certificate of Competence (operator's licence) or be under the direct supervision of the certificate holder.

For British citizens sailing outside the UK, certificates are recommended. The International Certificate of Competency (ICC), which has been issued since April 1999, is required by British citizens in some European countries for certain categories of pleasure craft for both coastal and inland waterways use. This is a qualification, primarily developed for use in Europe, that is a proven standard of competence in boat handling, navigation and knowledge of collision regulations. This must all be proven by test or previous qualifications. There is also an endorsement called CEVNI (the French acronym for European Inland Waterways Collision Regulations), which is required to travel on some inland waterways in Europe. This has to be issued by the national authority for the country of residence. The RYA have the latest information about the ICC and CEVNI, who needs them, and where and how to obtain them.

In the USA, certification for yachts is a state function, and the Coast Guard does not issue or require operator licences for recreational boats (any vessel used exclusively for pleasure or non-commercial purposes). Accurate, up-to-date State requirements can be obtained from your State Boating Law Administrator (http://www.nasbla.org/blas.htm). In US waters, a radio licence has not been required for pleasure craft since 1996, except for power-driven ships over 20m (66ft) in length on navigable waterways.

In Australia, all boats capable of travelling faster than 10 knots are required to be registered. Their drivers must hold a General Boating Licence and are expected to have a thorough knowledge of local rules and conditions. To operate a VHF radio, with or without DSC fitted, the minimum qualification required in Australia is the Marine Radio Operators VHF Certificate of Proficiency (MROVCP). VHF radios are covered by a class licence, but an individual station licence is no longer required. To operate an MF/HF radio (with or without DSC facilities) a Marine Radio Operations Certificate of Proficiency (MROCP) is the minimum qualification required and a Ship Station Licence is also required.

Safety and training Safety generally comes about through legislation, but truly only becomes effective through training. Not only does the Skipper have to be trained to command the yacht, but he also needs to train his crew on what to do in an emergency. MCA regulations for yachts with a professional crew greater than five demand that there is to be a training manual on board. However, just because the yacht does not carry paid professionals as crew, this shouldn't be an excuse not to create and use an On Board Training Manual.

The crew

The selection of a suitable crew can be one of the most difficult parts of advanced preparations. Without doubt, it is true to say that crew must always be considered the weakest link in any survival situation and the greatest strength in combating disaster. No matter how perfect the yacht, inadequate, incompetent or inexperienced crew will make the vessel unseaworthy. This is especially true when preparing to sail offshore. It is important to consider the training and experience of each member of crew to deal with the yacht in all likely weather. The skills and knowledge needed to handle a sailing vessel are generally greater than those required aboard a motor yacht, and the ideal crew for the yacht and the desired voyage may not be available or possible. Among the crew may be friends and family who will have to be regarded more as passengers than capable deckhands and watchkeepers, and it is the Skipper's responsibility to consider and privately evaluate each crew member and his potential usefulness before deciding to undertake a trip.

If possible, ensure all members of crew attend a sea survival course such as those run by the RYA, IYT, US Sailing or AYF, and that everyone has knowledge of basic first aid and resuscitation. Before a long passage, if time permits, and if some of the crew are unfamiliar with the boat, go out sailing for a day to familiarise everyone with the yacht and practise man overboard (MOB) drills.

Children Sailing with children can be challenging but also very rewarding – and it is never too early for them to learn to love sailing and become useful crew members. Youngsters can and should be involved as much as possible. Of course, a long passage can be boring, but given real responsibilities, commensurate with their age, children can achieve a great deal and feel a real pride in their accomplishments. Our own children were taking charge of a watch long before they could legally drive a car in the UK.

Crew responsibilities All new crew members should be given some form of familiarisation tour of the boat by the Skipper, and know where all the safety equipment is stored and how it works – even if they are more 'passenger' than 'competent crew member'. The General Familiarisation Checklist is an example of an aide-mémoire to ensure that nothing important is forgotten for the safety and enjoyment of everyone.

GENERAL FAMILIARISATION CHECKLIST

Welcome aboard
- General information about the yacht
- Planned voyage

Safety
- Calling the Skipper in an emergency
- Sending a MAYDAY
- Abandoning ship
  - Grab bag
  - Last minute grabs list
  - Liferaft
- Man overboard – button on GPS, equipment and procedure
- Location and use of
  - Firefighting equipment
  - First aid kit
  - Personal equipment – lifejacket, safety harness and thermal protective aid
  - Other lifesaving equipment – flares, etc
  - Yacht equipment – seacocks, bilge pump, fuel, etc
- Precautions on deck – one hand for self, one hand for boat
- Lifejackets and safety harness rules

The yacht
- Conservation of water
- Heads, shower and shower tray pump
- Using the cooker, including safety precautions
- Location of flashlights – spare batteries
- Introduction to deck gear
- Securing for sea – hatches and ports
- Stowage – in harbour and at sea

General
- Food and drink – location, rota, etc
- Seasickness – combating
- Garbage – disposal in harbour and at sea
- Smoking rules

A good crew member should:

- Do whatever the Skipper tells him – ask questions about it later if need be.
- Obey all safety rules at all times.
- Understand the use of all emergency and safety equipment.
- Be willing to perform the unpleasant jobs as well as the pleasant ones.
- Be tolerant of other people's foibles as long as they do not jeopardise safety.
- Carry a knife attached by a lanyard.
- Be able to tie basic knots – bowline, clove hitch, reef knot, round turn and two half hitches.
- Learn and fully understand the COLREGs.
- Keep the boat tidy – both personal gear and the boat's equipment.

◎ Dress sensibly and warmly.
◎ Never throw any rubbish over the side.
◎ Take a personal survival course.
◎ Take a first aid course.
◎ Only smoke with the captain's permission, and never when below.

The yacht

It is essential to ensure that the structure of the yacht and her fittings are in perfect working order before any passage, but especially when embarking on a long voyage such as an ocean crossing. The basic design and construction of the vessel must be suitable for the planned voyage – eg a flat-bottomed boat designed for shallow rivers is not likely to be seaworthy for an offshore passage. Any one of the following would be dangerous and might render a vessel unseaworthy: ✧ defective rigging, fittings or sails ✧ unreliable or neglected engine(s) ✧ inadequate, out-of-date navigation charts and nautical publications ✧ inadequate cooking facilities.

Good maintenance is vital, but even the best yacht can have a hidden problem. The checks listed here, where appropriate, should be attended to at the start of a sailing season and/or before an offshore passage:

◎ Get a professional survey of the engine, steering and rigging.
◎ Check the seacocks, cockpit drains, bilge pumps and plumbing.
◎ Service the main engine(s) and the generator(s).
◎ Ensure the engine oil and filler caps are kept clean and secure
◎ Check gas and liquid fuel pipes, cocks and joints.
◎ Test that the watermaker is providing uncontaminated water.
◎ Check lifelines, jackstays, reefing gear and heavy weather equipment.
◎ Check batteries and ensure that they are properly secured.
◎ Swing the compass and update the deviation card.
◎ Check that the navigation lights conform to international regulations.
◎ Create an inventory of the contents of lockers to facilitate finding spares in an emergency.
◎ Restock the bosun's locker and engine spares, including spare flashlight batteries.
◎ Ensure all yacht and equipment handbooks are filed on board.
◎ Check that all safety equipment is in good repair and, where appropriate, in date (see chapters 2 to 6).

In the UK, a Safety and Sea Check is a free service offered by the RNLI to owners of boats less than 13.7m (45ft) in length. A highly trained volunteer will check relevant levels of safety equipment. In the USA, the USCG similarly offers a free Vessel Safety Check and this checks most of those items listed above, plus a few additional items in relation to local regulations.

The On Board Training Manual The On Board Training Manual is a yacht-specific document. It does not contain details on firefighting per se, but it does give information on how to fight a fire on that particular yacht and will give the location of the fire locker – detailing its contents, and with information on how, when and why the equipment is to be used. It does not deal solely with fire, but covers a broad spectrum of safety issues aboard the yacht – from rigging the gangway to keeping a safe navigational watch.

Shoreside details Preparing the yacht will include checking that the insurance is up to date and adequate for the planned cruising area. If the voyage will be overseas, it is wise at this stage of the planning to check that the yacht, her equipment, documentation and crew conform to the entry regulations of the host country. Ensure that registration and all crew certifications, including passports and any necessary visas, are valid, as a few minutes' preparation at this stage can save hours, or even days, of bureaucratic nightmare on arrival. If sailing in UK waters, join the MCA's CG66 Voluntary Safety Identification Scheme. This is completely free, and gives the Coastguard details pertaining to the yacht and her likely whereabouts on a database that is accessible to all Coastguard Co-ordination Centres throughout the UK. It could save lives if the vessel gets into difficulty in British waters. Fill in and send off a Safety Identification Scheme form (CG66/MSF6000) keeping a copy for the yacht's records. At the start of the season and before any voyage, check that all the details are correct and that the shoreside contact is likely to be available and able to play his part while the yacht is sailing.

The Voyage Details Plan (see Appendix 2) is designed to be filled in and given to the Designated Person Ashore (DPA), with all the details he or she needs, to help set into motion a search and rescue in the event of the yacht failing to arrive at her destination at the expected time. Should efforts to call for help be unsuccessful in attracting attention, the shoreside contact is your lifeline to being rescued.

Specific preparations

With all the advanced preparations in hand, the actual planned voyage can be considered in detail. The majority of this planning can be done ashore if more convenient, and it is mostly concerned with navigation. For many people, this stage of passage planning is actually much more of a pleasure than a chore, but it is essential even for a short trip, especially in tidal waters.

The passage plan should aim to establish the most favourable route while maintaining appropriate margins of safety and safe passing distances offshore. When deciding upon the route, the following factors are among those that should be taken into account:

◎ The marine environment and its protection.
◎ The adequacy and reliability of charted hydrographic data along the route.
◎ The availability and reliability of navigation aids, coastal marks, lights and radar conspicuous targets for fixing the yacht along the route.
◎ Any routeing constraints imposed by the yacht, such as draught.
◎ Any precautionary areas or areas to be avoided along or close to the planned route.
◎ Areas of high traffic density.
◎ Any traffic separation schemes, inshore traffic zone, etc that must be obeyed.
◎ Weather forecasts and expected current, tidal, wind, swell and visibility conditions, especially bearing in mind tidal races, difficult headlands, etc.
◎ Areas where an onshore set could occur.
◎ Regulations such as yachts' routeing schemes and yacht reporting systems.
◎ The reliability and type of propulsion and steering systems on board.
◎ Possible alternative ports of refuge, plus restrictions on entry due to the tide or weather.
◎ The cruising range of the vessel and the availability of fuel both at the destination and along the way.
◎ The ideal departure and/or arrival time, bearing in mind:
  – tidal limitations such as bridges, locks or lack of water;
  – the difficulty of a night-time arrival at an unfamiliar place if there are likely to be lots of shore lights that might be confusing.

Before beginning the passage plan, gather together all the necessary documentation and tools, including:

◎ Clean charts, corrected up to date, covering the planned sailing area – and adjacent areas in the case of a weather diversion.
◎ Electronic charts suitable for ECDIS where fitted.
◎ Chart instruments, including soft pencils (2B), eraser, dividers, compasses and parallel rule, protractor or plotter.
◎ Relevant sailing directions (pilot books).
◎ Nautical publications including up-to-date tide tables, light and radio signals lists.

For coastal and pilotage planning and for plotting each course alteration point (or waypoint), large-scale charts should be used. For ocean passage planning or open water legs, smaller-scale charts should be used.

The route plan
The route plan should incorporate the following details:

◎ Planned track showing the true course of each leg.
◎ The compass course to steer on each leg.
◎ Details of lighthouses and/or signal stations on passage.
◎ Details of conspicuous points or relevant navaids such as RACON, etc.
◎ Leg distances.
◎ Any speed changes required on route.

At any time during the voyage, the yacht may need to leave the planned route temporarily at short notice. Marking on the chart relatively shallow waters and minimum clearing distances in critical sea areas will assist the watchkeeper when having to decide quickly to what extent to deviate without jeopardising safety and the marine environment. We find it helpful to draw circles around danger areas and to hatch them out with pencil marks. However, in using this technique, care should be taken not to obscure chart features. On paper charts, only pencil should be used.

The route plan should also take into account the need to monitor the yacht's position along the route, identify contingency actions at waypoints, and allow for collision avoidance in line with the COLREGs. Planning for anchoring off the port or aborting port entry in the event of problems arising should be included. The plan should also identify charted features that will assist monitoring progress and include contingency measures in the event of primary equipment failure, poor visibility, etc.

The main details of the route plan should be recorded using sketches, if appropriate, so that the plan can be readily referred to and easily used by all the watchkeepers. The more pre-planning that is done the less there will be to worry about at sea, especially if rough weather makes working at the chart table difficult.

Using GPS

The Global Positioning System (GPS) has changed navigation as dramatically as the telephone has changed long-distance communication. It is now possible to know exactly where you are to the nearest 100m anywhere in the world using equipment that can slip into a pocket, costs less than £100, and requires no particular skill to operate. Nothing is perfect though, and equipment can and does fail, and always at the most inconvenient moment. A second portable GPS set with spare batteries, if appropriate, is a small expense for peace of mind, because even with two sets things can still go wrong. Over-reliance on a GPS is very ill-advised and an example of poor preparation and planning. A Skipper should ensure that he can navigate safety without GPS and that he has kept a regular written record of the vessel's position at appropriate intervals during every passage.

Using electronic chart display systems

Passage planning can be undertaken using either paper charts or an electronic chart system. If a combination of electronic and paper charts is used, particular care must be taken at transition points between areas of electronic and paper chart coverage. Where there are distinct pilotage, coastal and ocean water phases, planning within any one part should be undertaken using either all electronic or all paper charts rather than a mix of chart types.

Where a passage is planned using paper charts, special care must be taken when transferring the details of the plan to an electronic chart display system or GPS way-point listing. In particular, the navigator should ensure that:

◎ Positions are transferred to, and are verified on, electronic charts of an equivalent scale to that of the paper chart on which the position was originally plotted.
◎ Any known difference in chart datum between that used by the paper chart and that used by the electronic chart display system is applied to the transferred positions.
◎ The complete passage plan as displayed on the electronic chart display system is checked for accuracy and completeness before it is used.

Transferring route plans to other navigation aids Care must be taken when transferring route plans to electronic navigation aids such as GPS, since the yacht's position computed by the navigation aid is likely to be in WGS84 datum. Route plans sent to the GPS for monitoring cross-track errors must therefore be of the same datum.

Special ocean passage planning considerations

In open waters, the route selected may well include a great circle, composite great circle or rhumb line route. When planning ocean passages, the following should be consulted:

◎ Small-scale ocean planning and routeing charts providing information on ocean currents, winds, ice limits, etc.
◎ Gnomonic projection ocean charts for plotting great circle routes.
◎ Charts showing any relevant yachts' routeing schemes.

Anticipated meteorological conditions may have an impact on the ocean route that is selected. For example:

◎ Favourable ocean currents may offer improved overall passage speeds, offsetting any extra distance travelled.
◎ Ice or poor visibility may limit northerly or southerly advance.
◎ The presence of seasonal tropical storm activity may call for certain waters to be avoided and an allowance made for sea room.

Details of weather routeing services for yachts are contained in lists of radio signals and in Volume D of the World Meteorological Organisation (WMO) Publication No 9. Long-range weather warnings are broadcast on the SafetyNET Service, along with NAVAREA navigational warnings, as part of the World-Wide Navigational Warning Service (WWNWS).

Landfall targets need to be considered and identified as to their likely radar and visual ranges and, in respect of lights, their rising and dipping ranges and arcs/colours of sectored lights.

Special coastal or restricted waters passage planning considerations

By comparison with open waters, margins of safety in coastal or restricted waters can be critical, as the time available to take corrective action is likely to be limited.

The manoeuvring characteristics of the yacht and any limitations or peculiarities that the yacht may have, including reliability problems concerning her propulsion and steering systems, may influence the route selected through coastal waters. In shallow water, particularly if the yacht is operated at speed, yacht squat can reduce under-keel clearances.

Coastal weather bulletins, including gale warnings and coastal navigational warnings broadcast by coast radio stations and NAVTEX, may require changes to be made to the route plan.

Non-navigational matters

Food, water, money, Customs requirements, etc must all be considered at this stage of the preparations. While not all of these items may be seen as directly concerned with safety and survival at sea, food and water are essential – not just to sustain life, but for the overall happiness and efficiency of the crew.

Water Careful management of fresh water is essential for the health and wellbeing of the crew. Aboard a yacht, a conservative average of 4.5 litres (1 gallon) of water is required for drinking and washing per person per day and new crew must be taught good conservation practices. On ocean passages, an additional 50 per cent reserve should be included in the total requirements. Two entirely separate supplies of water should be available in case of contamination and some portable containers should also be taken ready in the event of abandoning ship.

Watermakers are more common now on cruising boats, but often this means fewer water tanks are carried. Make sure you run the watermaker frequently to keep the tanks topped up, just in case of equipment failure.

Food Hot food and hot drinks are essential, particularly on a long passage. Even in the tropics it can be chilly at night, and a hot meal will be welcome and an excellent morale booster when the crew are tired and wet. The longer the intended passage, the more planning is required to provide a varied and interesting diet that caters for the tastes and dietary requirements of the entire crew. Feed the crew badly and next time they are offered a trip, they will likely make some excuse! Storage and refrigeration are important considerations as to what can and cannot be carried. The cook will certainly have a very unhappy crew if he gives them food poisoning as a result of a lack of attention to safe hygiene.

As well as planning for individual meals, snacks are needed, particularly for anyone on night watch. Food, especially sweet things, and caffeine-rich drinks provide lots of instant energy and help combat sleepiness and boredom when there may be little to see or do.

Alcohol and sailing

Alcohol can have a very debilitating effect so no crew member should perform any job while impaired by alcohol, or consume alcohol prior to duty. Alcohol impairment is defined as a blood alcohol content of 40mg/100ml or equivalent. It is not easy to determine how much can be drunk before the limit is reached. It varies with each person and depends upon weight, sex and age, what has just been eaten, and what sort of alcohol has been consumed. Some people would exceed this limit after 1.5 units of alcohol, which is the equivalent of one 440ml can of ordinary-strength beer.

UK legislation curbing excess drinking by professional crew means that yacht Skippers are not allowed ever to exceed 80mg of alcohol in 100ml of blood while on board their vessels, without being at risk of prosecution. These limits apply to all professional crew when they are on duty, and to Skippers of a yacht at all times when they are on board.

The law applies to professional mariners on UK-registered vessels around the globe, and to those serving on foreign vessels while in UK waters, and on unregistered vessels in UK waters. However, testing will be done by police, who would normally be called out by Maritime and Coastguard Agency officials.

The prescribed alcohol limits are not applicable to crew members who can properly be regarded as being off duty. Nothing in the legislation prevents yacht Skippers from adopting more stringent alcohol policies.

The STCW Code also advises governments to prescribe a maximum blood alcohol level of 0.08 per cent for personnel during watchkeeping, and to prohibit alcohol consumption within four hours of commencing a watch. Port states and flag state administrations may have more stringent policies.

Be safe – never drink alcohol immediately before sailing or when under way.

Final preparations

With just hours or minutes to go before sailing, the crew will be assembled and everything required for the passage should be on board. At this point, a crew briefing of some kind is essential. With new or occasional crew, the briefing must be much more comprehensive and include a 'Crew Familiarisation', and or a 'Watchkeepers Familiarisation'. The Skipper must detail the final allocation of duties and an explanation of the watch system. If crew are regularly aboard the yacht, the briefing will not need to be so thorough, but a recap of safety issues is never a waste of time.

Before actually getting under way there are various final checks to be made. Below is a list of those things, if fitted or appropriate, that should be tested and/or checked by the Skipper and made ready for use (the list is in alphabetical order rather than priority order).

Final checks

- Adequate provisions for the passage, including a margin for delays.
- Anchor made ready for immediate use.
- Ancillary watchkeeping equipment – binoculars, hand-bearing compass, etc.
- Barometer checked against reliable alternative.
- Batteries fully charged, including spares for accessories such as handheld GPS.
- Bilge clear and pump(s) working.
- Compass checked against known true bearing or gyrocompass (if fitted).
- Crew clothing, lifejackets and harnesses.
- Crew passports, visas, certificates of competency, etc.
- Echo sounder and lead lines.
- Ensign raised.
- First aid kit.
- Fog horn, whistles and bell.
- Gauges functional and reading correctly.
- Harbour/marina dues paid.
- Lubricating oil and engine coolant.
- Navigation equipment including: chart instruments; chart plotter; charts with courses laid off; electronic navigational position fixing aids, including GPS; log books; nautical publications; passage plan; sailing directions and pilot books.
- Navigation lights/shapes including: emergency lights and shapes for 'not under command' and at anchor.
- NAVTEX receiver/weatherfax, plus spare rolls of paper for each.
- Nearby yachts and harbour/marina authorities advised of departure.
- Personal needs and requirements such as prescription drugs or glasses.
- Radar.
- Radar reflector in position.
- Radio equipment.
- Shoreside contact updated of any changes of plan.
- Ship's papers and certificates of insurance.
- Steering gear including manual, autopilot and emergency.
- Ventilation operable and/or open and clear.
- Visual distress signals.
- Water, gas and fuel topped up.
- Watertight door(s) shut.
- Weather forecast and tide state.

Securing for sea

Securing for sea is a vitally important and easily forgotten job in the last-minute rush to get under way. In the calm of an anchorage or marina it is easy to forget how much things may move or where water might enter, especially in rough seas. Sailing yachts could well use this time to bend on the mainsail to the halyard, checking all sheets and cleats are free to run and operate. Where appropriate, headsails and mizzen sails should be prepared. Sailboats have different navigation lights to motor yachts and these should be checked prior to departure to avoid having to climb a mast while at sea. Make ready the cone day shape required by yachts when motorsailing. Down below, leeboards, lee cloths or any other appliance to secure people or equipment on alternating tacks should be prepared. Cookers, if gimballed, should be free to swing. Poor stowage can cause many problems, not just the obvious one of flying objects injuring crew, but also the difficulty of finding a particular item that may be crucial in an emergency. Special consideration must also be given to the position of the magnetic compass, and nothing metal or magnetic must be placed beside it or in an adjacent bulkhead.

The following list is a guide to those things that, while still the Skipper's responsibility, can readily be delegated to other crew members:

◎ All loose deck gear including ropes, warps, halyards, etc must be stowed or secured.
◎ Clocks and watches should be corrected and synchronised.
◎ Dinghy stowed or towing line should be made ready.
◎ Flashlights must be working with fully charged batteries.
◎ Galley equipment must be secured and the oven gimballed.
◎ Hatches and ports need to be secured, and deadlights fitted if appropriate.
◎ Loose gear should be stowed and lockers secured.
◎ Portable VHF(s) must be fully charged.
◎ Safety equipment, including the liferaft, must be secured to hand and any padlocks removed.
◎ Shore power and any other cables must be discounted.

Immediately after departure

Once the vessel is under way the anchor must be secured for the sea passage when clear of the fairway; and mooring lines and fenders must be stowed.

Passage planning checklists

Checklists are an excellent way of ensuring nothing is forgotten while planning – whether for an ocean passage, an extended cruise or a short day trip. The Passage Planning Checklist and the Individual Passage Plan (Appendix 2) are designed and included as examples that can be tailored to the individual yacht and her cruising area. What suits one Skipper aboard a small sailboat without an engine, planning a trip in an area with large tidal ranges, will probably not suit another captain with a large, fast motor yacht in the Mediterranean. These checklists are an addition to the entries required in the yacht's log books and navigator's notebooks.

Weather

The ease and safety of any voyage depends considerably on the weather. Heavy seas, adverse winds or fog are just some examples of conditions, especially if unexpected by the Skipper, that can potentially endanger or impede a safe passage. Therefore, every Skipper must:

◎ Know how weather works.
◎ Be knowledgeable about possible weather in his sailing area.
◎ Be able to interpret a weather forecast.
◎ Know where to obtain the best weather forecasts for his sailing area.
◎ Obtain a forecast immediately before sailing, ideally having monitored the weather situation for the previous few days.

2 Safety and Survival Equipment

This chapter is all about choosing safety equipment sensibly; it does not suggest the best manufacturer, but offers guidelines to help you make the right choice for the crew, the yacht and the sailing area. Equipment that forms part of the Global Maritime Distress and Safety System, including radio communication equipment, firefighting equipment, liferafts and grab bags are the subject of separate chapters.

RYA recommendations

The safety equipment that should be carried aboard the yacht is well detailed in a list prepared by the British Royal Yachting Association (RYA) who have produced an excellent list, reproduced here as Appendix 3. This list is designed to help small private yachts ensure that they carry adequate equipment, and does not take into account any regulations that apply to private vessels over 13.7m (45ft), commercially operated yachts, or those obliged to follow the US Coast Guard minimum requirements.

Class XII safety equipment

Regulations issued by the UK government, detailing certain safety equipment to be carried aboard Class XII vessels, pleasure vessels of 13.7m (45ft) or above, are included in Statutory Instrument 1998 No 1011, Statutory Instrument 1999 No 2721, and various Merchant Shipping Notices including 1665, 1676. These Merchant Shipping Regulations are summarised in table 2.1 Lifesaving Appliances Required on UK-flagged Yachts and table 2.2 Fire Prevention and Fire Appliances Required on UK-flagged Yachts.

In May 2002, the Maritime and Coastguard Agency (MCA) prosecuted the owner of *Mandator* a 15m (49ft) private motor yacht, for not keeping a proper lookout and having time-expired and insufficient lifesaving equipment aboard his vessel. The prosecution led to the British Marine Federation (BMF) consulting the MCA about the practical problems of complying with the Merchant Shipping Regulation without conflicting with the Recreational Craft Directive (RCD). The result of the meetings that followed between the MCA, BMF and RYA was the production of agreed equivalent standards of safety, which avoid possible conflict with the RCD, and take into account equipment readily available and commonly used by owners of private boats. The agreed equivalent standards require yachts to carry VHF radio, unlike the Merchant Shipping Regulations, and this means of summoning help is reflected in the scale of equipment carried. Like the Merchant Shipping Regulations, the equipment required varies with the distance from shore that the vessel is operating. Tables 2.3 and 2.4 summarise these schedules of exemption for fire prevention and for lifesaving appliances. Class XII vessels now have a choice of compliance with either the Merchant Shipping Regulations or the Exemptions.

TABLE 2.1 LIFESAVING APPLIANCES REQUIRED ON UK-FLAGGED YACHTS
Class XII – Pleasure Vessels of 13.7m/45ft in length or longer

Minimum requirements extracted from Statutory Instrument 1999 No 2721 and MSN 1676 for yachts which go to sea (*see Note 1*)

Length of yacht	> 21.3m/70ft — Not more than 3 miles from the UK coast and only at sea between April and October	< 21.3m/70ft — More than 3 miles from the UK coast or at sea between November and March inclusive	> or = 21.3m/70ft
Liferafts (*see Note 2*)	*Not required*	One or more SOLAS- or DOT-approved with aggregate capacity for the total complement	Two or more SOLAS-approved with aggregate capacity for twice the total complement
Lifebuoys – total	One for each person carried (minimum 2)	Two	Four
– with buoyant lifelines	*Not required*		Two
– with automatic light and smoke signal	One		Two
Buoyant lifeline	One, minimum 18m (59ft)		
Line-throwing appliance	*Not required*		One
Lifejackets – persons >32kg (71lb) **– persons <32kg (71lb)**	One for each person (*complying with MSN 1676 Schedule 9*)		
Lifejacket flashing light	One per jacket		
SOLAS parachute flares	Six		
Liferaft operation sign	On or near each liferaft and launch controls		
Training manual	*Not required*	One	
Maintenance instructions for lifesaving appliances	*Not required*	One	
SOLAS No 1 Table		One	
Rescue boat or inflated boat with launching appliance	*Not required*		One for yachts >25.9m/85ft

Note 1: Lifesaving appliances aboard yachts constructed before 1 July 1986 must comply with MSN 1677. As equipment is replaced or the yacht has major modification, the appliances must comply, like yachts built after that date, with MSN 1676.

Note 2: Liferafts must be stowed such that they can be transferred and launched either side of the yacht. The painter must be permanently attached to the yacht and the liferaft fitted with a float-free arrangement.

TABLE 2.2 FIRE PREVENTION AND FIRE APPLIANCES REQUIRED ON UK-FLAGGED YACHTS
Class XII – Pleasure Vessels of 13.7m/45ft in length or longer

Minimum requirements extracted from Statutory Instrument 1998 No 1011 and Merchant Shipping Notice 1665

Length of yacht	< 15m/49.2ft and open vessels < 21.34m/70ft	<21.34m/70ft	>21.34m/70ft	>21.34m/70ft
Gross tons		< 150 tons	< 150 tons	150 tons to < 500 tons
Fire buckets	Two, one fitted with lanyard	Two, one fitted with lanyard	Three, one fitted with lanyard	
or		or	or	
Portable fire extinguishers		Two	Three	Three, in accommodation and service spaces
Additional fire extinguishers for yachts with engine	Two portable extinguishers suitable for extinguishing oil fires	—	—	Two portable extinguishers suitable for oil fires plus one 45lt (10 galls) foam or one 16kg (35lbs) CO_2 OR If engines total less than 522.2 kW: One portable extinguisher suitable for oil fires per 74.6 kW engine power
Fixed fire-extinguishing system	Not required	Not required	Not required	One in each engine room and tank room
Fire pump	Not required	Pump must be outside engine. One hand- or power-operated with permanent sea connection; second pump may be required	One power-operated capable of delivering one jet of water from any fire hydrant, hose or nozzle aboard	—
Yacht with enclosed engine space	Not required		One additional pump outside engine spaces with separate power and sea connection; if necessary	One additional pump outside engine spaces with separate power and sea connection
Fire hose and fittings	Not required	One	Two	Three
Fire main	Not required	Not required	One	One
Hydrants	Not required	Not required	As required to permit jet of water to reach any accessible store rooms, passenger and crew spaces	—
Fireman's outfit with breathing apparatus	Not required	Not required	Not required	One
Fireman's axe	Not required	Not required	Not required	One

TABLE 2.3 SCHEDULE OF EXEMPTION FOR LIFESAVING APPLIANCES REQUIRED ON UK-FLAGGED YACHTS

Class XII – Pleasure Vessels of 13.7m/45ft in length or longer

MS 93/4/18 Part 5 Alternative to Merchant Shipping Regulations 1999 SI 1999/2721 (see Notes 1 and 2)

Length of yacht		> or = 13.7m but < 24m				>24m
Distance from coast		**< 3 miles**	**3 miles to < 20 miles**	**20 miles to < 150 miles**	**>150 miles**	**All areas of operation**
Liferafts	*Number and capacity*	Not required	One mor more with aggregate capacity for the total complement			Two or more with aggregate capacity for total complement if one is lost
	Stowage	Not required	Approved FRP containers on weather deck or in open space with float free arrangement and auto inflation			None
	– alternative	Not required	FRP container or valise stowed in dedicated locker opening onto weather deck			None
	Type	Not required	SOLAS, wheelmarked or DTLR approved with SOLAS 'B' pack			
	– alternative 1	Not required	ISAF OSR Appendix A Part 2 with SOLAS 'B' pack equivalent (see Note 3)		None	None
	– alternative 2	Not required	ISO Inshore Liferaft Standard		None	None
	– alternative 3	Not required	CE marked Cat C rigid or inflated dinghy ready for immediate use		None	None
Lifebuoys	*Total*		Two		Four	Four
	– with buoyant lifelines		Not required		One	Two
	– with automatic light		Not required		One	Two with self-activating smoke signals
Buoyant lifeline			Not required		One, minimum 18m (59ft) length	
Line throwing appliance			Not required			One
Lifejackets (Note 4)	*Persons >32kg (71lb)*		One for each person aboard – BSI 3595, CEN150 standard or DOT (UK) approved type with buoyancy provided by more than just oral inflation			
	Persons <32kg (71lb)					
	Light		One per jacket			
Flares	*Parachute*	Not required			Four	Four
	Red hand	Not required	Four			Four
	White hand		Four			Four
	Orange smoke		Two			Two
Training and maintenance instructions for lifesaving appliances						One
SOLAS No 1 or No 2 Table						One
Rescue boat or inflated boat with launching appliance		Not required				One for yachts >25.9m/85ft
	– alternative					
Maritime radio		Capable of transmitting and receiving, appropriate to sailing area				
Embarkation ladder (Note 5)		One at each embarkation station				
	– alternative	One approved device enabling access to survival craft in water at each embarkation station				None

Note 1: Lifesaving appliances on all vessels that proceed to sea are to be fitted with retro-reflective material.

Note 2: Servicing – inflatable liferaft, compressed gas inflatable lifejacket and hydrostatic release unit as recommended by manufacturer or their agents. Liferafts in valises should be serviced at least annually.

Note 3: ISAF OSR Appendix A Part 1 liferaft manufactured before 1 July 2003 permitted until replacement is due.

Note 4: Lifejackets for those on watch to be stowed in position readily accessible from the manned watch station.

Note 5: Only required if distance from embarkation point in the water exceeds 1m (3ft).

TABLE 2.4 SCHEDULE OF EXEMPTIONS FOR FIRE PREVENTION AND FIRE APPLIANCES REQUIRED ON UK-FLAGGED YACHTS

Class XII – Pleasure Vessels of 13.7m/45ft in length or longer

MS 93/4/18 Part 5 Alternative to Merchant Shipping Regulations 1998 (SI 1998/1011)

Length of yacht		> or = 13.7m/42ft but < 24m/78ft			
Fire buckets	**Fitted with lanyard**	Two			
	Type	Metal, plastic or canvas (suitable for intended use)			
Fire pump	**Number**	**EITHER** One		**OR**	
	Type	Fixed or portable		Not required	
	Capability	One jet of water with minimum throw of 6m (20ft) with 6 mm (2.4in) nozzle to any part of yacht			
	Style	Hand- or power-operated outside engine spaces with sea and hose connections or Hand-powered portable pump with throwover sea suction and hose connection			
	Fire hose and fittings	One with 6mm (2.4in) nozzle and spray			
		EITHER	**OR**	**EITHER**	**OR**
Fire extinguishers (see Note 1)	**Minimum number**	Two	Three plus	Four	Five plus
	Minimum fire rating of each extinguisher	13A/113B	None	13A/113B	None
	Minimum combined fire rating extinguishers	26A/226B		52A/452B	

Note 1: Fire extinguishers must be of approved types and/or technically equivalent to BS EN 3.

USCG requirements

Table 2.5 is a summary of the USCG minimum equipment requirements for recreational vessels, which varies depending upon the size of the vessel rather than the cruising area. The legal requirements for commercially operated yachts are not included in this book.

There really is no excuse for the Skipper, the rest of the crew or the yacht not to be prepared for sea. Free advice is available both in the USA, from the Coast Guard and, in the UK, from the Royal National Lifeboat Institute (RNLI). The RNLI is committed to making everyone a safe sea user rather than an accident statistic. Both the USA and UK have free sea safety publications, demonstrations of equipment and emergency procedures, and a free boat inspection service. In the UK, Sea Check is a face-to-face safety advice service carried out by an RNLI volunteer expert, at a mutually convenient time, aboard the yacht. It is not a test that can be passed or failed, but it will help a Skipper assess his own capability and ensure he has the correct equipment aboard the yacht. The USCG offers a similar service.

Maintenance and service of safety gear

It is easy to buy the correct safety gear, and even easier simply to stow it away and forget about it. What is important for every item of equipment aboard a yacht, and especially for safety gear, is that it is in good condition, that everyone knows how it works, and that it will function correctly. Draw up a safety equipment checklist (see Appendix 3) and display it in a prominent position. For all lifesaving appliances, the Skipper must:

◎ Read the owner's manual.
◎ File a copy of all instructions and information in the On Board Training Manual.
◎ Enter the item in the Maintenance Record Book, which should include, where appropriate, for each item:
 – a checklist for use when carrying out inspections;
 – maintenance and repair instructions;
 – a schedule of periodic maintenance;
 – a diagram of lubrication points with recommended lubricants;
 – a list of replaceable parts;
 – a list of sources of spare parts;
 – a record of inspection and maintenance.
◎ Fill in and send off any registration card supplied.
◎ Mark the equipment with the vessel's name.
◎ Mount or stow the item in its correct position immediately.
◎ If appropriate, practise using the item.

Having drawn up a Maintenance Record Book, the Skipper must consult it regularly and carry out the necessary checks. Any item that lives on deck is at the mercy of the elements and must be checked regularly for wear. The period of time between such inspections will depend mostly upon the location of the yacht – the tropical sun in particular is very harsh to all materials.

 Tip: Remember, some items like batteries and prescription drugs have long expiry dates, which are easy to forget.

TABLE 2.5 USCG MINIMUM EQUIPMENT REQUIREMENTS FOR RECREATIONAL VESSELS

Boat length (ft)	<16	16 to <26	26 to <40	40 to <65	65 to 165
Boat length (m)	<5	5 to <8	8 to <12	12 to <20	20 to 50
Lifejackets (PFD)	One, USCG approved, Type I, II, III or V wearable PFD for each person aboard				
	One throwable Type IV device				
Visual Distress Signals (VDS)	1 electric distress light or 3 combination (day/night) flares – only if operating at night	*Pryotechnic signal:* 3 orange smoke signals and 3 combination (day/night) red flares OR *Non-pyrotechnic substitute:* 1 orange distress flag and 1 electric distress light OR *Combination substitute:* 3 orange smoke signals and 1 electric distress light			
Portable fire extinguishers (USCG approved) *No fixed system*	One B-1 *(only required on boat with enclosed engine compartment, enclosed living space or permanent fuel tanks)*		Two B-1 OR One B-11	One B-1 and One B-11 OR Three B-1	One or more B-II (depends on weight)
Fixed system	No portables required		One B-1	One B-II or Two B-1	
Ventilation	All vessels built after 25 April 1940 that used gasoline as their fuel with enclosed engine and/or fuel tank compartments must have natural ventilation of at least two ducts fitted with cowls				
	In addition, all vessels built after 31 July 1980 must have rated power exhaust blower				
Backfire flame arrester	One approved device on each gasoline engine installed after 25 April 1940, except outboard engines				
Sound-producing devices	Some means of making an efficient sound signal			Signal device audible for ½ mile/4 to 6 seconds	
				One bell with mouth at least 7.9in in diameter	
Navigational lights	As per COLREGs, required to be displayed from sunset to sunrise and in or near areas of reduced visibility				
FCC radio licence	Not required				Required
Oil pollution placard	Not required		Durable placard at least 5in x 8in, posted in machinery space or at the bilge station		
Garbage placard	Not required		Durable placard at least 4in x 9in, displayed in conspicuous place		
Waste management plan	Not required			Required if vessel has galley	
Marine sanitation device	Vessels with installed toilet must have an operable, USCG-approved Type I, II or III marine sanitation device (MSD). Subject to local laws				Type II or III MSD only
Navigational rules (inland only)	Familiarity with rules is recommended			Copy of rules must be carried aboard the vessel	
Certificate of number (state registration)	All undocumented vessels equipped with propulsion machinery must be state registered. Certification number must be aboard when vessel is in use. Some states require all vessels to be numbered				
State numbering	Plain block letters/numbers not less than 3in high must be affixed on each side of the forward half of the vessel (contrasting colour to exterior). State validation sticker must be fixed within 6in of the registration number				
Certificate of documentation		Documented vessels must carry original and current certificate aboard. Vessel's name and hailing port must be marked on the exterior hull in letters at least 4in high. Official number must be permanently fixed to the interior in letters at least 3in high			

29

Mechanical failure is the main cause of distress at sea, so ideally every boat should have two independent means of propulsion. Most sailboats have a choice of engine or sails. On a motorboat, the ideal situation is two totally independent engine systems. A yacht with only one means of propulsion needs to be doubly careful about maintenance and must never set sail if there is any doubt about the condition or reliability of the equipment. Some measure of security is offered by carrying plenty of spares for emergency repairs under way – so long as there is a crew member who can use such paraphernalia!

Emergency steering

Every boat needs some sort of secondary steering in an emergency. If this has not been allowed for when the yacht was built, it should be retro fitted – especially if the Skipper is planning to cruise any distance. Ideally, emergency steering should be fitted in such a way that the helmsman can still see to steer. The larger the yacht, the less likely it is that this will be possible, but at least the large yacht will probably have a big enough crew to cope.

Rope cutters

Fouling a propeller is all too easy to do, especially at night in areas where there are lots of unlit fish traps or lobster pots. Unfortunately, this is also often in shallow water and close to shore where the loss of power, especially for a motorboat with no other means of propulsion, can be very dangerous. Rope cutters fitted around the shaft of the propeller are so efficient that a change in engine noise may be the only indication that something has been cut rather than wrapped. While rope cutters are useful and a very necessary safety item for a motorboat, this does not mean that running over a line is a good idea, because there is no guarantee that the rope cutter can cut a particular rope – and anyway, that rope may have been connected to someone else's livelihood.

Anchors

An anchor may not immediately spring to mind as a piece of *safety* equipment. However, while anchoring is usually a planned manoeuvre, it is also a very useful emergency option – by preventing further movement. In this scenario, anchoring can help the yacht regain deep water when aground or even prevent the grounding in the first place. When leaving a berth or manoeuvring at close quarters, have the anchor ready to let go in an emergency in case an engine fails or winds change unfavourably.

Tip: In poor visibility, when sailing in shallow water, anchoring may be the best option – rather than continuing and risking running into danger.

Anchor cable

Anchor cable can be made of chain, rope or a mixture of the two. As with the type of anchor, the choice may be a compromise, partly dictated by personal preference and partly by the size of the yacht. The elasticity of synthetic warps is a big advantage in preventing snatching and breaking out of the anchor in poor weather conditions. Rope is generally more convenient to stow but much more is needed to obtain the correct scope. The main advantage of chain is that far less is needed to obtain the necessary scope and, for larger yachts, over 20m (66ft), it is the only choice. A compromise for small yachts is a mixture of rope and chain. Where all chain is used, the inboard end of the anchor cable should never be shackled below decks. It should be secured with a stenhouse slip or a strong lashing so it can be quickly released. If an anchored yacht needs to be moved in an emergency, it is often quicker to let out and drop the entire anchor ensemble than to raise it out of the water. Better to lose gear than lose a boat.

 Tip: When the anchor cable is chain only, a piece of synthetic rope with good stretching abilities should be attached between the yacht and chain to act as a snubber. Snatching is uncomfortable, potentially damaging to the yacht, and can easily break out the anchor – with all the possible consequences of unexpected dragging.

Drag devices

No sane Skipper would choose to set out in a storm, but the further afield and the longer the passages undertaken, the higher the risk of getting caught out in one. In storm situations at sea, the Skipper must decide whether to continue to sail or slow the boat down in some way. Heaving-to or lying a'hull is a possibility, but most modern cruising boats will not do either safely. Without sails or engines, a yacht will tend to lie beam-on to the seas, or in light boats, the bow will tend to fall slightly beyond the beam reach. The yacht risks being rolled, pitchpoled or pooped, especially when the waves reach or exceed the beam width in height. In calm seas, lying a'hull can be a useful way to handle an emergency, but as the vessel is free to drift it can also be dangerous – especially if sea room is limited. In gale force winds, a sea anchor and a drogue are two items of survival equipment that can greatly help the Skipper to maintain control of his vessel. These drag devices can help a yacht ride out a major storm in relative comfort and safety. Like all safety devices, though, it is essential that the crew know how to use them properly and have practised rigging them. While a drogue and a sea anchor both add drag to the yacht, they are very different devices.

Sea anchors

A modern sea anchor is a large parachute-like device deployed over the vessel's bow, where it opens underwater and forces the bow back into the seas. It is the offshore equivalent of a ground anchor, helping a yacht to hold her position, though not attaching her to the ground. A full-sized sea anchor reduces drift to less than 1 knot, excluding any current.

A sea anchor has more use than just storm handling; it can:

◎ Let a singlehander take a rest.
◎ Buy time for the crew to jury-rig a dismasted yacht.
◎ Help prevent a yacht losing ground if she is unable to make way.
◎ Allow a vessel to wait in position for daylight to make a tricky entrance.
◎ Create smoother conditions to facilitate rudder repairs.

Tip: Small conical-shaped devices advertised as sea anchors are not suitable for survival use by a yacht.

Drogues

A drogue is a much smaller device than a sea anchor and there are a number of designs available. Unlike a sea anchor, a drogue is not designed to stop a boat, but instead to slow it down. A drogue can be used in the following ways:

◎ When towed off the stern, it can stabilise a vessel in a strong following sea.
◎ When towed off the stern with a bridle, it can be used as an emergency steering device to yaw the boat if steering fails.
◎ When towed off the stern of a vessel in tow, it can limit the 'whiplash' effect and give the towing vessel better control.
◎ When towed off the windward quarter, it can help to maintain directional stability while negotiating a dangerous harbour entrance.

There are a variety of drogues available for yachts up to 20m (65ft) and there are arguments for and against each type. In an emergency, it is possible to jury-rig a drogue from anything that will sink and provide drag, but it will not perform nearly as well – especially in severe weather conditions – as a purpose-made one. The low pull that allows steering control may also allow the boat to broach, capsize and/or pitchpole in the heaviest seas, but it can still be a very valuable piece of safety equipment for survival at sea.

Bailing and bilge pumps

Water aboard the boat is inevitable, and generally not a problem when confined in a tank or washing across the deck. The problem comes when the water escapes or enters below deck. Water mostly gets inside a yacht because of indifferent maintenance, but problems can occur in any boat.

All through-hull fittings must be fitted with a seacock, which can be shut in the event of any failure of the pipe or fitting. Ensure all seacocks are kept clear and can be accessed easily. A tapered wooden plug of sufficient size should be attached with a lanyard to each and every seacock as double security. Hose and hose clamps, especially those connected to any through-hull fitting, must be checked regularly to ensure they are in good condition. Hose clamps are a weak point and very prone to breaking. They should always be made of stainless steel and, if there is room, a second one should be fitted.

Every yacht should have at least two suitable bilge pumps. An ideal set-up will have two separate bilge pumping systems, each with their own suction and discharge lines – one on deck and one below. An electric pump with a float control switch is a very good idea as it can automatically pump any rising water before it is seen flooding over the cabin sole. It is important to include some sort of alarm to alert the crew that the automatic pump is in operation, as any water ingress needs to be checked as soon as possible. One or more of the pumps aboard the yacht must be a powerful manual version, in case no power is available. It is essential to check that the manual bilge pump is sited in a position where it can be used easily; potentially, it might be needed for a prolonged period in an emergency.

An additional portable electric pump that can be taken to the site of any water ingress is an excellent back-up and support to the main pump. Finally, some sort of simple portable hand pump – such as the stirrup-pump style used to bail a dinghy – provides added comfort at a very cheap price – and in fact *saved* our 60ft (18.3m) boat!

 Tip: Always stow the handle close to the bilge pump and, if the set-up is on deck, attach the handle with a lanyard to prevent it being accidentally knocked overboard.

Bilge and bilge-pump maintenance

Bilges should always be clean and free of oil, and special attention must be paid to this area after any engine work or haul-out as dirt and debris in limber holes and bilges can easily cause a blockage. All pumps should be tested very regularly; no one can predict when they may be needed in an emergency. Electric float switches and alarms are very prone to failure, so should be checked at least monthly – and *always* tested before leaving the boat unmanned.

The diaphragms, seals and valves of manual pumps should be serviced once a season, or every six months on a cruising boat. Spare parts and/or service kits for all pumps should form part of the yacht spares inventory. Seacocks should be opened and closed regularly and kept closed when the boat is unattended. Whenever the yacht is out of the water, grease all the seacocks and check they are firmly attached to the hull, are in good condition, and move freely.

 Tip: Before testing a bilge pump, ensure the bilge is free of oil. Apart from being environmentally unfriendly to pump oil or fuel overboard, it is also against the law.

Flood prevention equipment

The single most important aspect of a vessel's construction is the ability to maintain watertight integrity and thus improve the ship's chances of survival. A yacht's structure and hull may suffer damage, but if sufficient watertight integrity is maintained, the ship will stay afloat. A crack or, worse still, a hole in the hull, particularly below the waterline, can allow water inside the vessel and, if unchecked, the ship will sink.

Plugging and patching

Water ingress can be controlled in a number of ways, and these are to an extent dependent upon the type and scope of the damage. The majority of the repairs will be a temporary measure to keep the boat afloat until she can be hauled out of the water for proper repairs. The ideal is to stop all the water ingress, but reducing the rate of flow to something that the pumps can handle successfully will be acceptable. Temporary repairs to a hole in the ship's hull, or indeed any of her piping system, involve either putting something in the hole, or putting something over the hole.

Temporary repairs need not involve sophisticated tools or expensive equipment, just the practical application of the two principles of plugging and patching. Remember, though, in an emergency it is much better and quicker to grab a plugging kit than scrabble around looking for things to use.

Something in the hole: softwood plugs and wedges

The quickest and easiest way to plug a hole in an emergency is to put something in it, such as a pillow or cushion from a bunk. To effect a more permanent repair, a softwood wedge or plug wrapped in a rag is a simple and cheap option. Large holes may require a group of wedges and plugs to fill the hole. A plugging kit should therefore contain: ✧ assorted softwood plugs in various sizes up to 25cm (10in) ✧ assorted softwood wedges ✧ a bag of rags ✧ hammer, maul or mallet. Larger yachts may want to include more of the above items, plus: ✧ hatchet ✧ cold chisel ✧ handsaw to cut wood.

Something over the hole: patch repair kits

Patching is a good temporary repair method, especially for cracks in glassfibre, and also for holes, both those that can be reached from inside the yacht and those that cannot.

Patch repair kits consisting of underwater epoxy, mixing sticks, gloves and some sort of matting or material to epoxy bond over the crack or damaged area can be purchased or self-assembled. The epoxy acts as underwater glue for the patch material, which is applied like a band-aid over the damaged area. Some repair kits use a 'wad' of foam or sponge rubber, which is saturated with epoxy and crammed into the hole as a plug. Patch material such as rubber or vinyl needs to be flexible but watertight.

> **Tip:** Epoxies do not stick well to most plastics.

Repairs from both inside and outside the yacht can easily be performed using a proprietary product that is essentially a variation of an umbrella. Push it through the hole, and then open it, whereupon the pressure of water acting against the hull forces it to spread the patch over the hole and provides an excellent temporary repair.

Collision mats are a good choice for external hull repairs, especially when it is impossible to reach the damage from inside the yacht. Traditionally this is a section of old sail canvas with ropes attached to each corner; they can be purchased or made easily. The mat is drawn over the outside of the hull until positioned over the hole and then the pressure of the water holds it in place. Getting the material quickly over the hole can be a problem, especially when there is any debris in the water.

Emergency non-radio signalling equipment

Signalling equipment is not only required in distress situations, it is also used to attract attention and quickly communicate intentions. In a distress situation, pyrotechnics and some sort of radio signalling device are the obvious way of signalling and these are dealt with in separate chapters. Annex 4 of the COLREGs, which lists all the recognised visual and sound distress signals, includes various other methods of communication that may be used in an emergency.

Sound

All yachts must have some means of making a sound signal in restricted visibility and to make manoeuvring and warning signals. Yachts less than 12m (40ft) need any effective means of making a sound, while larger yachts need a whistle and a bell and, if over 100m (330ft), they will need a gong as well. It is essential that any sound-producing equipment is loud enough to be audible from the bridge of a large ship. Portable gas and air horns are available from chandlers, and many yachts have a permanent installation. Automatic fog horns are available to make the restricted visibility sound signals, and so allow the crew to concentrate on navigating in difficult conditions.

 Tip: Sound-signalling equipment is also very effective as a means of summoning the entire crew in an emergency; however, agree on a sensible signal.

Lights

At night, a light is a very effective method of indicating position or conveying a warning. An electric distress light can be substituted for pyrotechnics under USCG minimum equipment requirements. To attract attention, a handheld or mounted searchlight with a powerful halogen bulb is far more efficient than a flashlight. Strobe lights should be avoided for signalling from the yacht, as these can be confused with a north cardinal buoy.

Flags

A set of international code flags is not only useful for dressing the yacht overall; they still have a very practical purpose for communication. A set of flags of appropriate size for the yacht should be carried, plus a reference book listing the hoists.

Flashlights

Flashlights have numerous uses on board a yacht, and there can never be too many to hand, along with spare batteries. Waterproof torches are good, and submersible ones are the best as they can double up as dive lights if it is necessary to go underwater to check the hull. While not as efficient as a searchlight for signalling from the yacht, a flashlight can be used in an emergency. They are ideal for providing a less intense light on deck at night to identify unlit channel marks, or prepare an anchor for dropping without totally destroying night vision. Every crew member should have a personal submersible torch kept on their person at all times as a means of attracting attention in a man overboard situation. Flashlights with red bulbs or lens covers are best for working or moving around the yacht at night, as night vision is not impaired by their use.

 Tip: A disposable chemical lightstick gives cheap and effective location lighting at close quarters. One should be attached to every lifejacket and oilskin.

Navigation Lights

Correct navigation lights are fundamental to safety at sea, and the COLREGs give detailed information as to what must be displayed where, when and how. Tenders with outboard engines also require navigation lights. Spare bulbs and other electrical spares should be carried as part of the spares inventory in case of breakdown. High masthead tri-lights reduce electrical drain on a sailboat, but close to the shore and among other yachts they can be confused with shore lights. Ideally, sailing yachts should also be fitted with deck-mounted navigation lights. In the event of power failure, some form of emergency navigation lights should be available – such as oil lamps. An oil lamp may also be a good alternative anchor light for a small yacht with limited electrical power.

Radar reflectors

There are two varieties of marine radar: X-band and S-band. X-band radar operates at a frequency of approximately 9.4 GHz, with a wavelength of 3.2cm, while S-band operates at approximately 3 GHz, with a longer wavelength of 10cm. Ships will typically carry both, while small vessels usually carry the smaller X-band units. X-band radar offers greater resolution and detection of smaller targets, but is more susceptible to sea clutter (interference from rain and seas). S-band radar has longer range and less interference from rain and sea clutter, but has less sensitivity for small targets. A ship will typically use her X-band unit near shore, while in offshore waters they commonly use the S-band unit set to a 24-mile scale.

With fewer watchkeepers on the bridge, officers aboard merchant ships place more reliance upon ARPA systems. These systems automatically capture and track radar targets, and provide a warning to the watch when a close approach is predicted. An ARPA system will only work with targets that are visible on the radar, and typically a minimum of three consecutive 'hits' is required on the ship's radar before a blip is acquired as a target. This means the return must not only be strong, but also consistent.

Passive reflectors

Most passive reflectors are octahedral in form: three metal surfaces mounted at right angles to one another, forming eight trihedral reflectors. To give a good radar response, the octahedral reflector needs to be quite large – ideally with a $10m^2$ (108 sq ft) radar cross-section, correctly mounted and fitted at a height of at least 4m (12ft) above the waterline. More sophisticated and expensive radar reflectors are available – one with an array of reflecting corners stacked vertically within what looks like a large fender; another has layers of plastic inside a sphere and works by focusing the radar energy to a reflective band around the 'equator' of the lens and then back to the source of the energy. There is much debate about exactly how effective all these devices are, but the bottom line is: something is better than nothing. The one thing key to the performance of any reflector design is size. The reflective performance of any type of reflector is proportional to the fourth power of its linear size. Doubling the size of a reflector results in an increase of an effective area of 16 times.

 Tip: Biggest is very definitely best, at least in radar reflector terms.

Active reflectors

Radar Target Enhancers (RTEs) are permanently mounted, powered units that detect radar illumination and return an exact copy as a strong and consistent contact on the radar screen. However, they have a couple of disadvantages: they need power, and so won't work in the event of a power failure on board; and they do not show up on S-band radars.

The perfect choice?

Neither active nor passive radars are the perfect answer to being seen by other vessels, so the obvious choice would be to fit one of each. But having one of each is not an excuse for complacency to overtake the crew; nothing matches a good lookout at all times for collision avoidance. The large ship may not 'see' the small yacht, but the watchkeeper on the small vessel, in good visibility, can visually see the ship a long way off and take appropriate action.

Pyrotechnics

Flares, also called pyrotechnics, are visual distress signals designed to alert people that someone is in trouble; they also provide a location signal for would-be rescuers to home in on. SOLAS, an IMO convention, stipulates the performance standards for flares designed for commercial vessels. There are other flares on the market, though, that do *not* meet that same standard of burn time or brightness. In a distress situation it makes sense to have the maximum signalling power possible, so buy flares that match the SOLAS requirements, and buy at least the number recommended in the RYA list. The pyrotechnics carried depend not upon the size of the boat, but on the distance it is likely to go.

Orange smoke canisters
SOLAS-specified buoyant smoke signals burn for not less than three minutes and will not ignite oil or fuel. They should be carried for all offshore passages. For yachts that never go far from shore, handheld orange flares, which burn for about one minute, may be sufficient.

Red handheld flares
SOLAS-specified red handheld flares have a minimum burning period of one minute and a luminous intensity of 15,000 candela, and *nothing less* should be carried. A minimum of three such flares should be carried aboard all yachts.

Red parachute flares
SOLAS-specified red parachute flares, with self-contained launchers, reach 300m (1,000ft) in altitude and burn for a minimum of 40 seconds. Pack plenty for any trip to sea; they can attract the attention at great distances, including those ships that are over the horizon.

Using pyrotechnics

Flares must be stored in a watertight container and kept in a readily accessible place. All flares come with instructions on how to use them, which should be read and memorised. Everyone aboard the yacht must know where pyrotechnics are stored and how to fire them *before* an emergency arises – it is too late to be hunting around or to start studying the instructions on a dark night in extreme conditions.

 Tip: White flares should be kept near the steering position, and stored separately from the other colours to avoid confusion.

Pyrotechnics maintenance

Flares deteriorate with time but, if properly cared for and correctly stowed, they should have an effective life of three years from the date of manufacture. Pyrotechnics should be inspected at least twice a year and always before any off-shore passage, replacing any that show signs of decay. They should be stored in a watertight container. White flares should be kept separated from the other colours to avoid confusion.

On no account use out-of-date distress rockets or flares for testing or practice purposes or just for fun, people have been killed this way. Special care should be taken regarding the disposal of obsolete pyrotechnics. These may not be dumped at sea or sent through the post. They should be disposed of ashore by returning them to the supplier or their representative. You can ask a liferaft service station to accept them as they all have to have an arrangement to deal with expired pyrotechnics. Alternatively, contact the local Coastguard.

Lifejackets and buoyancy aids

Without a lifejacket, even an Olympic swimmer would have difficulty in staying afloat in cold water. This is because of the disabling effects of cold, shock and cramp. A lifejacket is designed to keep a person afloat without effort or swimming. It must be self-righting, turning the wearer onto his back so that his mouth is held clear of the water even when unconscious. Suitable lifejackets must be carried for everyone aboard the yacht, including any children. Exactly when to wear a lifejacket is often a personal decision, but they must always be worn:

◉ When there is a high risk of collision or foundering.
◉ In heavy weather, fog and at night.
◉ By non-swimmers and children when on deck (at all times).
◉ When working forward on deck, unless using a safety harness.
◉ When in a dinghy (this is the law in many places).

All lifejackets and buoyancy aids in the EU must comply with European EN standards. If the lifejacket has an integrated safety harness, it must also comply with EN 1095. There are four categories defined by buoyancy for an 'average' wearer weighing 70kg (11 stone), with buoyancy measured in Newtons where 10 Newton equals 1kg (2.2lbs) of flotation.

Categories of buoyancy for lifejackets

♦ 50 Newton (EN 93). Only for use by competent swimmers in sheltered waters when help is close at hand. This style is not guaranteed to turn a person face-up. It is a buoyancy aid, not a lifejacket.

♦ 100 Newton (EN 395). For use in sheltered waters, but where help is further away. It is unlikely to self-right an unconscious survivor.

♦ 150 Newton (EN 396). For general offshore and rough weather use. It may not immediately self-right an unconscious person wearing heavy waterproof clothing.

♦ 275 Newton (EN 399). For offshore and extreme conditions and those wearing heavy protective clothes to ensure self-righting an unconscious survivor.

In the USA, lifejackets – commonly called PFDs (personal flotation devices) – are required aboard all boats regardless of size. PDFs are divided into four categories relating to design rather than buoyancy: Type I offshore lifejacket; Type II near shore life vest; Type III recreational vest, float coat, inflatable vest; Type V special use device, inflatable vest with harness.

What to look for in a lifejacket

Like everything else in life, choosing a lifejacket is about compromise. While there is no question that the safest lifejacket if someone falls overboard unconscious has 275 N buoyancy, it is not the most comfortable. The 275 N jacket is huge; swimming is difficult and climbing into a liferaft or up a ladder almost impossible. For this reason, a 150 N lifejacket tends to be the most popular choice. But buyer beware – always check the label; a 150 N jacket does not necessary supply 150 N of buoyancy! Some companies deliberately provide significantly more buoyancy, while others provide less by labelling the jacket suitable for someone less than 70kg (11 stone).

The primary function of a lifejacket is to protect a casualty who has fallen into the water. Hoods or spray masks provide a very valuable shelter from spray, which in even

moderately choppy water can result in drowning. Saving from drowning must obviously be followed by safe retrieval, and for this reason every lifejacket should be highly visible, fitted with a whistle to attract attention, and have a strong ring or loop to facilitate rescue. Retro-reflective tape and an easy to activate automatic or manual flashing light are highly recommended and are required on Class XII yachts.

It is of the utmost importance that a lifejacket is the correct size and fits tightly. Many deaths have occurred from a broken neck caused by jumping into the sea with a loosely tied lifejacket, which has been driven upwards on impact with the water. Crutch straps stop the lifejacket from riding up in the water. Like the jacket itself, they must be tightly fitted to function properly.

By far the most popular choice for active boating is the automatic gas inflation lifejacket, which inflates using a water-dissolving capsule or cartridge or a hydrostatic mechanism. Manual-inflation jackets using a cord to fire the CO_2 cylinder are better for foredeck crew who may occasionally be immersed. Inflatable jackets are usually so small in their uninflated state that they would never interfere in any deck activity, and essential if they are to be worn at just the time there is the most risk of falling overboard. Lifejackets fitted into the lining of a jacket are very comfortable, and one way of ensuring this lifesaving piece of kit is always worn in rough weather. Most inflatable lifejackets are available in an integrated harness version, which is a big plus for safety and convenience. These jackets are made with adequate resistance and a proper fitting for attaching the tether.

Tip: A lifejacket that has not been sold as a combined harness must not be used in that way; it may not hold under tension.

Lifejacket maintenance

All lifejackets and buoyancy aids should be examined at least once a year for any wear or damage. Inflatable models will require regular maintenance and this should be detailed in the documentation that came with the lifejacket. Always keep at least one spare re-arm kit for each type of automatic inflatable lifejacket aboard the yacht.

Every six months and before a long passage:

♦ Ensure that the personal emergency locator light is functioning and the battery is in date.
♦ For inflatable lifejackets:
   – undo the Velcro closures and lay the jacket flat;
   – unscrew the CO_2 cylinder, and check it is sound and that the tip is not punctured; set it aside;
   – orally inflate the lifejacket fully and leave it for a few hours. It should remain hard; if not, return it to the manufacturer for investigation;
   – deflate the jacket, re-install the CO_2 cylinder, screwing it tightly into place, and refold the jacket according to the instructions;
   – replace the hydrostatic devices at the prescribed intervals.

Children's lifejackets

Children's lifejackets are rated in exactly the same way as those for adults, and are sized according to the child's weight. Traditional foam lifejackets are the best choice for children who cannot yet swim, and for those younger than six or seven. The jacket not only provides flotation if the child falls over the side, but also acts as a bumper to protect them from hard knocks. As an added bonus, the jacket definitely slows down the movements of an inquisitive and adventurous child.

Automatic inflation lifejackets give a child a much greater freedom of movement and undoubtedly enhance their enjoyment of sailing. They are ideal for a child who can swim, is already familiar with life on a boat, and reasonably aware of danger. It is important that the child is old enough to understand that a lifejacket is for emergency use and must only be inflated if such a situation arises.

Children should wear their lifejackets at all times on the deck of the yacht, including in the cockpit. They should also wear them when they go ashore in a marina or port until they are well clear of the water. A young child just back from a sail is unlikely to walk sedately down a pontoon, and that is just when they are most likely to fall in the water – we had to retrieve ours by the back loop on the lifejacket more than once! Wet, bedraggled and bawling, but very much alive and well.

Flotation vests for dogs and cats
Flotation vests are also available for dogs and cats, though whether you can persuade your cat to wear one is another matter! But these are excellent for hooking man's best friend out of the water, whether he went in intentionally or not. They also supply a very secure and safe handle to transfer an animal from boat to dinghy or shore.

Clothing

It may be hot and dry ashore, but it will always be cooler and wetter at sea, so clothing in temperate and higher latitudes is about preventing hypothermia. A cold, wet crew is a demoralised crew, and in grave danger of moving from merely uncomfortable, to hypothermic, then to dead. Foulweather gear must not only keep the wearer dry from rain, spray and solid water, but also allow ease of mobility. It must be durable to withstand the marine environment of rough surfaces, chemicals and salt, but also comfortable to live in for extended periods of time.

More generalised sailing books will provide much helpful information on the subject of specific clothing, so only a few points will be mentioned here.

All foulweather clothing should be of a conspicuous colour such as yellow to make it easier to locate the person in the event of a man overboard accident, for example. Strips of reflective tape are also very important for night-time visibility. Some top-of-the-range jackets have a built-in harness and lifejacket, ensuring these items of safety equipment are not left in a locker in an emergency.

For the extreme conditions of ocean racing, dry suits made of breathable materials are commonly worn. While not truly survival suits, they are insulated for flotation and heat retention.

An uncovered head leads to a significant heat loss, hence the importance of hats – and in a hot climate the person's head (and any other parts of the body that are exposed) needs protection with a full UV filter sunblock.

Proper sailing gloves not only keep hands warm, but also protect against rope burn and other possible injuries.

Suitable footwear provides protection from the cold, wet and injury on deck, and must give a good grip in wet and dry conditions.

 Lots of thin layers are far more efficient than one thick one. Wear a scarf to prevent water dripping inside your clothes. On really rough passages, consider wearing a wetsuit under your wet weather gear.

Guardrails, lifelines and safety harnesses

A lifejacket is a means of preventing the loss of life of anyone who falls overboard, but it is obviously far better to prevent the accident in the first place and to stay safely on board. In the open sea, a person falling into the water, especially in rough conditions, has a poor chance of survival. It is all too easy to forget that the old sailor's maxim 'one hand for yourself and one for the ship' is especially important on a heeling sailboat. Unfortunately there are often jobs that need both hands, and this is where lifelines, safety harnesses, etc can save a wetting – or far worse.

Guardrails

Guardrails running along both sides of the yacht are fundamental equipment for any vessel voyaging outside sheltered waters. This should comprise metal stanchions securely through-bolted at their base with a top rail (wire on small yachts) and a mid-height rail. Ideally, the top of the guardrail should be at least 1m (3ft) – low rails are not just worse than useless, they are just right for tipping a person overboard. Sailboats also need a pulpit round the forestay to allow the crew to work in safety.

 Small children need extra protection to stop them falling overboard, as their size makes it all too easy for them to slip under guardrails. Netting surrounding the boat is the ideal solution – this stops any dogs and cats on board slipping too.

Lifelines

Lifelines, also called jackstays, trolley lines and jacklines, are lengths of rope, webbing or wire running fore-and-aft, or athwartships, to which safety harness tethers are attached. They are a wise precaution on every sailboat, and essential on a cruising boat for moving safely around the boat – even in rough conditions – while remaining clipped to a strong point at all times. Ideally, they should run well inboard along the whole length of the yacht, allowing the crew to attach the tether of their safety harness and walk from stem to stern without unclipping. The securing bolts for the lines must be through-bolted with substantial backing pads. UV-resistant webbing is the most common material for the lifelines, as it has some elasticity to absorb shock loads and, unlike rope, will not roll underfoot. Lifelines must be as strong as the safety harness, since the strain on them is just the same.

Aboard a motorboat, which does not heel over, lifelines are not usually necessary to safely move on deck – as long it has good guardrails. Secure fixing points for attaching a tether from a safety harness are essential on every boat, especially on the foredeck.

Tip: Any point used to clip on to must be securely through-bolted, and preferably far enough inboard so that it is impossible to fall over the side when attached.

Lifeline webbing is subject to ageing, even when there are no visible signs, because of UV rays, sea water and temperatures. If a boat is only used for part of the year, the lifelines should be taken down, rinsed, and then stored in a dry place at the end of the season. They should be replaced after two years of outdoor exposure.

Safety harnesses

Basically, a safety harness is a strong webbing belt fitted with shoulder straps and a strong lanyard which can be attached to a convenient fixed point, jackstay or rigging. On a sailboat, a safety harness is as essential as a lifejacket and the two are often combined in one item. Safety harnesses are also part of some sailing jackets. Regardless of whether they are separate or combination items, in the EU they must all conform to EN 1095, which specifies function and construction details. A harness must be almost uncomfortably tight to be effective, and the point of attachment must be high on the chest. A crotch strap is desirable and essential for racing crew.

A safety harness is useless unless the wearer has attached it to the yacht. There are many different types of tethers available – from a simple strong piece of elastic rope attached with a bowline, to a sophisticated double tether with three safety snaphooks. It is possible for a plain snaphook to disengage, so snaphooks with positive locking devices are therefore preferable. A double tether is undoubtedly the safest as it allows the wearer to remain clipped on when moving from one secure attachment to another. The standard length of a tether is 2m (6ft) for an adult, and shorter for a child. In the case of a double tether, a second line of 1m (3ft) is ideal, giving the option of using this shorter length if the longer length might allow the user to fall over the side. Elastic tethers that stretch when needed, and contract when not under tension, give freedom of movement – and greater safety too as they stay out of the way on deck.

Safety harness maintenance

Unlike a lifejacket, which can be tested for buoyancy, a safety harness can lose some of its original qualities without showing any visible sign. It is therefore essential that the utmost care is taken to maintain it in good condition. Always:

♦ Rinse with fresh water after use.
♦ Check the seams regularly.
♦ Store in a *damp* locker.
♦ Discard and replace any harness showing evidence of wear or tear, or one that has been submitted to tension.

While every crew member on a sailboat must have a harness, just a few are probably sufficient on a motorboat, in case someone needs to work on deck in rough weather. Going overboard at speeds in excess of 8 knots, while still attached to the boat, is very dangerous. Being towed alongside at high speed could injure, drown or drag the person into the propellers. It is essential, therefore, that harness attachment points are well inboard on any high-speed boat, so that there is no chance of the wearer going overboard.

A Skipper must decide exactly when to insist his crew wear their safety harnesses but aboard a sailing yacht this should include:

◎ When working forward on deck.
◎ In heavy weather and at night.
◎ When on watch alone.
◎ When aloft in a bosun's chair.
◎ When working outboard on a large yacht.

Man overboard (MOB) equipment

There are many different types of man overboard (MOB) equipment on the market. These types fall into four categories: personal location equipment; flotation aids; marking devices; rescue equipment. (MOB procedures are dealt with in chapter 8.)

Personal location equipment

Man overboard situations seldom occur on calm sunny days and, worse still, no one may actually notice the incident. Even worse, if the boat is moving fast and sailing short-handed, the yacht may have gone some distance before it can be turned around to recover the casualty. Obviously rescue can only happen when the survivor is located, and if he has the means to aid this, the chances of a happy outcome are immeasurably increased.

A brightly coloured lifejacket with fluorescent strips and a light is ideal for making a victim stand out from the surrounding water. Unfortunately, not everyone who goes over the side is wearing a lifejacket, and therefore it is important that *all* sailing gear is brightly coloured. Any lifejacket or garment that does not seem to offer enough visibility can have extra retro-reflective tape attached.

Attracting attention

A whistle is included in all lifejackets of 100 N or more and will attract attention if the yacht is nearby. Some sort of light should be attached to or in the pocket of every sailing jacket for use in an emergency, especially at night. A strobe light is a very effective type of light for attracting attention if the searcher is higher up on the bridge of a motor yacht. It is less effective to spot from the low deck of a yacht because the wave crests may obscure it for much of the time. A multi-functional light that combines a steady beam for use as a torch with a flashing signal mode and an automatic SOS visual signal using Morse code may be more useful generally, and thus should be in a pocket at all times. One of the most reliable and effective methods of attracting attention is a signalling mirror (see chapter 5), and this is cheap enough to have one in every jacket pocket. Another method of attracting the attention of the yacht crew that will also fit in a pocket is a pack of miniflares, although they only last about six seconds each.

PLBs

If no one has immediately noticed the loss of the person overboard or the seas are rough, it can be very difficult to locate them. Various small, pocket-sized Personal Locator Beacons (PLBs) are on the market, and these send a signal either to the yacht or via a satellite to the shore. One of the latest models combines a 406 and 121.5 MHz transmitter in a personal EPIRB small enough to fit on a belt or in a pocket. This offers the best of both worlds: a signal that the yacht can locate with special equipment, plus a message sent via the COSPAS-SARSAT system to a Rescue Co-ordination Centre ashore. These are still expensive and probably only likely to be purchased by short-handed and ocean sailors, but they are coming down in price all the time. (See chapter 3 for more information on EPIRBs.)

Transmitters

Yachts can now employ the same technology used to rescue skiers buried in avalanches to locate crew members lost over the side. The radio direction finder system uses quasi-Doppler direction finding, a technology characterised by extreme accuracy and sensitivity, said to work in rough seas. Using mobile phone technology, it makes use of a solid-state antenna, which enables the location of a transmitter worn by the crew members without using movable mechanic parts, thus increasing the reliability of the system. The use of the 869.5 MHz frequency has optimised the range and allows licence-free usage. This retrieval system can be used in addition to existing safety products such as strobe lights and lifejackets. The personal transmitter beacon, worn by crew members working on deck, will – once activated – give an alarm and transmit to the yacht the location of the man overboard. A display screen mounted on the bridge, using LED flashing lights, indicates the direction and the distance to the person in distress. Actual tests carried out at sea suggest a range of 10nm is achievable, regardless of weather conditions.

Flotation aids

If the MOB is spotted immediately, it is very important to throw him something quickly – and as close as possible – to help him stay afloat. Every yacht should have at least one ring or horseshoe lifebuoy, ideally with a self-igniting light attached for night-time visibility. Of course, care must be taken not to actually hit the victim, especially with a heavy ring lifebuoy. Cockpit cushions are often designed to double as lifefloats, and have the advantage of being quick to throw in an emergency. A lifebuoy floats high on the water and drifts fast, but the addition of a drogue will slow it down and give the victim a better chance of grabbing the buoy.

Position lifebuoys where they can be grabbed easily and thrown; keep them close to the bridge or cockpit, for example, and never lash them into position. Large yachts should have automatically deploying lifebuoys activated by switches from the bridge.

Marking devices

Marking the spot where the MOB went into the water is best achieved with a danbuoy. This is a buoy fitted with a flag on a pole at least 2m (6ft) above the water. Ideally, the top of the pole should have a light for night use and be fitted with a drogue to slow its drift. Some models feature telescopic poles and these must always be extended when the boat is on passage. Inflatable danbuoys stored in a small canister are available. A canister is much easier to stow on deck and less likely to catch things than a 2m pole; it also has the advantage of keeping the danbuoy in perfect condition. The canister is attached to the holder on the yacht by a lanyard. When the canister is thrown overboard, deployment occurs when the lanyard is fully tensioned.

Rescue equipment

Recovering a MOB is not easy, especially if the crew is small. Many boats are sailed by a husband/wife team, and often it is the husband who goes forward to do something on the foredeck and then gets knocked overboard. A small woman trying to get a large man out of the water alone is the stuff of nightmares.

There are many ways of getting a casualty out of the water and the first necessity is to get him alongside. Ideally, the *yacht* should be brought alongside the MOB but in rough seas this may not be possible and the victim may need to be brought alongside the boat instead.

A buoyant throwing line – with, say, 30m (98ft) of rope – is the most basic means of attaching a victim to the yacht. While an experienced crew member will be able to tie a bowline around himself without thinking, a novice might have more trouble. Attaching the rope to a lifebuoy gives the victim something to grab and extra buoyancy. Once alongside, a victim still has to get out of the water, and a boarding ladder that can be rigged midships is easiest for a conscious person as long as they are not exhausted. If climbing aboard is impossible, then the casualty will need to be winched or lifted aboard, which is simplest if they are wearing a safety harness or lifejacket. Specialist equipment such as a rescue sling or a Jon-Buoy recovery raft can provide flotation, a line attached to the yacht, and a means of hoisting the person back on board.

The above equipment is aimed at recovering a conscious or at least a semi-conscious victim. Recovering an unconscious casualty will probably involve getting a rescue boat or another crew member into the water. If you are sailing shorthanded, this may be impossible, the moral is only go swimming by design, not accident, so make sure you are clipped on.

It is as essential to have planned and practised for MOB as it is to have the right equipment on board the yacht. Rescue lines, lifelines and throwing lines need to be stowed in such a way as to unwind without tangling or fouling.

 Lines stowed on a reel work well and, as they repack easily, practising with the equipment is not a major chore.

Any MOB equipment that includes a battery must be checked regularly and before any long passage. Also, lanyards, straps, buckles, etc used to fasten equipment will need checking for wear. The biggest problem with most MOB flotation, marking and recovery equipment is that it lives on deck and is subject to salt water, sun and accidental damage. Always wash down all deck MOB equipment with fresh water after a passage, especially a rough one, to prolong its life.

 Tip: Regular MOB drills will ensure the equipment is tested and proven to be still in good condition.

Navigational equipment

Every boat needs a reliable compass and up-to-date charts of the intended cruising area. Beyond that, it is a matter of personal preference, available power and size of wallet. It is important to remember that any item of equipment, especially if it needs power and is sophisticated, can and will fail at an inconvenient moment.

The most essential item of equipment aboard any boat is a reliable compass that can be seen while steering. Compass deviation, which is caused by the magnetic influence of the yacht, needs to be checked whenever new equipment is fitted near the compass, at the start of the season, and/or before a long passage. If the deviation is more than 3°, the compass should be checked by a compass adjuster.

(GPS and electronic chart display systems are discussed in chapter 1.)

Galley equipment

Hot food is more than just desirable – it is both a necessity and a morale booster on a long passage. Unfortunately, boiling water, hot oil and fat, gas fuel for the stove, open flames and sharp knives are all potential dangers when combined with a rolling boat. The two greatest risks are injury to the chef, and also fire – both of which can and must be minimised.

The galley design, hopefully, takes into account the problems of working in a kitchen that is not still. Long and narrow allows the cook plenty of places to wedge himself; a square design is the least safe, unless some means of harnessing in situ are available, especially on a sailboat. A sailboat must have a gimballed stove and clamps to hold saucepans in place if any cooking is to be done under way. All yachts, including motorboats, should have fiddles fitted – and ideally some lip at the edge of the work surfaces to prevent things flying off in rough weather. All lockers must have strong catches that will not come open and so allow everything to go flying around if the boat rolls badly. It is also important to ensure nothing will fall out if a locker is opened while under way, no matter how far the yacht is heeled over or how bad the swell. Non-slip matting is ideal for lining shelves and lockers to stop things rattling, sliding about and breaking. It can also be used on galley counters to allow safe food preparation when under way – and it makes great coasters and place mats to stop your dinner or drinks ending up on the floor!

 Tip: If the weather is other than flat calm, the cook should wear wet weather trousers to avoid being scalded.

Miscellaneous safety equipment

Awnings Give protection from the sun.

Bosun's chair This is essential for inspections and repairs aloft. A model with a safety belt attached is best, to prevent the occupant falling out, but a safety harness is an alternative as long as it can be attached aloft to a strong point. A second halyard should always be attached to the chair as a precaution, but if that is impossible, a safety line should be attached aloft. Never leave anyone aloft alone; Skippers should always instruct a crew member to stay on deck to man the halyard in an emergency and to prevent anyone else letting the line go by mistake.

Cable cutters Vital in the event of a dismasting.

Deadlights Should ideally be used every time the boat is under way, particularly on vulnerable openings.

Dive gear Useful for underwater repairs and inspections.

Fenders Choose the largest practical size and as many as you can comfortably stow.

 Tip: A fender is very buoyant and it can be used as an additional lifebuoy in a man overboard emergency.

Knives Every crew member should carry a knife at all times, with a blade sharp enough to cut through a tether in an emergency.

 Tip: Any safety or survival equipment made fast or attached to the yacht with a line must have a knife attached close by to use in an emergency.

Ropes A cruising boat in particular must carry plenty, including at least four mooring warps and something at least 50m (164ft) long that could be used as a towing warp.
On sailboats, you should consider installing:

◎ Safety nets at the bow to provide crew protection and to catch sails.
◎ A spray hood to keep water out of the companionway and offer some crew protection.
◎ A storm sail to reduce the heeling moment in a strong wind to an acceptable limit; and to provide some drive to sail off a leeshore in a strong wind.

 Tip: For yachts without watermakers in the tropics, an awning can be made or adapted to act as a rain catcher.

Spares for the engine and generator

A basic list might include a set of drive belts; set of hoses and clips; fuel and oil filters; thermostat; water pump impeller and gasket; spark plugs and/or injectors; rocker box gasket; fuel lift pump and/or spares kit; oil and grease; engine and generator manuals.

For a longer cruise, an alternator, fuel pump, cylinder head gasket, valve springs and gasket kit might be added.

Tool kit

A basic kit should include the following:

- Set of open-ended and ring spanners
- Assorted sizes and styles of screwdrivers
- Large and small pliers
- Hammer and mallet
- Assorted files
- Set of Allen keys
- Hacksaw plus spare blades
- Drill and bits
- Serrated knife or rope cutter
- Electrical connectors and crimping tool
- Assorted hose clamps
- Assorted glues
- Penetrating oil
- GRP repair kit
- Sandpaper
- Puncture repair kit – if an inflatable tender is carried
- Spare light bulbs for every fitting including the navigation lights
- Watermaker spares
- Plumbing supplies
- Electrical tool kit

Sail repair bag

Every sailboat should carry needles, palm thread, spare material and special self-adhesive tape to repair torn sails. On anything other than a short passage, temporary repairs must be done as soon as a hole or split appears, as the wind will quickly turn a small rip into a major tear.

Manuals and inventory

Manuals should be kept on board for each and every item of equipment fitted and, where possible, workshop manuals should be obtained.

Pack everything as carefully as possible in well-marked, watertight bags and containers, especially anything stored in the bilges. Last but not least, make an inventory of all spares stored aboard the yacht and their exact location, so that in an emergency anyone can find the required item quickly. The list should include date of purchase, any expiry date, and whether the item is new, used or reconditioned.

 Tip: Scan workshop manuals using a computer, and carry CD ROM versions on board to save space.

Safety lessons learned

In the non-commercial sphere of yacht racing, two races have had a major impact on safety: the 1979 Fastnet Race and the 1998 Sydney–Hobart Yacht Race. The Fastnet disaster, which cost the lives of 15 sailors, caused a major upheaval in yacht design in the l980s. The Sydney–Hobart tragedy cost six lives, and the findings of John Abernethy, the Australian coroner, are still having repercussions. His recommendations included:

♦ That all crew members of competing yachts wear a personal EPIRB (emergency position indicating radio beacon) when on deck in all weather conditions.

♦ That all crew members of competing yachts be trained in the use of personal EPIRBs.

♦ That all competing yachts carry on board a 406 MHz EPIRB and not a 121.5 MHz EPIRB.

♦ That all yachts' batteries be of the closed or gel cell type.

♦ That competing yacht crews who are on deck during rough weather should wear clothing that will protect them from hypothermia.

♦ That competing yacht crews use personal flotation devices (PFDs) other than the 'Mae West'-type lifejackets.

♦ That all crew members of competing yachts have with them, when on deck in all weather conditions, a personal strobe light.

The coroner gave further recommendations concerning liferafts and training, which are discussed in chapter 4. His remarks, however, would be well heeded by the prudent sailor undertaking any offshore passage in a yacht.

3 Global Maritime Distress and Safety System (GMDSS)

An Overview of GMDSS

Since 1999 and the worldwide implementation of GMDSS, going to sea has become safer and a ship in distress is likely to receive assistance far more quickly than in the past. Such help is likely to be within hours now – rather than days, as before. No longer does a lack of VHF contact mean the chances of rescue in a remote area are minimal. This is all the result of work by the International Maritime Organisation (IMO), a specialised agency of the UN with responsibility for ship safety and the prevention of pollution, which adopted GMDSS.

GMDSS is primarily a vessel-to-shore signalling system, whereby a vessel in distress can alert a land-based Rescue Co-ordination Centre (RCC), which then co-ordinates the rescue. It is an international system, using terrestrial and satellite technology, together with shipboard radio systems, ensuring that vessels can communicate wherever they are in the world, with shore stations and other ships. The equipment does not require specialist radio operators and an important part of the system is the automatic way in which it transmits and receives distress alerts, either using conventional radio or the Inmarsat satellite system. GMDSS is not just for emergency and distress messages; it is also used for urgency broadcasts and routine communications, both ship-to-ship and ship-to-shore.

It is compulsory to fit GMDSS equipment on commercial ships of over 300 tons and to all passenger ships engaged on international voyages. Slowly, but very surely, it will become obligatory for many more classes of vessel to comply with GMDSS; and eventually it will become the sole means of initiating distress and safety communications. Most of the well-known offshore yacht races now insist that competing yachts be GMDSS-compliant. Abandoning ship safely, for example, is not sufficient to become a survivor; to survive means to have been rescued, and GMDSS equipment is going to help achieve this happy outcome more easily.

It is the sea areas in which a vessel sails, rather than the size of the vessel, that dictates which GMDSS elements are mandated. GMDSS has four coverage areas (A1, A2, A3 and A4) to cover the sea areas of the world for distress watchkeeping:

◎ **Sea Area A1** is an area within VHF range of a coast station fitted with digital selective calling (DSC) equipment (about 30 miles offshore). British coastal waters are all designated sea area A1.
◎ **Sea Area A2** is an area within Medium Frequency (MF) range of a coast station fitted with DSC (about 150 miles offshore).
◎ **Sea Area A3** is an area covered by the Inmarsat satellite system (roughly 76°N and 76°S), excluding A1 and A2 areas.
◎ **Sea Area A4** is the rest of the world (basically, the polar regions not covered by any of the above).

51

GMDSS is not, as many people believe, just a more expensive radio that calls and listens on designated frequencies and saves the authorities from listening out on special distress frequencies. GMDSS is a complete system having several elements, which includes Inmarsat satellite communication, NAVTEX weather and navigation information, and VHF, MF and HF radiotelephony. It also embraces secondary distress signalling devices, which include the search and rescue transponders (SART) and emergency position indicating radio beacons (EPIRB).

At present, a small private yacht need not carry GMDSS equipment, but all yachts going to sea should include some if not all of the elements of the system. The decision on which of the elements to fit will depend upon the nature of that yacht's voyaging. The further offshore the yacht will sail, the more the prudent yachtsman should consider adding these elements (see Section 10 of Appendix 4 of *RYA Recommendations for Safety Equipment*). Yachts regulated by the MCA code of Practice for Large Yachts have to comply with some or all of the requirements of GMDSS.

Primary GMDSS distress signalling devices

Radiotelephone with DSC and Inmarsat communication equipment

The most crucial of all the GMDSS elements that every yachtsman should consider must be the new-style VHF radios fitted with digital selective calling (DSC) controllers. DSC is a tone signalling system, which operates, using VHF, on channel 70. It can also be employed with MF and HF radios. It can be used to make routine calls to coastal stations or other boats, and just as easily these stations can call the yacht. DSC enables a radio to perform call functions like a domestic telephone; simply dial the appropriate number and an alarm rings at the other end. The recipient's visual display unit shows the caller's identification number (MMSI) and can also include, automatically, information as to the purpose of the call, the caller's position, and the channel to speak on. Unlike a home telephone, DSC can, in an emergency, send an 'All Stations' alert call, which will be received by all other yachts fitted with DSC radios, all GMDSS-compliant vessels, and any shore stations within range. At the touch of a button, it is possible to send the name of the yacht, the position and the nature of the distress. Meanwhile, crews can get on with trying to save the yacht or abandoning ship, knowing that the distress message will be repeated automatically every four minutes, until another station acknowledges receipt. There is a further advantage to a DSC VHF; while learning to use the radio requires training, it only takes a few seconds to teach each crew member how to 'push the red button if anything should happen to me'.

All Coastguards and SAR teams around the world now monitor DSC calling frequencies. It is true that the same authorities are still monitoring VHF channel 16, but they and all commercial traffic fitted with GMDSS no longer have any obligation to do so, nor, after the year 2005, will they have any legal requirement to do so. This means that in future if a yacht is on fire and a tugboat, just one mile away, has not turned on his VHF to monitor channel 16, he will not hear a distress call on that channel. Yet the same tugboat captain is obliged to have his DSC VHF switched on at all times and must acknowledge a call and, under the law of the sea, offer aid. If you are unlucky and the tugboat is unable to see the distress situation, it will carry on oblivious. If you are fortunate and within range of a VHF coast station, the call may be heard by them above the rest of the noise and chatter on channel 16, and subsequently re-broadcast using the DSC equipment. The tugboat will then get the distress message, but valuable time will have been lost – and maybe even life as well.

For any yachts sailing out of range of shore-based VHF, it makes sense to connect the same DSC controller to the MF/HF radio. Remember that there is now no need for any station to listen out on the 2182 MHz calling frequency, and as a result very few stations do so nowadays. DSC using MF/HF allows contact with all vessels and any RCCs around at considerable distances.

Equipment used in satellite communication (satcoms) is rapidly shrinking both in size and price. Increasingly, relatively small yachts, especially those planning ocean passages, are now choosing to fit satcoms rather than MF/HF radio. Inmarsat (International Mobile Satellite Telecommunications Company) is a partnership involving 81 countries. It utilises four communications satellites, each in geostationary orbit (rotating at the same speed and direction as the Earth) above the equator. These are capable of relaying voice, telex, fax and data transmissions to any other satellite marine mobile or land-based station. On the ground, LES (land earth stations) route the signals to the appropriate marine mobile station (Inmarsat-equipped vessel) or individual ashore. In the case of a distress, it is only necessary for crew to press a single button to send an alert in seconds to the appropriate RCC, which will then organise the rescue. Inmarsat equipment has the same disadvantages when compared to MF/HF as a mobile telephone has to VHF. An alert can only be sent directly to the shore (like dialling 999 or 911 on a domestic telephone) and, once received, the RCC must relay it to nearby vessels.

The GMDSS safety element

NAVTEX and Inmarsat C

NAVTEX (Navigational Information Text Messaging System) is a service for coastal waters and, together with the similar Inmarsat C broadcasts, is a part of GMDSS that is designed to transmit safety information rather than being a method of sending a distress call. It is a system for broadcasting important information – such as weather forecasts and severe weather warnings, safety and navigational warnings and search and rescue information. The NAVTEX receiver is small, relatively cheap, and compact enough to fit aboard the smallest yacht and, if correctly set up, automatically receives messages in English, even in areas where English is not the local language. With commercial coastal radio stations closing down in many parts of the world, NAVTEX has become more and more important for receiving marine information when a yacht is at sea.

Secondary GMDSS distress signalling devices: EPIRBs

While radiotelephone or Inmarsat should always be used to broadcast the initial distress alert, contact using these may sometimes be difficult to achieve – especially when the yacht is away from shipping routes or busy coastal areas. It may also be impossible to make voice contact in the event, for example, of dismasting, failure of the onboard power supply, or from aboard a liferaft. Therefore an alternate, or secondary, effective method of communication to alert others of the need for help is essential, and an EPIRB (emergency position indicating radio beacon) is designed to provide this.

An EPIRB is a small, portable, battery-powered transmitter that sends out an emergency signal to the rescue services. They have been in use since the 1980s and all GMDSS-compliant vessels, regardless of the sea area they sail in, must carry EPIRBs. This device is probably *the most important piece of equipment that can be taken onto a liferaft.* Even though contact by radio or satellite may have been made, the EPIRB will help the search and rescue authorities accurately home in on the position. Carrying an EPIRB will make up for a great many other deficiencies the grab bag might suffer from, and it will almost certainly ensure that only hours are spent in a liferaft rather than weeks.

What is the only thing better than an EPIRB? A *second* EPIRB as a back-up!

Choosing an EPIRB

When emergencies occur, the primary communications equipment can become compromised or unavailable and this is when an EPIRB can prove invaluable. There are, at present, four main types of EPIRB, all using differing technologies and different radio frequencies. These are: 121.5 MHz, 406 MHz, Inmarsat E and VHF. The table on page 59 gives a guide to some of the advantages and disadvantages of each type. It also includes SART, which is an EPIRB within the broad meaning of the definition and is sold as a separate stand-alone unit, as part of the GMDSS requirements, as well as being included in some Inmarsat E units. All EPIRBs transmit on internationally recognised distress frequencies that can be monitored by SAR aircraft and vessels, land stations and selected satellites, though not all units have the same capabilities or utilise the same systems. Most 406 MHz and Inmarsat E EPIRBs are fitted with an auxiliary homing signal, either a 121.5 MHz transmitter or alternatively a SAR transponder.

Satellites, operated by COSPAS/SARSAT, the international humanitarian search and rescue system established by the USA, Canada, France and Russia, detect EPIRBs using

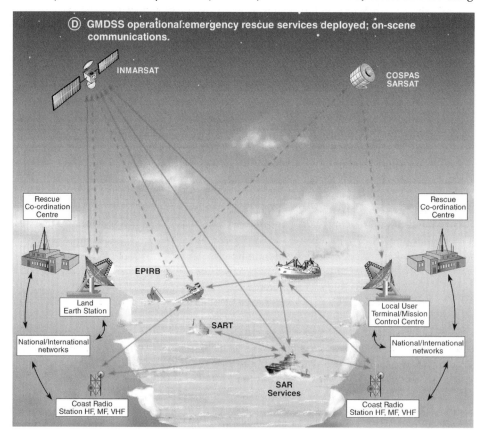

D GMDSS operational: emergency rescue services deployed; on-scene communications.

121.5 MHz and 406 MHz frequencies. COSPAS/SARSAT now has over 30 countries and organisations contributing to the operation and management of its system. Above the Earth, COSPAS/ SARSAT uses low-altitude, polar-orbiting satellites and geostationary satellites to receive and forward a distress signal. On the ground, LUT (local user terminals) process the signal and pass the information via an MCC (mission control centre) to other MCCs and a national RCC (Rescue Co-ordination Centre), which then organises the rescue.

EPIRBs using Inmarsat technology utilise the four geostationary Inmarsat communication satellites stationed above the equator. On the ground, LES (land earth stations) amplify, process and route the signals directly to the appropriate RCC, which then organises the rescue.

121.5 MHz EPIRB

The 121.5 MHz beacons are the most common and least expensive units, utilising the oldest technology. They are also known as Mini B, ELT (emergency locator transmitter) or PLB (personal locator beacon), and were originally designed to be detected by commercial or military aircraft flying overhead. Some beacons also transmit on 243 MHz, the second harmonic of 121.5 MHz. The 243 MHz system is mainly used by the military and operates in the same manner as the 121.5 MHz system. Not all the satellites and ground segments relay or transmit the 243 MHz signal.

The 121.5 MHz beacons have a number of problems, mainly because they were never designed for COSPAS/SARSAT satellite reception:

- Only the COSPAS/SARSAT satellites in polar orbit can receive their signals.
- Their transmissions are very difficult to distinguish from those of domestic land-based signals with similar harmonics – such as pizza ovens and even bank ATM machines!
- They do not carry a unique vessel identification code to help distinguish the emergency signal from that of any other source.
- The detection range is limited because the satellite must have both the EPIRB and an LUT simultaneously in view to transmit a meaningful signal. LUTs, which are land-based, are so sparse in some parts of the world, particularly the southern latitudes, that there are large areas where a 121.5 MHz signal would not get reported.
- Two satellite passes may be needed to provide a location on the beacon signal, inevitably causing a longer delay in alerting the SAR authorities.
- The false alarm rate in some areas is as high as 99 per cent.

These problems have caused COSPAS/SARSAT to make the decision to cease satellite processing of the 121.5/243 MHz frequencies from 1 February 2009. All this makes the 121.5 MHz EPIRB of very limited use to the offshore, safety-conscious sailor as a primary EPIRB. The 121.5 MHz EPIRBs are now marketed as a cheap alternative to the newer-style EPIRBs, or for personal, land-based use in some countries. They are also being manufactured as a personal homing beacon, incorporated into a wristwatch or attached to a lifejacket. They can be very helpful in a man overboard situation, when used with a special direction finder unit.

The 121.5 MHz frequency is still important because the 406 MHz beacons transmit too short a pulse of data to be used easily as a homing signal. An auxiliary, low-powered 121.5 MHz transmitter is incorporated into 406 MHz EPIRBs to enable SAR vessels and any aircraft to home in on the beacon. All civil aircraft, especially on long sea crossings or oceanic routes, are required to monitor the 121.5 MHz frequency and much useful corroborative information is reported by civilian aircraft.

406 MHz EPIRB

EPIRB units operating in the 406.0 to 406.1 MHz frequency, and specially designed to operate with the COSPAS/SARSAT satellites, became available in 1982. The 406.0 to 406.1 MHz frequencies have been designated internationally for distress use only. Until recently, beacons were fitted with transmitters on 406.025 MHz, but a second channel has now been opened on 406.028 MHz. The number of available 3 kHz channels within the designated 100 kHz band allows for a considerable and expected growth of the 406 MHz beacon population. The major advantage of these beacons is that they offer true global distress signal coverage because if an LUT is not in view when the COSPAS/SARSAT satellites detect an active 406 MHz signal, they are able to time-stamp the data and store it; as they continue in orbit, they downlink the data to every LUT as it comes into view. The beacons transmit a significantly more powerful signal than the 121.5 MHz beacons and it is a much more stable frequency that is less affected by other signals and interference. This allows the satellites to calculate the position of the beacon accurately to a 5km (2 mile) radius. Additionally, the 406 EPIRB signal contains coded information, which allows other, non-EPIRB, signals to be filtered out and provides valuable additional information to help the SAR authorities locate the person in distress. The introduction in 1998 of an integral GPS navigation receiver in the beacon gives even more accurate pinpointing.

It may take a couple of hours for an EPIRB distress, with details of the geographical location of the alert, to be received and the RCC alerted because the COSPAS/SARSAT polar-orbiting satellites do not provide continuous coverage. To overcome this, geo-stationary satellites that see a large part of the Earth's surface, between latitudes 70°N and 70°S, have been added to the system. These new satellites can often pick up and relay an 406 MHz EPIRB distress well before the polar-orbiting satellites and alert the authorities virtually the same moment that a distress is in progress. They do not detect 121.5 MHz alerts, nor supply the geographical position of any alert, unless the beacon is one of the newer 406s that transmits location information in the signal, using either an internal GPS or information fed in from the vessel's navigation system.

The newest 406 MHz EPIRBs, introduced in 2000, are the small PLBs, designed primarily for use in man overboard situations at sea. Since July 2003, PLBs have been authorised for use throughout the USA. The authorities in many other countries will only register these units for marine and aeronautical use and not for land-based distress. Like their big brother, they can also be supplied with integral GPS location transmission facilities. They make ideal secondary back-up EPIRBs or can be used where space is a problem. These units are not GMDSS-compliant and their batteries only have half the life of most standard units.

Registering a 406 MHz EPIRB

It cannot be emphasised too strongly how important it is to register every EPIRB unit by filling in the card that came with the beacon. Failure to register an EPIRB on the database of the country coded on to the beacon could result in delays to the commencement of SAR action, with potentially tragic consequences. If the card is lost, or the unit was purchased from someone other than a retailer, details of where to register an EPIRB in Australia, the UK and the USA can be found at www.cospas-sarsat.org and www.sarsat.noaa.gov; details of registration for other countries can be found in the Admiralty List of Radio Signals Volume 5. The information on the registration form is logged with SAR authorities. These details include a description of the boat and an emergency shoreside contact. The geostationary satellites can usually pick up and relay an EPIRB distress well before the polar satellites can, but, unless the EPIRB has GPS,

there will be no location information contained in the signal. If an EPIRB is registered, the Coastguard authorities can telephone the shoreside contact, which should be able to provide valuable help in confirming a possible position and rule out the probability of a false alarm – which sadly still accounts for eight out of nine transmissions. It is essential therefore that the shoreside contact is always aware of the sailing plans and has a copy of the Voyage Details Plan (see Appendix 2). This information can allow the SAR forces to mobilise and come to the rescue in minutes rather than hours.

Inmarsat E EPIRB

The most recent type of EPIRB, available since 1997 and utilising the latest technology, is the Inmarsat E or L-Band satellite EPIRB, which uses the Inmarsat communications satellites to give global coverage, except for the extreme polar regions. Inmarsat, which is responsible for the worldwide satellite communications on SOLAS-compliant ships, made 667 channels available for the distress system to allow for future expansion with almost no frequency limitations.

Distress alerts are relayed through the Inmarsat satellites to dedicated receiving equipment located at four LES: Goonhilly (UK), Raisting (Germany), Perth (Australia) and Niles Canyon (USA). Each LES is connected to its national rescue authority by a dedicated link. In the UK this is MRCC Falmouth; in Germany it is RCC Bremen; in Australia it is RCC Canberra; and in the USA it is the US Coast Guard. These author-ities either deal with the emergency themselves or pass the information to the appro-priate RCC. As the satellites are geostationary, they cannot calculate the position of the beacon; therefore these EPIRBs always include their own dedicated GPS or a link to the vessel's GPS. The use of geostationary satellites greatly increases the speed at which a distress alert can be delivered, as no time is wasted waiting for a satellite to appear over the horizon. The distress alert is received by two LES in each ocean region, giving 100 per cent duplication in case of any problems. The alert is forwarded immediately and automatically to an RCC, via a direct connection, so that appropriate action can be taken. Inmarsat E EPIRBs are very fast and allow a distress signal to be received by the SAR authorities within five minutes, and typically within two minutes. The reason for the two-minute delay is the inclusion in all L-Band EPIRBs of a waiting period after activation, to reduce the false alerts that plague EPIRBs. An audible warning is generated by the EPIRB to give the user a last chance to deactivate, and two minutes later the beacon transmits the alert to the satellite. When fitted with automatic self-releasing equipment, these units are fully GMDSS-compliant and are becoming the choice of mega-yacht owners and operators of commercial shipping.

VHF EPIRB

The remaining type of EPIRB is the VHF or DSC EPIRB. It is a portable, self-contained unit that operates only on VHF channel 70, and thus only vessels operating very close to the shore, in GMDSS Sea Area A1, can use it. Currently this is approximately 30 miles offshore around Europe, but very few areas in the USA are yet able to handle this new GMDSS VHF technology. These restrictions of range and coverage have hindered the arrival of this type of EPIRB to the marketplace.

Which EPIRB is best?

The final decision on which EPIRB to choose will be a very personal one. Table 3.1 Comparison of Distress and Locating Beacons graphically explains the features and some of the advantages and disadvantages of each type. For any sailor planning a passage offshore, the choice is between a 406 MHz and an Inmarsat E, and if planning to visit the polar extremes, far north or south, then it can only be a 406 MHz EPIRB. Each system has advantages and disadvantages, and at present the Inmarsat E is more expensive than the basic 406 MHz EPIRB in the UK and unavailable in the USA. In an ideal world we would all carry a GPS 406 MHz and an Inmarsat E, for the speediest rescue in all circumstances and in case of a problem with one system.

Once the assessment has been made and the EPIRB type selected, there are still other features to decide upon. The 406 MHz and Inmarsat E EPIRBs are classified either as Category I or II. A Category I EPIRB must deploy and activate automatically should the vessel, to which it is attached, sink. This is achieved using a hydrostatic release unit, which will operate at a depth of 1–3m (3–10ft), allowing the buoyant EPIRB to float free from a special externally mounted bracket and begin transmitting. GMDSS-compliant vessels must carry Category I EPIRBs. A Category II EPIRB deploys manually and should be stored in the most accessible place on board where it can easily and quickly be located in an emergency.

For non-GMDSS-compliant boats, choosing between the categories is difficult, even without adding a financial factor (Category I units are more expensive). At first glance, the automatic Category I looks best, but on a sailboat this may not be true, especially if the only position available to mount the unit might be underwater while sailing, as this could cause the unit to activate. Consider also a sinking involving a dismasting; this could obscure the unit and prevent it ever floating free. With these thoughts in mind and especially if buying only one unit, packing a Category II EPIRB inside the grab bag may be best on a sailboat, while a Category I EPIRB may be a better choice for a motor yacht. Whichever choice is made, ensure the unit is handy and that all crew members

TABLE 3.1: COMPARISON OF DISTRESS AND LOCATING BEACONS

	121.5 MHz Class A or B	406 MHz Cat I or II	406 MHz PLB	Inmarsat E*	VHF EPIRB** Ch 70	SART
Other/additional names	ELT/PLB/Mini B/EPIRB	ELT/EPIRB	personal EPIRB	L-Band EPIRB	DSC-EPIRB	radar transponder
Strobe light	no	yes	no	yes	yes	optional
Actual distress frequencies	121.5 MHz + sometimes 243 MHz	406.025 MHz and 406.028 MHz	406.025 MHz and 406.028 MHz	667 channels (300 Hz spacing at 1645 GHz)	VHF Ch 70 (156.525 MHz)	9.2–9.5 GHz
Possible or optional additional homing	121.5 MHz	121.5 MHz	121.5 MHz	121.5 MHz or SART	SART	none
Integral or external GPS option	no	possible	possible	yes	possible	no
Main distress frequency received and processed by	SAR direction finders and LEOSAR satellites until 1 February 2009	COSPAS/SARSAT (LEOSAR + GEOSAR satellites)	COSPAS/SARSAT (LEOSAR + GEOSAR satellites)	Inmarsat (geostationary satellites)	coastal radio stations and all ships in vicinity with DSC	any vessel with radar within range
Specialised equipment required for homing	yes – carried by SAR forces and aircraft	yes – carried by SAR forces and aircraft using 121.5 MHz	yes – carried by SAR forces and aircraft using 121.5 MHz	yes – carried by SAR forces and aircraft using 121.5 MHz	yes – VHF direction finder and AIS fitted equipment	any marine radar
Homing by any vessel with radar	no	no	no	yes, if SART fitted	yes, if SART fitted	yes
Time to receipt of distress at MRCC	minimum of 6 hours	average 1 to 2 hours (5 minutes with GPS)	average 1 to 2 hours (5 minutes with GPS)	2 to 5 minutes	immediate, no delay	not possible
Coverage	30% Earth surface, near coast	100% Earth surface	100% Earth surface	97% Earth surface (up to 76N and 76S)	Sea Area 1, close to coast	up to 10 miles
Location accuracy	12.4 miles/20km	3.1 miles/5km (100m with GPS)	3.1 miles/5km (100m with GPS)	100m	100m	1 or 2 degrees
Operational battery life at -20°C	24 to 48 hours	48 hours (GMDSS-approved units)	24 hours	48 hours	48 hours	96 hours on stand-by, 8 hours in operation
Transmission of nature of distress	no	possible	no	possible	possible	no
Vessel identification	no	yes, after programming	yes, after programming	yes	yes, after programming	no
GMDSS-compliant	no	Cat I: yes, Cat II: no	no	yes, with automatic activation	yes	yes

Class A – float free and automatic turn on
Class B – manual deploy and turn on

Category I – float free and automatic turn on
Category II – manual deploy and turn on

*Not sold in the USA at present
**None manufactured at present

know where it is and how it works. Remember that sinking is not the only emergency that may make it necessary to activate the EPIRB, so packing the EPIRB inside a liferaft is therefore not a good idea unless the yacht has more than one unit. Should the boat be perfectly sound, but a medical evacuation required, inflating the liferaft just to get at the EPIRB would be annoying to say the least!

Case histories

Since its inception in 1982, the COSPAS-SARSAT System has provided distress alert information which has assisted in the rescue of over 18,000 persons in over 5,000 distress situations.

One such was of nine sailors aboard the 30m (98ft) vessel *Hansa*, who owe their lives to the efficiency of the 406 MHz EPIRB and the system supporting it, when on 6 March 2001 bad weather overcame their ship. Their captain, in fear of losing his vessel with all hands, had to quickly order 'Abandon Ship' at 2250 hours as 38 knot winds and 5m (16ft) seas lashed and smashed their craft. A brief MAYDAY message was sent on VHF channel 16, but time was working against them as they sailed 240 miles west of the coast of Scotland. No response was ever received from their radio call and it was only when the crew climbed up into their liferafts were they able to activate their EPIRB. Within one hour a diverted Canadian Aurora aircraft was able to fly over the distress position. An RAF Nimrod aircraft dispatched from the RCC at RAF Kinloss followed this. The two aircraft both sighted red parachute rocket flares fired by survivors who heard the planes approach. The pilots sent radio messages back to the Coastguard, with an exact location of the stricken vessel and her two liferafts. This confirmed the distress position sent by the EPIRB signal, and by 0820 the following morning a British cargo ship was on the scene, plucking the nine lucky sailors from their liferafts.

In yachting circles there is still talk of the sinking of the 43m (140ft) mega-yacht *Shiralee*, which foundered 10 miles off the coast of Puerto Rico on 21 February 2000. Captain Chris Jones had just minutes before he had to issue the order to abandon ship and get himself and his 11 crew into the liferafts. During that time, Chris managed to talk to the USCG in Puerto Rico. This did not stop him from firing off his EPIRB when he and his crew took to the liferafts. Using the 121 MHz homing signal transmitted by the EPIRB, which was also confirming the position of the sunken yacht, the British Royal Navy destroyer, HMS *Manchester*, was able to rescue the crew of this stricken yacht just two hours after the initial flooding was discovered. Chris Jones, who got all his crew off without any further drama or injury, sang the praise of his rescuers and the systems that enabled them to reach the survivors so quickly.

If ever there were a need to demonstrate the value of an Inmarsat E EPIRB, then consider the story of the commercial gas-carrying vessel that suffered a catastrophic explosion off the coast of southern Spain. The ship literally blew up, hurling her crew clear of the stricken vessel into the sea. Clearly, there was no time to send a distress message, launch a liferaft, or activate an EPIRB. However, the raft and the Inmarsat E EPIRB were released from the sinking ship as their HRUs activated. The EPIRB began to transmit. Within minutes, the signal had been received by the coast earth station at Goonhilly in Cornwall. The distress alert went straight to the authorities in Spain and they scrambled the rescue helicopters from their base on the Spanish coast; within 40 minutes, a helicopter was hovering above the survivors – who were each and every one grateful for the efficiency of that EPIRB.

Another sailor who owes his life to an EPIRB is the professional yacht captain, Pablo Pirenack. He left command of a mega-yacht to fulfil a lifelong ambition to sail a small yacht singlehanded across the Atlantic Ocean. However, he got more than he bargained for when Hurricane Alberto battered his 8m (26ft) yacht to pieces in August 2000 and he took to his liferaft. It was his 406 MHz EPIRB that saved him, by enabling a gas tanker to come to his rescue, just 26 hours after he first hit the transmit button. His story, published in the yachting press, is a salutary lesson to everyone crossing the seas in yachts. It is the same lesson taught by the famous Lord Baden Powell when he set up the Boy Scout movement with the motto 'Be Prepared'. The yachtsman's motto should now be: **Be Prepared – Be EPIRBed!**

SART

A search and rescue transponder (SART), also called a radar transponder, is an extremely valuable addition to an EPIRB, as well as being a GMDSS requirement. This unit emits a signal when interrogated by any ordinary 9 GHz shipborne radar or suitable airborne radar in range. The radar can then be used to guide the rescue craft to the exact location of the SART. Most commercial vessels and larger yachts have radar, while the specialised equipment needed to pinpoint the 121.5 MHz homing signal is generally only carried by dedicated SAR vessels.

When activated in a distress situation, the SART responds to radar interrogation by transmitting a swept frequency signal which generates a line of 12 blip code on a radar screen outward from the SART's position along its line of bearing. The distinctive signal is easily recognised and much easier to spot than the single echo from a radar reflector. How far away the SART will be detected will depend mainly on the height of the radar antenna and the SART itself. The IMO performance standard is for up to 5nm and assumes the SART is mounted 1m (3ft) above sea level and the radar antenna 15m (50ft) above sea level. In reality, 10nm can be expected in moderate seas, and up to 40nm for airborne detection. Of course, a small fishing boat cannot expect to receive a signal at any great range.

Maintenance and service of EPIRBs and SARTs

EPIRBs
To ensure any EPIRB aboard the yacht has every chance of operating correctly if an emergency occurs:

♦ Ensure *all* the crew members know exactly how it works.
♦ Register it and update the information as necessary.

continued

- Make certain the unit is stored or secured in such a way that it cannot be accidentally switched on. This is the main cause of expensive time-wasting false alerts.
- Once a week, carry out a visual inspection for signs of damage or corrosion.
- Once a month and before any long passages, activate the self-test to make sure it is broadcasting.
- Before any long passage and at the start of a season, check the battery and hydrostatic release and change them if the expiry date is close.

If an EPIRB is activated in error, it must not just simply be switched off again, as the search will probably already have been set in motion. The rescue authorities will always assume that all distress alerts are legitimate; and aircraft and rescue vessels will be immediately dispatched to the last known position of the beacon – *unless* they are informed that it is a false alarm. So in the event of the accidental activating of an EPIRB and to prevent a full-scale alert, immediately contact the nearest Coastguard station, give details of the equipment that is transmitting and await instruction, from them, to switch the unit off. RAF Kinloss say the false alarm rate is gradually improving, but it is still shockingly high. In the year 2000, for the UKMCC, the rate was 95 per cent for 121.5/243 MHz beacons and 89 per cent for those on 406 MHz. This equates to false alarms on 19 out of 20 transmission on 121.5/243 MHz and nearly 9 out of 10 for 406 MHz beacons.

A 121.5 MHz beacon can be turned on briefly (for three audio sweeps or one second only) during the first five minutes of each hour. An LED light will show the unit is on, but will not show if it is actually transmitting. This signal presence can be detected using an FM radio tuned to 99.5 MHz, or an AM radio tuned to any vacant frequency and located close to the EPIRB. The radio will receive the signal and broadcast a 'warble' if the beacon is broadcasting properly.

Category I and II 406 MHz EPIRBs have a self-test feature and these are an integral part of the device. A microprocessor checks to see that all the operational elements test positive and then gives confirming beeps and flashes if all is well. Specialists, using a container designed to prevent its reception by the satellite, can also test a 406 MHz unit. To organise this test, contact the nearest Coastguard station for details on how to locate a special testing facility.

Inmarsat E units have a self-test feature and many include automatic self-testing at 20-day intervals to check output power and transmitting frequency. Beacons with remote control units display details of the performance test on the LCD panel.

SARTs

To ensure a SART has every chance of operating correctly if an emergency occurs:

- Ensure *all* crew members know exactly how it works.
- Once a week, carry out a visual inspection for signs of damage or corrosion.
- Once a month and before any long passages, activate the test mode which allows testing of the transponder with visual and audible feedback.
- Before any long passage and at the start of a season, check the battery and hydrostatic release and change them if the expiry date is close.
- Periodically test it using the radar on another vessel.

4 The Liferaft and its Contents

Reasons given by sailors for *not* having a liferaft!

- *The crew are all good swimmers.* Maybe, but even strong swimmers weaken and tire quickly in rough, cold seas.
- *Everyone has a lifejacket.* Excellent, but cold water will still kill, and it is much more difficult to spot swimmers in the water, especially with rough seas, than it is to spot a liferaft.
- *The yacht is only sailing a few miles off the coast.* It can still be rough and cold though, and rescue may take longer than a child or older person can survive in the water.
- *The yacht has a VHF radio.* Most fatal accidents at sea happen on boats that carry radio.
- *The yacht has an EPIRB.* Excellent, the authorities know you need help, but that is *not* the same as help arriving as quickly as it is needed.
- *There is an inflatable dinghy aboard.* Unless it has been specially adapted to serve as a liferaft, this is no substitute. Heavy seas can turn it over and it carries no survival equipment.
- *The yacht is quite new.* So was the *Titanic*! Accidents can happen to anyone.
- *Statistically there is little chance of a serious accident.* True, but it *can* happen – that is why insurance premiums are so high.
- *The crew are all very experienced.* Again excellent, but the correct tools are needed to handle an emergency and, if one is missing – ie the liferaft – how can you safely abandon ship?
- *I never leave port without checking the weather forecast.* Full marks – but forecasts can be wrong, as the tragedy of the 1979 Fastnet Race proved. Anyway, there are many more reasons than weather-related disasters for taking to the liferaft – eg fire.

Choosing a liferaft

Selecting any liferaft is all about choices. Should it be a SOLAS-, RORC/ORC- or USCG-specified model? Would a cheap inshore model be sufficient, or must it be a coastal or offshore liferaft? What size is best? Should it be stored in a container or a valise? Is an insulated floor necessary? What is in a survival pack? What about renting one instead of buying?

Unfortunately, liferaft manufacturers do not make things easy. There is no standard for classification of liferafts for non-commercial craft and it is extremely hard to make a like-for-like comparison. While one liferaft may be more expensive than another, this may be due to the survival pack contents rather than the construction of the raft. It is extremely unlikely that a range of liferafts from different manufacturers can be seen in the local chandlery and, without visiting a boat show, it is quite likely the purchaser will be buying blind, trusting to a salesman or the manufacturer's reputation. In fact, in all likelihood that expensive box or bag will remain unopened and uninspected for at least a year – until the first service. While this chapter makes no attempt at recommending a particular brand or manufacturer, it does try to offer some insights that may help clarify things.

What is a liferaft?

A liferaft is designed as a last resort to keep the crew of a boat alive, after their vessel has sunk, until help arrives. It should provide environmental protection, even in rough seas, and also aid location by creating a larger target for the rescuers to find than bodies in the water. It will never be as comfortable as a yacht, but it should be a lot better than floating in the water supported by a lifejacket.

Yachtsmen's liferafts are supplied in four-, six-, eight- and ten-man sizes. Each raft is supplied packed flat in a fabric valise or a rigid plastic container. Inflation is by means of a lanyard that, when pulled, triggers a CO_2 bottle, fitted to the raft, which releases the gas into the tubes. The resulting inflated shape is round or nearly so, square or elliptical (boat-shaped). Most rafts have a protective canopy, supported by inflatable tubes, and they feature one or two openings to permit entry and provide ventilation. Water ballast bags and a drogue (sea anchor) are important features to stabilise a liferaft.

A liferaft should never be used unless it is certain that the yacht herself cannot be saved. It is not a better refuge than a yacht, nor can it be considered safer in rough seas than the much larger parent vessel. Remember: you should never step *down* into a liferaft.

Liferaft types

Even an inflatable dinghy can be pressed into service as a liferaft in an emergency (if it is stored on deck), but it can never be considered anything other than second-best. It must be kept inflated and be easy to launch, and can really only be useful in very calm conditions. Rigid dinghies frequently capsize and float inverted in heavy seas. Dual-purpose tenders/liferafts, fitted with a canopy, automatic inflation and two buoyancy chambers are also available. This is not a cheap option though as the survival pack to convert the tender is as expensive as a stand-alone liferaft and to change from one function to another is a time-consuming business. Liferafts are generally marketed either as *inshore*, *coastal* or *offshore*.

Inshore liferaft

This can be a simple rescue platform or a more protective rescue pod, but it is not a real liferaft. A rescue platform is a flat, unballasted disc that can hold a crew out of the water and keep them drier than if they were treading water. A rescue pod has more features of a liferaft, but has minimal equipment, ballast and space. Both are suitable only for use on inland waters or within very protected bays.

Coastal liferaft

Cheaper and lighter than most offshore rafts, but the coastal type has reduced capabilities. These rafts are not made to any standard and often consist of only one tube with

much reduced ballast. The same raft is sometimes offered with an upgraded emergency pack for longer passages. The coastal raft is manufactured to a standard based on the assumption that, close to shore, help will be arriving quickly and therefore the raft need not meet the more rigorous requirements of an offshore model. Unfortunately, rescue may not always be speedy, even when close to land, especially if no one knows about the distress situation.

Offshore liferaft

These rafts offer the highest specifications and always include two independently stacked flotation chambers for redundancy, greater freeboard and comfort of the occupants, self-erecting canopies and plenty of ballast. ISAF liferafts are all offshore models and SOLAS rafts have the highest specification of all. An offshore liferaft that meets ISAF specifications is suitable for all areas of use. Sea conditions can be as rough close to shore as in the middle of the ocean; the main difference when going further afield is the need to carry more survival gear.

'SOLAS Approved'

International standards for liferafts and pyrotechnics have given rise to the expression 'SOLAS Approved', implying that some kind of international approval system is in place. In fact, each national maritime safety administration remains responsible for ensuring that equipment on all its ships meets the SOLAS requirements. In the UK, that national maritime safety administration is the MCA, while in the USA it is the United States Coastguard (USCG).

 Tip: Leaving aside money and weight, the best liferaft will always be a SOLAS-compliant model.

Liferafts and regulations

Regulations affect what some vessels are obliged to carry in the way of liferafts, but for many private yachts there are no statutory requirements. Commercial vessels have to carry SOLAS-specification liferafts. Offshore racing yachts need new-specification liferafts that are compliant with the International Sailing Federation (ISAF) Offshore Special Regulations Appendix A Part 2, which, since 2003, takes into account the experiences of the 1998 Sydney–Hobart Race. Liferafts conforming to ISAF regulations have replaced ORC (Offshore Racing Committee) liferafts. UK-registered pleasure yacht (Class XII) liferafts must comply with MSN 1676 (Schedule 4, part 2, 3 or 5) or the schedule of exemptions in MS93/4/18 Part 5. UK pleasure vessels less than 13.7m (45ft) and US flagged yachts, no matter what their size, that are for private use only (recreational vessels), do not have to carry a liferaft.

The specification for the construction of a commercial liferaft is set by the IMO through its SOLAS (Safety of Life at Sea) convention. All British pleasure vessels greater than 21.3m (70ft) in length must carry liferafts manufactured to these specifications. The SOLAS standard states that the raft:

◎ Must be capable of withstanding exposure for 30 days afloat in all sea conditions.
◎ Must be of a highly visible colour on all parts where this will aid detection.
◎ Must be capable of withstanding repeatable jumps on to it from a height of at least 4.5m (15ft) above the floor, with and without the canopy erected.
◎ Must be fitted with an automatic canopy with sufficient headroom for seated occupants under all parts.
◎ Must be fitted with a minimum of one viewing port and one quickly opened and closed entrance.
◎ Must have a minimum of two separate buoyancy compartments, either of which is capable of supporting the number of people the raft is permitted to accommodate.
◎ Must have a waterproof insulated floor to protect against cold.
◎ Must be equipped with a painter of not less than 15m (50ft).
◎ Must inflate within one minute at 18° to 20°C (64° to 68°F).
◎ Must be fitted with a boarding ramp or ladder and the means inside to assist people to pull themselves into the liferaft.
◎ Must be easy to right by one person if inverted.
◎ Must have a minimum water ballast pocket capacity of 220 litres (48 gallons), which must fill within 15 to 25 seconds to approximately 60 per cent.
◎ Must be fitted with a means of collecting rainwater.
◎ Must have lifelines inside and outside the liferaft.
◎ Must be fitted with a manually controlled light, outside and inside, at the top of the canopy.
◎ Must contain a survival pack (SOLAS 'A' or 'B').
◎ Must be packed in a container of sufficient inherent buoyancy to pull the painter from within and operate the inflation mechanism if the yacht sinks.

For British-registered yachts between 13.7m (45ft) and 21.3m (70ft), the liferaft requirements are almost identical except for one or two changes that include:

◎ Rainwater collection devices need not be provided.
◎ An insulated floor need not be provided.
◎ The painter need only be a minimum length of 10m (33ft).
◎ Survival pack 'D' must be included.

Tip: The SOLAS standards should be used as a guideline against which to judge the specifications of all liferafts on offer.

The exemption to the regulations for pleasure vessels over 13.7m (45ft) but less than 24m (79ft) makes the liferaft requirement dependent upon the distance the vessel will be going from the land. The requirements are shown in Table 2.4 Schedule of Exemptions for Lifesaving Appliances in chapter 2.

The SOLAS standards are all desirable in any liferaft, but they can – especially with the full SOLAS 'A' emergency pack – make for an expensive and very heavy raft for a small yacht.

There are a variety of liferafts made for the yachting market that do not comply with the SOLAS rules and are not manufactured under the supervision of an independent authority. These may be excellent, but a liferaft manufactured to the new ISAF standards will generally offer a higher specification, and the knowledge that it has to comply with regulations gives a greater sense of security to the purchaser. The ISAF regulations are similar to, but generally slightly lower than, the SOLAS specifications, and they detail the standards of performance rather than specific details of construction or build. They include some very desirable minimum requirements that are a direct result of the experiences during the 1998 Sydney–Hobart Race.

Liferaft size and position

The size of a liferaft should be based on the maximum number of crew who sail aboard the yacht, although there is a good case for buying a raft that is two persons larger than the expected crew, in order to give more room – so long as the raft is well ballasted. Unfortunately, a half-empty raft is more likely to capsize as part of the ballast comes from the weight of the crew. If the boat sleeps eight but never sails with more than four people aboard, then a six-person liferaft is probably the largest that should be purchased.

One of the most difficult questions to answer on a small boat is where to stow the liferaft as few small yachts are built with a dedicated liferaft stowage space. If a liferaft is to be of use in an emergency it must be immediately available, which implies that it should be stowed on deck or in a locker that opens from the deck. Tied in with the decision about location is the choice between container and valise. A liferaft kept on deck should be inside a rigid plastic container to protect it from the weather and from knocks, but this can make a raft impossibly heavy for a small person to move. A hard case is not impervious to water. The two halves of the case have a gasket to keep out water, but the painter, which protrudes from the unit, allows water to penetrate. To let water out, all rigid containers have small drain holes in the bottom. It is essential that a liferaft on deck be strongly secured to withstand heavy weather. A fabric valise is lighter, less bulky and slightly cheaper, but it must be better protected from the elements and therefore should be stowed down below or in a deck locker.

Most manufacturers now vacuum-bag their liferafts; this protects the raft from water ingress and damaging changes in the environment, gives longer life expectancy, an increased protection of the safety equipment packed in the raft, and results in a smaller package. An additional monetary gain can be made in the long term as vacuum-packed liferafts usually need servicing less frequently than the standard annual requirement.

A hydrostatic release unit (HRU) can be used to secure a liferaft stowed in a container on deck, so that it will be automatically released when the yacht sinks below

Lessons learnt from the 1998 Sydney–Hobart Race

The disastrous Sydney–Hobart Race in 1998 resulted in a number of racers abandoning their vessels and taking to liferafts. Because so many liferafts were used at the same time, and there was an inquest afterwards as to why six sailors lost their lives, there was a great deal of information around as to what made a good raft. And as a result of the disaster, the coroner made a number of recommendations relating to liferafts. Perhaps the most important of these was that he felt that all liferafts should meet the SOLAS standard. He said: '…the recommendation of a liferaft complying with the SOLAS requirements is not, as one submission states, for "A possible slight gain in people comfort in the unusual circumstance of a crew having to take to the raft". It is so that, if the unusual circumstance does arise, the crew will have the best opportunity of survival and they are entitled to that.'

The coroner raised a number of points as a result of the testimony of various survivors – in particular, the evidence from the survivors from the yacht *Winston Churchill*. He felt that liferaft manufacturers should address certain aspects not covered by the SOLAS regulations, and that:

♦ Paddles, torch, emergency leak stopping plugs and seasickness medication, all items likely to be required immediately upon boarding the liferaft, should be stowed separately attached with a lanyard.
♦ An equipment pack should be attached to the liferaft with a permanent lanyard that is easy to operate with cold hands.
♦ The equipment bag should be easy to open and reseal by people with cold hands, eg Velcro or a plastic zipper.
♦ It needed to be recognised that cotton ties that seal liferaft entrances are impossible to undo by survivors.
♦ Buoyancy tubes and floors of liferafts should be made of a highly visible colour to aid rescuers.
♦ Manufacturers should discontinue the rope ladder entry in favour of the much easier ramp entry design.

The coroner's recommendations have resulted in the new ISAF minimum specifications for liferafts for Category 1 and 2 races, long distance races offshore and close to shore, but not transoceanic races. Category 0 races, transoceanic sailed under adverse conditions, require SOLAS liferafts to be carried. Gradually, changes are filtering through to liferafts manufactured for the pleasure yachting market. The changes are often seen in the top-end model or in the introduction of a new model, but in the USA one large chandlery chain has taken at least one recommendation to heart by changing the colour of all its liferaft bottoms to orange.

about 3m (10ft). The liferaft painter must be secured to a strong point on the yacht so that when the HRU releases the raft it will inflate and float to the surface. On a sailboat, with the possibility of lines and shrouds tangling up the liferaft, an HRU may offer a false sense of security.

Wherever the liferaft is stowed, make sure it has instructions to inflate it clearly written on it, or on an attached waterproof sticker, with the print large enough to be read without glasses.

Liferaft emergency packs

Survival equipment supplied and packed inside a liferaft ranges from minimal to good, and horror stories about the survival gear found in liferafts abound. It's not just the lack of equipment, or the missing items, but also the quality of the supplies. In general, the cheaper the liferaft, the less equipment is included. Table 4.1 lists the contents of five standardised emergency packs available for liferafts. Most manufacturers will include virtually anything in a liferaft – for a price of course. Unfortunately, the more included inside the liferaft, the bigger and heavier the container or valise must be and the more expensive it becomes. The most basic emergency equipment includes only items to repair the raft, but even the most comprehensive SOLAS 'A' pack will need to be augmented with a grab bag. In the very worst scenario – a yacht sinking in seconds and with no time to grab anything – the crew may be forced to survive with just what has already been packed in the raft.

Liferaft packs are generally stored inside a waterproof bag attached within the raft to prevent everything coming loose upon launching and inflation. The knife for cutting the painter is stowed separately, as are such items as a drogue and a rescue quoit.

The ISAF general requirements for equipment packed inside the liferaft are a model for all non-commercial liferaft packs. The specification states that:

◎ Every package must open and re-seal easily – even with cold, wet, numb hands, and without using an implement of any kind.
◎ Portable items must have lanyards or tape tails with Velcro self-sealing strips so that the object can be fastened to the liferaft without tying a knot.
◎ The equipment pack must be inherently buoyant, brightly coloured and tied by a line to the inside of the raft.

TABLE 4.1 LIFERAFT EMERGENCY PACKS

ISAF Offshore Pack	Following Sydney–Hobart 1998 Race recommendations	'D' Pack	SOLAS 'B' Pack (up to 12-person size)	SOLAS 'A' Pack (up to 12-person size)
Category 1 & 2 racing yachts	*Offshore racing*	*Class XII <21.3m (70 ft) in length*	*Leisure/commercial coastal*	*Leisure/commercial offshore*
Bailer	Bailer	Bailer	Bailer	Bailer
Hand flare x 3	Hand flare x 4	Hand flare x 3	Hand flare x 3	Hand flare x 6
Paddle x 2	Paddle x 2	Paddle x 2	Paddle x 2	Paddle x 2
Pump	Pump	Pump	Pump	Pump
Repair kit	Repair kit	Repair kit	Repair kit	Repair kit
Rescue line and quoit	Rescue line and quoit	Rescue line and quoit	Rescue line and quoit	Rescue line and quoit
Safety knife	Safety knife	Safety knife	Safety knife	Safety knife
Sea anchor	Sea anchor	Sea anchor	Sea anchor x 2	Sea anchor x 2
Signal card (SOLAS 2)	Signal card (SOLAS 2)	Signal card (SOLAS 2)	Signal card (SOLAS 2)	Signal card (SOLAS 2)
Sponges (1pp)	Sponges (1pp)	Sponges x 2	Sponge x 2	Sponge x 2
Survival instructions	Survival instructions	Survival instructions	Survival instructions	Survival instructions
Flashlight, waterproof x 2	Flashlight, waterproof + spare batteries and bulb	Flashlight, waterproof + spare batteries and bulb	Flashlight, waterproof + spare batteries and bulb	Flashlight, waterproof + spare batteries and bulb
Whistle	Whistle	Whistle	Whistle	Whistle
Antiseasickness tablets (6pp)	Antiseasickness tablets (6pp)	Antiseasickness tablets (6pp)	Antiseasickness tablets (6pp)	Antiseasickness tablets (6pp)
	Plus	*Plus*	*Plus*	*Plus*
	Parachute flare x 2	Parachute flares x 2	Parachute flares x 2	Parachute flare x 4
First aid kit	First aid kit	First aid kit	First aid kit	First aid kit
Signalling mirror	Signalling mirror	Signalling mirror	Signalling mirror	Signalling mirror
		Graduated drinking cup		Graduated drinking cup
	Fishing kit	Fishing kit		Fishing kit
	Buoyant smoke signal x 2	Buoyant smoke signal x 1	Buoyant smoke signal x 1	Buoyant smoke signal x 2
			Radar reflector or SART	Radar reflector or SART
Seasickness bags (1pp)		Seasickness bags (1pp)	Seasickness bags (1pp)	Seasickness bags (1pp)
Thermal protective aids x 2		Thermal protective aids x 2	Thermal protective aids x 2	Thermal protective aids x 2
		Can opener		Can opener x 3
				Scissors
Drinking water (0.5 litres (1 pint) pp)	Drinking water (0.5 litres (1 pint) pp)	Drinking water (0.5 litres (1 pint) pp)		Drinking water (1.5 litres (3 pints) pp)
	Food ration (1 tin per person)	Food ration (3,333 kj per person)		Food ration (10,000 kj per person)
Sunburn cream x 1	Sunburn cream x 2			
Sunscreen x 2				
Buoyancy tube leak plug x 6	Buoyancy tube leak plug x 6			
'Wet' notebook and pencil	Plastic bags (5pp)			

Note: pp = per person

Points to look for

Having made the decision to buy a liferaft, what makes a good choice? In practice, boat shows are generally the only opportunity available to most boatowners to study what various liferaft manufacturers have available. Even if the yacht requires a SOLAS or ISAF model, there are still choices to make as the regulations only dictate minimum standards, which some manufacturers exceed while others just meet. The SOLAS standard (listed under the heading 'Liferafts and regulations' on page 66) makes a good list to take with you at the time of purchase so you can use it for comparison. In addition, particularly for non-regulated liferafts, there is a need to check and compare:

◎ The construction, particularly at the seams.
◎ Is the opening in the canopy large enough and can it be closed and opened even with cold hands?
◎ How easy is it to get into from the water, assuming that the crew are wearing foul-weather gear and inflated lifejackets?
◎ Internal handholds – are any fitted?
◎ Is the drogue well made and securely fastened with at least 30m (98ft) of line?
◎ Is there good ventilation?
◎ Is the bottom of the raft brightly coloured to assist rescuers if it is overturned?
◎ Does the righting system look easy to use?
◎ Are there at least four water ballast bags to give a minimum total capacity of 25 litres ($5\frac{1}{2}$ gallons) per person or 160 litres (35 gallons) in total, whichever is larger?
◎ Are the ballast bags securely fastened to the raft?
◎ Is the gas bottle on the opposite side to the opening, so that on righting the raft the opening will be immediately in front?
◎ What is in the survival pack and are the items well made?
◎ Is the pack easy to open and close even with cold hands?
◎ Is the pack attached with a permanent lanyard that is easy to operate with wet hands?
◎ Are there pockets inside the raft to store survival gear?
◎ Are items likely to be needed immediately – such as paddles – stowed separately and tied to the raft?
◎ Is the repair kit capable of repairing punctures even if the buoyancy tubes are wet with fresh or salt water?

Liferaft maintenance and service

Like most things on a yacht, a liferaft can't be 'a buy and then forget about it item' until the day arrives when it becomes 'a needed item'. Handle a liferaft carefully whenever it is placed on or removed from its stowage position and do not roll or drop it. Liferafts should never be hosed down during routine deck washing. Regular washing by hand with soapy fresh water is recommended, providing unnecessary wetting is avoided. Washing down is the ideal time to check that:

♦ the container is free of any obstacles, especially if fitted with a hydrostatic release.
♦ the container is undamaged.
♦ the section of painter outside the unit is undamaged.
♦ the sleeve protecting the painter line is undamaged and firmly fits and seals the opening.

- the liferaft is firmly fastened in its stowage position and the fastenings are undamaged.
- the hydrostatic release is correctly fastened and is in date.

If any problems are found with the liferaft, make temporary repairs if you can, and have the unit serviced as soon as possible. It is important that a liferaft is landed ashore as required by the manufacturer or regulations, to be inspected by a qualified agent approved by the manufacturer. The label on the front of the container shows the date the next service is due. Servicing is expensive but necessary – and extending the period between services beyond that recommended only makes it more likely that the raft will require more costly repairs later or even be condemned before its expected life-span. Servicing should be undertaken to:

- Inflate the raft to check for airtightness of the chambers.
- Check the general condition of the raft structure and valves.
- Replace dated items like flares, batteries and water.
- Make sure that the inflation cylinder is full and undamaged.
- Inspect the firing head.

Tips:

If possible, visit the service centre to see the liferaft while it is unpacked during its service.

Take pictures of the raft and the equipment and include it in the On Board Training Manual.

When the liferaft returns from its service, check very carefully that the raft is correctly re-secured to the yacht via the HRU.

Many service centres like to leave the raft inflated for 24 hours to check that it remains firm, to stretch the material, and to ensure it is completely dry before re-packing. Always choose a service centre that will allow the crew to be present, so everyone can watch as the raft that they might one day need is opened. This may be the only chance you ever get to see the raft; this can be a big eye-opener, especially if it was bought unseen from a brochure.

Vacuum-packed liferafts produced for the leisure market often have extended periods between servicing, but they should have a yearly visual check to ensure the packaging is intact and undamaged. The older the raft, the more important the annual service, to be sure it is still in perfect order.

When the liferaft is due for its annual service, check the hydrostatic release unit, if fitted, to see if it also requires servicing. Disposable or non-servicing types usually need replacing every two years.

5 The Grab Bag and Its Contents

It would be nice to think that if the yacht sinks and the crew take to the liferaft, then the worst is over. With modern-day communications this may be true, but although help could be on its way, unless the yacht is close to land, surrounded by other vessels, it may still be some time before rescue arrives. Surviving for any length of time with just the items packed inside the liferaft will, at best, be uncomfortable if the raft contains a SOLAS 'A' pack and, at worst, could leave the crew swimming if the liferaft has only a basic pack.

Every yacht, no matter how small or large, needs some kind of grab bag (also called a ditch bag, ditch kit, abandon ship bag, emergency bag or flee bag) to supplement the liferaft emergency pack. Even in the best situation of abandoning ship, with a little notice of the event, these precious minutes are far more likely to be spent trying to save the yacht rather than choosing what to take to the liferaft. No one is likely to be in the best frame of mind to make sensible decisions, nor will the equipment that will best aid the crew in a liferaft necessarily be there – unless the Skipper thought about it while the yacht was still attached to the shore and he was able to go shopping. Sailing organisations such as the RYA include a grab bag on their recommended equipment lists. British vessels over 13.7m (45ft) but less than 24m (79ft), voyaging less than 150 miles from shore, need one if the liferaft does not carry a SOLAS 'B' pack. The ISAF require racing yachts to have a grab bag to supplement their required liferaft emergency pack or SOLAS 'B' pack. We have written a whole book (*The Grab Bag Book*, Adlard Coles Nautical) on the subject of grab bags, and much – but not all – of the information in this chapter comes from this.

A grab bag should contain everything essential to survival in a liferaft. Even if the yacht does not have a liferaft and it is proposed to use the dinghy in an emergency, there should be some form of 'abandon ship bag'. In fact, it is even more important to have some survival gear packed and ready to go, as a dinghy is very unlikely to contain even the most basic of emergency supplies. The starting point of deciding what to pack in the grab bag must be dependent on what is, or is not, already contained in the liferaft emergency pack – and its quality. Other factors to consider are: the area in which the yacht sails or plans to sail, and the maximum crew numbers carried. The less in the emergency vessel and the farther from shore the yacht will travel, the more a grab bag is needed.

Packing the grab bag

A grab bag container can be rigid or soft; purpose-made or simply any old waterproof bag; it can be one large container or a number of smaller ones. The style and type of bag depends upon where it will be stowed on the yacht, how much it has to store, and personal preference. A soft dry bag is a good choice on a small yacht as it is easier to store, but it will need to be padded to protect the contents. A waterproof, rigid bag will keep the contents safer, and if it floats it can be towed outside the liferaft leaving more space for the crew.

Check that every crew member can handle the fully laden bag. It may be better to split the load into two smaller bags.

Whether large or small, there are certain common properties that every grab bag and items inside it should have. These include:

◎ Bag clearly marked with the name of the yacht and 'GRAB BAG'.
◎ Bag ideally brightly coloured, waterproof and able to float.
◎ Duplicate grab bags to match the number of liferafts aboard the yacht.
◎ A list of all packed items on waterproof paper at the top of the bag.
◎ A lanyard attached to the bag and every item inside to prevent loss.
◎ Small items stored inside in plastic boxes or jars with secure lids.
◎ Larger items should be vacuum packed or stored in re-sealable plastic bags to reduce their size and protect them.
◎ Contents of all sealed items listed on the outside with waterproof ink.
◎ Instructions for all equipment on waterproof paper.
◎ All sharp items that could puncture the raft fitted with a protective cover.
◎ Stowing the grab bag to hand – eg cockpit on a sailboat, wheelhouse on a motor-boat.

A copy of the grab bag contents list should be included in the On Board Training Manual and used as part of the general familiarisation given to every crew member sailing aboard the yacht. Another copy of the contents list must be given to the emergency contact ashore with the Voyage Details Plan, so that rescuers understand the potential of the crew aboard the liferaft to survive a long time.

The ISAF regulation grab bag

There are plenty of lists out there written by professional sailors and issued by various sailing authorities with suggestions as to what to pack in the grab bag. In the end it comes down to personal choice, unless the yacht has to obey any regulations. The ISAF regulation grab bag must contain:

◎ Watertight handheld marine VHF transceiver plus spare batteries.
◎ Watertight flashlight with spare batteries and bulb.
◎ Two red parachute flares and three red hand flares and cyalume-type chemical light sticks.
◎ Watertight handheld EPFS (electronic position-fixing system), eg GPS.
◎ SART.
◎ Dry suits or survival bags.
◎ Second sea anchor for liferaft unless spare already in raft.
◎ Two safety tin openers.
◎ 406 MHz or 'E' EPIRB registered to the yacht.
◎ First aid kit.
◎ Water.

◎ Signalling mirror.
◎ High-energy food.
◎ Nylon string, polythene bags, seasickness tablets.
◎ Watertight handheld aviation Air Band VHF transceiver (if race area warrants this).

When considering the relative merits of packing one item over another, it may be worth thinking about each item and asking the question 'Does it have a multiple function?' An item that can double up for two or more tasks is more valuable than one that cannot. Of course, some items only have one function, eg an EPIRB summons help, but it still remains top of our list. The whole list creates our idea of the perfect bag for sailing worldwide, the 'Ocean Grab Bag'. For yachts travelling less far, a shortened list is suggested, the 'Coastal Grab Bag'. For those with plenty of money and a full range of GMDSS equipment aboard their yacht, there is the 'Minimalist Grab Bag'.

The majority of the items in a grab bag can be divided into categories, though a few things are unclassifiable and others, such as duct tape, overlap several groups. With limited space, it may help to rate an item to help decide what to pack. The categories, more or less in order of priority, are: 1 Search and rescue (SAR); 2 Maintenance and protection; 3 Medical; 4 Food and drink; 5 Survival and morale; 6 Personal.

1 Search and rescue (SAR)

Items in this category include EPIRB, pyrotechnics, SART, etc. Stories abound of survivors watching SAR authorities fly overhead or sail by without spotting them in their tiny liferaft. In fact, it is extremely difficult to spot a liferaft – especially in rough seas. The more the crew can do in the liferaft to attract attention and the more methods of signalling available, the more likely it is that someone will come to their aid. The more items in the grab bag in this category, the less should be needed from other categories.

2 Maintenance and protection

Items in this category include a bucket, cushions, repair kit, spare sea anchor, etc. The better the quality of the liferaft, the fewer of these items should need to be used. Even so the longer the crew have to survive in the raft, the more items will be needed.

3 Medical

A liferaft with a SOLAS 'A' or 'B' emergency pack will have a good selection of first aid supplies; but if the raft hasn't got one of these, the grab bag must include something similar. Like most items, the farther off the beaten track the yacht sails, the more of these items must be added to the grab bag.

4 Food and drink

A yacht sailing close to the coast, especially in well-populated areas, probably does not need to put food or water in the grab bag, especially in temperate zones. A yacht sailing farther offshore or in sparsely populated areas, with few other vessels around, should add at least some water – and food too if search and rescue equipment is limited. Yachts crossing an ocean or sailing far off normal shipping routes may have to wait some time for rescue, even when the rescue services have been notified, and should therefore consider adding these items. In the medium term, water is needed for survival, especially in hot climates, and in the long term, food will be needed – plus a means of gathering more.

5 Survival and morale

Items in this category include short-term and long-term living inside the liferaft. Items that can be put in this category include charts, lighter, land survival book, towels etc. Things that will help morale, such as a pack of cards, are a very important factor in survival after the first few hours.

6 Personal

Items in this category include personal identification documents, money, prescription glasses, etc. These are items that, realistically, the Skipper or the crew could do without if push came to shove, except in the case of personal medication for life-threatening conditions.

Grab bag categories

Minimalist grab bag

The 'minimalist grab bag' presumes that we are talking about a yacht with all the latest GMDSS-compliant communications and distress equipment designed for the vessel's sailing area plus a SOLAS liferaft. With an automated distress message having been sent using the onboard DSC radio and satellite communications equipment, and the crew comfortably settled in a top-of-the-range liferaft, the only extras that will be required are:

◎ Inmarsat E EPIRB.
◎ 406 MHz EPIRB with GPS.
◎ Manual watermaker.
◎ Portable satellite phone.
◎ Handheld GPS.
◎ SART (if not included in the liferaft).
◎ Immersion suits for each member of crew.
◎ A good book of short stories.

With that combination, wherever the disaster happens in the world, help should arrive quickly – but just in case it is delayed for any reason, the book of short stories is included to occupy the minds of the survivors.

Coastal grab bag

The 'coastal grab bag' presumes that we are referring to a yacht that sails close to shore and in well-populated areas where rescue will be measured in hours rather than days. For this reason, items for long-term survival, such as food and drink, are excluded. This grab bag could also be used for short passages farther offshore, with the addition of some water. See items listed below.

Ocean grab bag

The 'ocean grab bag' is the ultimate bag for round the world cruising and ocean passagemaking. It includes *all* the items listed in the next section.

Items for a grab bag

The following items are listed in alphabetical order. Items with a † are those that are found in a SOLAS 'A' emergency liferaft pack. Any item already packed in the liferaft and known to be well constructed and supplied in sufficient quantities can be safely left out of the grab bag. Items suitable for a 'coastal grab bag' are indicated by *.

*Antiseasickness tablets†** The uncomfortable movement of the raft, the strong probability of the abandonment of the yacht having taken place in rough weather, the confined, enclosed nature of the liferaft plus the sight of others close by being sick, and even the strongest stomach is likely to suffer from *mal de mer*. Seasickness is very debilitating; it causes the loss of valuable fluids that may be extremely difficult to replace in a raft, and in general it makes people more prone to hypothermia. This can eventually kill the sufferer. There are many different antiseasickness preparations available over the counter and some of these are discussed in the next chapter. Pack plenty of the medication of choice and include prescription anti-emetic drugs in the first aid kit. Antiseasickness tablets are included in many better liferaft emergency packs, but view these as extras and not the sole supply.

Tip: Pack antiseasickness tablets at the very top of the grab bag and ensure that all crew in the liferaft take them as soon as possible. They work best if used *before* anyone starts to feel seasick.

*Bailer†** A liferaft, especially in rough seas, is unlikely to remain dry, so every liferaft emergency pack should include a bailer. Even if the bailer is of good quality, more than one is a good idea. A plastic dinghy bailer with a handle is cheap enough and makes a good container in the grab bag to protect small items, so pack a couple.

Tip: If the grab bag is large enough, include a dinghy hand pump as they are very efficient.

*Batteries** Including spare alkaline batteries for all electrical equipment has been mentioned with individual items, but it is reiterated here as a reminder. Rotate these batteries with the yacht's regular supply to ensure they are always fresh.

*Binoculars** A spare pair should be packed in the grab bag, and those used on the yacht noted on the Last Minute Grabs List (see page 88). They will help ensure that you see what is a genuine rescue craft before you set off a pyrotechnic.

*Bucket** A bucket has many uses – from additional bailer to makeshift privy. A collapsible model or a folding bowl will fit inside a grab bag. Failing this, pack a small children's seaside bucket. Add the location of the ship's buckets used for washing down, etc to the 'extra grabs list'.

Tip: Use buckets as carrying containers at 'abandon ship' time.

Can opener† * A can opener is included in liferaft packs that contain water and food. But even if food is not packed in the grab bag, include a can opener to undo any tins taken from the galley.

Camera* A disposable waterproof camera may help morale – and show friends what life in the raft was really like.

Charts* Ship routeing, current and wind charts are not actually for navigation, which is almost impossible in an inflatable liferaft, but for morale. Drift, possible landfalls and sources of rescue can be estimated with the addition of a compass.

Tip: If the charts are not on waterproof paper, laminate them.

Cellular telephone* Most crew carry a mobile phone; select one that is fully charged and pop it in the grab bag in a waterproof case before setting sail. Do not forget to retrieve the phone at the end of the passage. While a cellular mobile phone should not be the only means of making a call for help, it may be a valuable additional method of making contact when in a liferaft and close to shore.

Chemical heat pack Hand and body chemical heat packs can help offset hypothermia, a real possibility after a very short time in almost any waters. The hand packs give six hours of gentle warmth, the body packs give 20 hours. The higher the latitude, the more packs should be included in a grab bag.

Compass* A small plastic model to go with the routeing charts takes up little room, and will be useful if the liferaft reaches the shore.

*Containers** Use various sizes of containers, with watertight lids, to pack items in the grab bag. The containers can serve double duty as water collectors or bailers. Also include collapsible water carriers in which to store collected or made water.

*Contents list** A contents list should be at the top of the grab bag just under the anti-seasickness tablets. Print the list on waterproof paper or laminate it. The list should have brief instructions on how to use each item and when to replace it (where appropriate).

*Credit card** A credit/debit card can ease things ashore, especially in a foreign country. Ensure the card is the type that can access cash from a bank, ATM or cashpoint machine.

Cutlery Add some camping or plastic picnic cutlery to make everyone feel more civilised – it costs little in money or space.

Cutting board It is difficult and dangerous to cut anything in a liferaft without a firm surface. Liferaft paddles can be used as an alternative as long as they are not the canvas-style ones. A polyethylene antibacterial kitchen chopping board is ideal as water will not hurt it. A small 'backpackers' chopping board takes up little space, or use a larger board to provide a firm bottom or side for a soft grab bag.

*Diving mask** This is not only useful if repairs are needed under the raft, but is also protection for the lookout in driving rain or heavy seas.

Drinking cups† Liferaft equipment that includes water also includes a graduated drinking cup to divide up the water fairly. Add extra plastic cups to serve a double function as bailers or water catchers.

Drinking water† Any ocean-voyaging yacht should have at least 0.5 litres (1 pint) water per person in the liferaft if possible. Even if a portable watermaker is included in the grab bag, extra water should be added to the bag. Before any long passage, fill as many large plastic bottles as possible 80 per cent full of water; alternatively, empty 20 per cent from large plastic bottles of mineral water and reseal. Tie together with a floating line and store as near the liferaft as possible. The partly filled bottles will float in sea water, and can be trailed behind the liferaft – leaving more space inside.

*Duct tape** Choose the best quality and check it will stick in the wet, as some brands are better than others. The tape has endless uses including: ✧ mending liferaft leaks above the waterline ✧ securing a bandage or splint to a patient ✧ covering the strobe light on an EPIRB ✧ making a watertight seal on a container.

Enema kit If a crew member is suffering from severe seasickness and unable to keep down anything taken by mouth, dehydration becomes a major problem. This could easily happen in a liferaft, and an enema kit or rectal drip is the only way to rehydrate the victim.

*EPIRB** An EPIRB registered to the yacht, quietly talking to the satellites, is the most important piece of equipment that can be taken to a liferaft. Fortunately, the purchase price and size of an EPIRB has dropped rapidly since their introduction, and to suggest having one for the yacht and one for each liferaft is no longer beyond most sailors' pockets. For more about EPIRBs and which type to choose, read chapter 3 and look at Table 3.

If you are buying more than one EPIRB, consider purchasing two different models, eg a 406 MHz and an Inmarsat E – or at least choose different manufacturers, so there is no chance that a design fault or manufacturing defect could cripple both. For busy coastal waters, one EPIRB is probably sufficient, especially with a portable VHF radio and a mobile phone. Pack a Class II, manual deployment 406 MHz or Inmarsat E EPIRB as the final item at the top of the grab bag, so it's always handy for other emergencies.

First aid kit†* British SOLAS-specified liferaft packs and 'D' packs must include a Category C first aid kit packed in a sealed, re-usable container, together with first aid instructions printed on waterproof paper. The Category C medical supplies are listed in Appendix 4. If the liferaft emergency pack does not include this, or its equivalent, consider having a Category C kit packed inside the liferaft or included in the grab bag. It may be impossible to grab the yacht's medical kit, so duplicate a few items in the grab bag, especially when sailing offshore:

◎ Prescription topical anti-bacterial ointment because germs breed quickly in a liferaft.
◎ Aspirin as a first aid, initial treatment for heart attacks.
◎ Transparent waterproof and breathable adhesive bandages.
◎ Prescription anti-emetic drugs in suppository or injectable form for severe seasickness.
◎ Inflatable splints for broken limbs.

Fishing kit† A very limited fishing kit is included in many offshore rafts. No bait is supplied, and since fish should not be eaten without a plentiful supply of water, the inclusion of fishing gear may be questionable – though in the long term, food will be as important as water. But fishing is fun and passes the time. A grab bag fishing kit should be designed to catch small to medium fish only – large game fish could damage a vulnerable liferaft. Only pack the highest-quality item and ensure that any metal is stainless steel. Visit a fishing shop and select or get help to choose a small, but comprehensive, kit to include: ✧ 100m (300ft) of light fishing line ✧ 2 small hand winders; if they are too big for the bag, consider a kite winder ✧ wire leaders with clip-on swivels ✧ clip-on swivels ✧ assorted sinkers ✧ plentiful supply of assorted hooks ✧ various lures ✧ a small gaff or net to help land fish ✧ waterproof instruction booklet.

Flashlight/torch†* All standard liferaft emergency packs include a waterproof flashlight to be used for signalling as it is a very effective method of attracting attention at night. Many liferafts have no internal light, so pack at least two waterproof flashlights near the top of the grab bag in case you have to abandon ship at night. An additional hands-free waterproof light is a plus. Try to ensure all flashlights use the same size batteries and pack plenty of spares. Stock rotate all batteries with the yacht's regular supply and include the grab bag flashlights on the list of items to check before a passage.

 Tip: Diving lights are the ideal choice aboard a boat, as they are waterproof, generally float and have a lanyard fitted.

Foil A large sheet of thick aluminium foil, folded up, takes little room and has many uses – including radar reflection and fishing lures.

Food rations The 10,000 kilojoules per person ration in a SOLAS 'A' liferaft pack is approximately three days of food in mild or warm weather. In cold weather and cold waters, where more energy – and thus food – is necessary to keep warm, this ration will not last as long. Although these rations are probably not very tasty, they are the best food choice for a liferaft as they are specially designed for consumption with minimal water. If the liferaft does not include any or only a limited amount of rations, include them in the grab bag. Any food you catch will be mostly protein, which requires much more water to digest. Extra items to pack should be high carbohydrate and high sugar, and low protein, such as: boiled sweets (hard candy); chocolate; dried fruit; energy bars; glucose tablets; tinned fruit; tinned sweetened milk.

Funnel This is useful for transferring water between containers and to make sure that water is not wasted.

Gloves A couple of pairs of thick gloves, either of leather or man-made material with non-slip palms, are invaluable for protecting hands – especially when fishing.

Immersion suit In cold waters, those less than 21°C (70°F), an immersion or survival suit is highly recommended. Immersion suits are not insulated, though, and it is essential that warm clothing is worn under the suit. In theory, survival suits should be inside the grab bag; but as they are usually large, each must be considered as a separate stand-alone grab bag.

Inflatable cushions Some sort of inflatable cushions or mattress will make life very much more comfortable, especially if the liferaft has no additional insulated floor, either inflatable or foam. They will help to keep the crew above any water that inevitably finds its way inside a raft.

 Tip: Sailboat crews can grab the cockpit cushions as they leave.

Kite* A highly visible kite attracts attention, pinpoints location, and as a bonus it is fun to fly! A special rescue parafoil kite is available in bright orange with the international distress signal of a black ball and square printed on it. It will fly in winds from 5 to 25 knots and can even lift a strobe light or radar reflector.

Knife* Pack in the grab bag a large, sturdy, fixed-blade knife, with a plastic sheaf (well-coated with petroleum jelly to prevent rust). A dive knife is a good choice, but some survivalists suggest avoiding a double-edged knife.

Knife sharpener* A stone or ceramic sharpener is best as it will not be adversely affected by salt water.

Land survival book* The *SAS Survival Book* (Collin's Gem series), for example, is small enough to fit into a corner of the grab bag and yet it is very comprehensive. Ashore in a desolate part of the world, it can really help to keep the crew live. Pack it inside at least two sealed plastic bags to keep it dry until the liferaft reaches shore.

Land survival kit* Pack a few things for landfall. Make sure they are in a pocket-sized watertight container and include firelighters, matches, a magnifying glass, water purification tablets, a wire saw and a snare.

Light sticks* A SOLAS liferaft will have a manually operated interior light, but other rafts often have no light at all or, at best, one that cannot be turned off and thus will quickly go out. Light sticks are ideal as they offer a gentle light that can last all night. Battery-operated waterproof light sticks are sold in dive shops, as an alternative to chemical sticks for night dives. They have the advantage of lasting much longer than the chemical sticks, plus being able to be switched on and off. Their disadvantage is the same as for any electrical item in a water environment. A selection of both kinds is ideal, plus spare batteries.

 Tip: Pack chemical light sticks very carefully in the grab bag to stop them activating in error.

Lighter* A windproof refillable lighter (with spare butane) can be used for sealing things like polypropylene rope in the liferaft and to start a fire ashore.

Money* Cash will be very useful after rescue or landing. Pack the local currency or, if sailing abroad, US dollars are generally a good choice.

Multipurpose tool* Everyone aboard a yacht should carry a knife, but pack at least one multipurpose tool in the grab bag. Choose one with a good assortment of extras such as pliers, bottle opener, scissors, screwdrivers, wire cutter, serrated knife, file, awl/punch, etc. Use petroleum jelly to coat the blades, etc and, if possible, vacuum-seal the tool to prevent rusting.

Multivitamin tablets For long-term liferaft survival, include 30 days' supply per person of chewable multivitamin tablets.

Pack of cards A pack of waterproof playing cards are ideal to while away the hours of waiting.

Paddles†* A pair of paddles should be included in every liferaft, to assist with moving away from the mother ship. Check the quality of the model packed inside the liferaft and, if in doubt, place instead a full-sized, buoyant set inside, or add a pair to the grab bag.

Pens and pencils* Pack a few writing implements that work on waterproof paper – they are needed to write a log, or keep score of that poker game!

Personal hygiene items Personal cleanliness boosts morale and helps to keep everyone healthy. Brushing your teeth makes most people feel much better, especially if they have been seasick, so pack travel sets of toothbrushes and toothpaste. Moist wipes instead of precious water will help to remove salt from the skin and to reduce the likelihood of saltwater boils. Remember to include a few feminine sanitation items.

Personal identification documents If the yacht is travelling aboard, include a photocopy of everyone's passport and other relevant ID in the grab bag. Photocopy the documents onto waterproof paper or laminate ordinary paper copies.

Personal inspiration This may be a religious book, a collection of poems, something for meditation or whatever else is appropriate to the crew's beliefs or views and will help pass the time.

Personal medicine†* Any medication required by crew members must be included in the grab bag and rotated regularly. Drugs kept in the fridge should be stored in an accessible position, inside a watertight container and add it to the 'extra grabs list'. It is difficult to know exactly how much to pack, especially as lack of food and water can affect the actions of drugs, perhaps 30 days for an 'ocean grab bag' and five days for a 'coastal bag'.

Petroleum jelly This is an extremely versatile product for use as a lubricant; it is not only a valuable medical addition but can also be used for protecting metal objects.

Plastic bags†* It would be difficult to pack too many plastic bags to use as seasick bags as well as storage. Include a selection of sizes – re-sealable heavy-weight freezer bags are the most useful. Zipper style bags are the easiest to use.

*Portable VHF** Special waterproof survival-craft VHF radios (also called 'survival craft radios') are readily available, because they are required aboard fishing and commercial vessels, and the *ultimate* grab bag – if money were no object – would include one of these. It is far more likely, though, that the 'last minute grabs list' will include collecting the yacht's handheld waterproof VHF. A lithium ion battery – the expensive sort that can be recharged at any time without waiting for the battery to run down – is much superior to a Ni-Cad. If the VHF can use alkaline batteries as well, this is a big bonus – but of course means that spare batteries for it should be stored in the grab bag.

*Prescription glasses/contact lenses** Crew with less than perfect vision will really appreciate some glasses or contact lens if they had no time to fetch their normal ones during the abandonment. So pack a spare pair of glasses in a rigid case, and spare lenses and lotions, for each member of crew that needs them. Even a not quite current prescription is better than nothing. Include some cheap glasses for the longsighted; they can be very useful for magnifying things.

Pump†* A bellows or hand pump should be part of every liferaft equipment bag for topping up the buoyancy chambers, but the quality of these is often miserable. This item should be in one piece ready for use without any assembling; if not, pack one that is inside the grab bag. The longer the liferaft is in use, the more a pump will be needed, so an 'ocean grab bag' should include a second one.

Pyrotechnics†* The yacht's flare kit should obviously be grabbed and taken to the liferaft, but extra flares should also be included in the grab bag, and this is an ideal place to put the out-of-date flares. Many liferaft emergency kits include at least some pyrotechnics but, if not, add them at the next service and beef up the grab bag supply to at least match the SOLAS 'A' pack if the yacht is staying close to shore, or the SOLAS 'B' pack if going further afield (see page 70). Always choose flares that meet the SOLAS specification for burn time and brightness, to ensure the maximum signalling power.

Radar reflector†* This is a SOLAS requirement if an efficient radar transponder (SART) is not included in the liferaft. A raft does not reflect radar waves, and unfortunately it is hard to get a reflector high enough to be effective – especially in a big sea. If the emergency pack includes one this is good; if not, seriously consider purchasing a SART instead. If money is very tight, a radar reflector is better than nothing.

Repair kit†* Liferafts all come with a repair kit of some kind, but not necessarily a useful one, so check it carefully. If in doubt about the quality of the liferaft kit, or if travelling far offshore, add extra supplies in the grab bag. Ensure that the equipment is suitable for the liferaft and pack it near the top of the grab bag, with:

- a spare canopy and raft material;
- glue that will work in a wet and salty environment;
- a variety of needles, including sail repair needles, waxed thread and a sewing awl;
- assorted sizes of leak stopper plugs to effect a temporary repair;
- assorted sizes of hose clamps to tighten the raft material around a plug;
- assorted sizes of raft repair clamps. These are included with a few liferafts and are the easiest way to repair a hole with an airtight seal;
- spare plugs for pressure release and topping up valves.

Rescue line and quoit†* This should be included in every liferaft with not less than 30m (100ft) of buoyant line, and fastened to the raft. It is designed to throw from the liferaft to a survivor in the water, to help them to reach the raft.

Rope* Pack a large assortment of long lengths of rope and twine in the grab bag to use as lashings, lanyards and general improvisation.

Safety knife†* A blunt-tipped blade, supposedly incapable of harming the raft or a person, is included with a liferaft, stored near the entrance, to cut the painter if necessary. A knife meeting SOLAS specifications will have a buoyant handle.

Sail repair tape† Heavy-duty sail tape is designed for the salt environment and is very useful for quick repairs. This makes a valuable addition to duct tape.

SART* A Search and Rescue Radar Transponder (SART) is a GMDSS requirement for many vessels. A SART's ability to alert and guide *any* passing vessel that is using radar – not just one searching for the liferaft – makes it a very valuable addition to an EPIRB, which can only be homed in on with specialised equipment. It is expensive, but so important that some liferafts include it in their emergency pack. (More information about how it works is given in chapter 3.)

Satellite mobile phone Satellite phones are becoming more and more common and soon may be even as cheap as a cellular phone is today. This really is a possible life-saver, as it can be used to talk to potential rescuers who are far away from the liferaft.

 Tip: If you have a satellite mobile phone, keep it beside the grab bag when on passage.

Scissors* A strong pair of kitchen scissors are extremely useful, especially when conditions are too rough to use a knife safely. Coat the blades in petroleum jelly.

Sea anchor†* A sea anchor, also called a drogue, is needed to reduce the drift rate of the liferaft and to lessen the risk of capsize. Every liferaft needs one – especially boat-shaped rafts – and a self-deploying version is best. They are all too easy to lose in rough weather, so more than one should be included in the liferaft and grab bag. SOLAS 'A' and 'B' packs include one sea anchor permanently attached to the liferaft with a shock-absorber painter with swivels at each end of the line to prevent fouling, and they include a second as a back-up. The coroner reporting on the disastrous 1998 Sydney–Hobart Race recommended fitting a minimum of 15m (49ft) of attachment line, and stated that even more would be a good idea. A sea anchor has an additional use – which is to help the paddles move a circular liferaft in the desired direction.

Seasickness bags†* It is bad enough being seasick, but having nothing to be sick in results in total misery! Obviously it is no good packing an aircraft-style sick bag made of paper for use in a wet environment; instead, add a roll or two of cheap plastic bags to the grab bag.

Signal card†* A waterproof copy of the illustrated table of SOLAS lifesaving signals should be included in every liferaft. These visual signals are used between shore stations in the UK and ships in distress. Include a photocopy on waterproof paper as a back-up.

Signal mirror†* Also known as a heliograph, this will reflect the sun's rays into the direction of rescue personnel. In theory, it can be used to transmit Morse code, but in an unsteady liferaft it would probably be better employed to create a simple flash. In normal sunlight the flash from a good signal mirror, generally the bigger the better, can be seen from at least 10 miles away. A buoyant waterproof marine model, with instructions for use printed on waterproof paper, is best. As it takes little room and is perhaps the cheapest all-round signalling device on land or sea, pack at least two – and ideally one for every crew member.

Spare clothing Everyone should be wearing as many layers of clothing as possible before taking to the liferaft, but in a very rapid exit some people might not have time to put on warm clothes. Extra clothes packed in a watertight bag are a bonus, especially if it is necessary to enter the water.

 Tip: A vacuum-bagging machine can reduce a large woollen sweater or fleece to a very small size and ensures that it stays completely dry.

*Sponges** Sponges are cheap and are included in many liferaft packs. SOLAS packs include two, while the ISAF offshore pack has one per person. In theory, they are for drying and mopping up residual water from the floor of the raft. They are also very useful for collecting condensation to drink from the inside of the canopy, so keep at least one free of salt water for this purpose.

*Strobe light** A rapidly flashing strobe light stands out in open water. It is blindingly bright at close range, but further away it is less obvious because the light is dispersed rather than directed. Its major advantage is that it can operate unattended, but the directed light from even a very small flashlight will be visible at a much greater distance.

 Tip: If the raft is not already fitted with one, attach a strobe to the outside of it for added visibility at night.

Sunblock cream†* A sunblock cream is important protection against the misery of sunburn when on the water. It is very easy to underestimate the power of the sun, even on an overcast day, and burn a pale skin. So pack a high-SPF waterproof sunblock and also zinc oxide or special ultra-protection cream for the lips and nose, no matter how close you are to shore. Pack at least one tube, more for large crews.

*Sunglasses** A pair of sunglasses for each crew member will not cost a lot, but will be very welcome if it is warm and sunny. One pair for the watchkeeper is vital.

Survival instructions†* Every liferaft should come with some basic instructions about survival. Add a photocopy of the relevant sections of this book – or, better still, the *Grab Bag Book* (Adlard Coles Nautical) – and include them in the liferaft and every grab bag.

 Tip: Either laminate your photocopied pages or use a waterproof paper in a photocopier.

*Thermal protective aid (TPA)** A TPA is specially designed to fully enclose a person, covering them from head to toe, and keeps a survivor warm by reflecting back the body heat. TPAs are available with arms and legs, or as one big bag – and both sorts have a hood. The outer edges are sealed, except the ends of any arms, which makes the TPA impermeable up to the zip or Velcro, so even in a partly water-filled liferaft a person's feet will remain dry.

TPAs with arms and legs have the advantage of enabling the wearer to carry on various activities while remaining inside the suit. On the other hand, the bag style is more efficient at retaining heat and could accommodate two people for re-warming. Pack one for each crew member, no matter how little else is packed in the grab bag – perhaps include a selection of both styles.

TPAs are lifesaving pieces of kit in the treatment of hypothermia. A space blanket is not a substitute for a thermal protective aid in a liferaft.

Towels A couple of hand towels, well sealed in bags against water, can be used in many ways – eg as a pad to stop bleeding, protection against chafe, for cleaning, collecting water, as well to dry people and objects.

*Umbrella** This might seem a strange item to include in a grab bag, but it can be very useful! A small folding umbrella is light and cheap, and can be used by the watchkeeper, with his head out of the liferaft, as a sunshade or rain cover. If the raft lacks a canopy, include one umbrella per person to provide valuable shade.

Tip: Umbrellas can also be used to catch rainwater.

*Watch hat** Pack a hat to protect against sun or cold, depending upon the sailing area, to give the watchkeeper a measure of comfort. If the liferaft is a basic inshore model, without a canopy, include a hat for every crew member.

Watermaker A reverse osmosis watermaker is the only reliable way of making drinking water from salt water and they are included in some liferafts as part of the standard equipment. With the EPIRB and SART, this is top of the list to pack in a grab bag and, like those items, it is not cheap. There are, at present, only two choices of manual watermakers on the market, both made by PUR: Survivor 06 and Survivor 35. The Survivor 06 is the smaller model, able to produce just over 1 litre (2 pints) of fresh water per hour. The Survivor 35 is a little bigger and more expensive; it can make 5.5 litres (1.2 gallons) per hour, and is preferable for crews of eight or more.

*Waterproof paper** It is important that a log is kept in a liferaft, both as a memory aid and for morale.

*Whistle†** A whistle will not attract the attention of a ship or passing aircraft, but it can help anyone in the water to locate the liferaft. They are cheap and small, so pack a couple of powerful ones. In theory, everyone in the liferaft should be carrying one, attached to their lifejacket.

*Yacht's papers** Include a copy of the yacht's registration and any other official documents, photocopied onto waterproof paper or laminated ordinary paper. Make sure another copy of everything is kept ashore, including insurance documents, and consider filing a second set with the holder of the Voyage Details Plan.

Climatic variations to the grab bag

The climate of the cruising ground will create the need for some variations to the grab bag. However, the specific items may not differ so much as the *numbers* of the items. To create a 'cold weather variation' it will be necessary to add warm hats, one per person; gloves, one pair per person; extra chemical heat packs; more food; additional spare clothes; immersion suits.

The same bag will have little or no need for sunglasses, sunblock or sunburn cream, although these items may well be of use in the polar regions. To create a 'warm water variation', it will be necessary to add sunhats, one per person; extra sunblock; extra sunburn treatment creams; extra water; sunglasses, one pair per person.

Similarly it will be possible to eliminate chemical heat packs and inflatable cushions from the grab bag.

Last Minute Grabs List

The purpose of a grab bag is to make it available to grab in an emergency situation where time is limited and sinking is imminent. During a controlled evacuation there are additional items that should also be taken to the raft. These are items that are likely to be in everyday use around the yacht, and could in turn become life preservers if carried to the raft. Remembering what they are and where to find them in an emergency is the trick. It makes sense, therefore, to think about what is available before these things are needed, then to list which of them should be taken if there is time. This Last Minute Grabs List should then be pinned up in a prominent position aboard the yacht; Table 5.1 is an example of such a list.

 Tip: A copy of the Last Minute Grabs List is a useful addition to the On Board Training Manual.

Maintenance of the grab bag's contents

With everything shut away inside a bag or box, it is easy to forget to check the contents of a grab bag for servicing or replacement. A grab bag needs to be emptied at least once a year and have every item unpacked and checked to ensure it is in good working order and, where appropriate, that items are in date and batteries fully charged. The bag and contents should also be checked before any long passage. Keep annotated copies of the grab bag contents list noting, where applicable, the expiry dates of items, and include this in the Maintenance Record Book or log book.

TABLE 5.1 LAST MINUTE GRABS LIST

EQUIPMENT	LOCATION
Binoculars	*Wheelhouse*
EPIRB	*By wheelhouse door in float-free holder*
Portable GPS	*Wheelhouse*
Pyrotechnic container	*Under wheelhouse seat*
Sextant and tables	*Wheelhouse*
Portable VHFs (2)	*On charge in workshop*
Medical kit	*Skipper's cabin*
Portable satellite phone	*Skipper's cabin*
Cellular phones	*Individual cabins*
Fleece blankets	*Individual cabins*
Heavy weather gear	*Individual cabins*
Immersion suits	*Individual cabins*
Lifejackets	*Individual cabins*
Spare warm clothing	*Individual cabins*
Portable shortwave radio	*Main saloon*
Food and drink – galley	*PRIORITIES: cookie jar, fruit, chocolate, breakfast cereals, tinned food, dried fruit, milk and soft drinks*
	NOTE: Pack in shopping bags under sink
Prescription drugs	*Galley fridge, top shelf*
Buckets	*Aft deck locker*
Man overboard buoy	*Aft deck, port side*
Extra water	*Sundeck tied beside liferaft*
Soft drinks	*Sundeck locker and fridge*
Sunlounger cushions	*Sundeck locker*

6 Medical Training, Equipment and Advice

Preventing illness

Prevention is always better than cure, and the chances of injury and illness occurring must always be reduced as much as possible. The possibility of accidents can be minimised (but unfortunately never entirely prevented) by making sure that safety precautions are taken – such as wearing safety harnesses, clipping on, using a preventer when downwind sailing, fitting gas and smoke alarms, etc. The chances of illness can be minimised by following medical advice, taking prescribed medicines as required, and following good hygiene practices. Generally, cruising yachts have very healthy crew, partly due to the most popular sailing locations being where the climate is warm and there is plenty of sun and fresh air. Of course, there are usually additional hazards in these parts of the world, including infectious diseases and malaria, but the chances of getting these illnesses can be reduced by immunisation and preventative medicine.

Immunisation

Vaccination is a highly effective method of preventing certain infectious diseases. If sailing in north-western Europe, North America, Australia and New Zealand, the risks of catching an infectious disease are no greater than if the sailor were living ashore in any of those countries, and therefore no immunisations beyond those given to the general population are needed. If the yacht will be sailing outside of these countries, the Skipper needs to ensure that all the crew have had the appropriate vaccinations in plenty of time before the departure date, and that the immunisations are kept up to date as long as they are relevant.

Routine vaccinations

No matter where the yacht is going to sail, there is still a risk if vaccines that are routinely administered in childhood are not up to date. Adults in their country of residence often neglect to keep up the schedule of booster vaccinations, particularly if the risk of infection is low. Some older adults may never have been vaccinated at all. Therefore pre-sailing precautions should include booster doses of routine vaccines if the regular schedule has not been followed, or a full course of primary immunisation for crew who have never been vaccinated. Outside of Europe, North America, Japan and Australasia, diseases such as diphtheria and poliomyelitis, which no longer occur in most industrialised countries, may be present, and therefore updating routine immunisation is even more important. These vaccinations include: ✧ diphtheria/tetanus/pertussis (DTP) ✧ hepatitis B (HBV) ✧ haemophilus influenzae type B (Hib) ✧ measles (MMR) ✧ poliomyelitis.

Special vaccinations

If sailing outside of north-western Europe, North America, Australia and New Zealand, a wider range of immunisation is likely to be needed. It is important to consider not just the countries that you plan to visit, but also those that you *might* visit – as a result of weather conditions, changes of itinerary, etc. International vaccination requirements and recommendations can be ascertained from the World Health Organisation (WHO).

In deciding which vaccines would be appropriate, the following factors should be taken into account for each vaccine: ✧ risk of exposure to the disease ✧ age, health status, vaccination history ✧ special risk factors ✧ reactions to previous vaccine doses, allergies ✧ WHO recommendations.

Mandatory vaccination, as authorised by the International Health Regulations, nowadays concerns only yellow fever. Yellow fever vaccination is carried out to protect individuals in areas where there is a risk of yellow fever infection and to protect vulnerable countries from importation of the virus. If the yacht will be visiting a country where there is a risk of exposure to yellow fever or going to a country that requires yellow fever vaccination as a condition of entry, all the crew must be vaccinated.

Despite their success in preventing disease, vaccines do not fully protect 100 per cent of the recipients, so you must not assume that there is no risk of catching the disease if you have been vaccinated. All additional precautions against infection should be followed carefully, regardless of any vaccines or other medication that have been administered.

Medication for malaria

Malaria is a common and life-threatening disease in many tropical and subtropical areas, and it is currently endemic in over 100 countries.

Falciparum malaria kills. Initial symptoms, which may be mild, may not be easy to recognise as being due to malaria. These include fever, chills, headache, muscular aching and weakness, vomiting, cough, diarrhoea and abdominal pain. These symptoms can lead to acute renal failure, generalised convulsions, circulatory collapse, followed by coma and death.

Protection against HIV and other blood-transmitted diseases

Human Immunodeficiency Virus (HIV) and other infections, such as hepatitis B and hepatitis C, can be transmitted by non-sterile equipment that punctures the skin. Unless *absolutely certain* that the equipment being used is sterile, skin-damaging procedures such as ear piercing, tattooing, acupuncture, manicure and shaving with open razors should be avoided.

In most of western Europe, North America, Japan and Australasia, all donated blood is now screened for HIV antibodies. However, in most developing countries there may only be the most basic blood transfusion services and much of the blood donated is unscreened. The risks from blood transfusion in such circumstances are high. All crew members should be aware that:

◎ Accidents are the most common reason for needing a blood transfusion.
◎ Blood transfusions should only be accepted when absolutely essential.
◎ It makes it much easier to find a blood donor in an emergency if someone already knows their own blood group.

In many developing countries, re-use of medical supplies – including needles and syringes – is common, and the risk of blood-transmitted diseases being passed on is high. Prevention of this risk – particularly in the case of HIV, which has no known cure at present – is essential for anyone needing treatment ashore. Suture/syringe packs are available from some chemists and travel specialist shops, containing sterile injecting equipment for use in an emergency (eg when skin cuts need suturing, an intravenous drip is necessary, or injections are required, or in the case of dental surgery). The MCA Category 'A' medical stores includes a recommended kit if a vessel will be in a malarial area where medical facilities are limited. It is designed to be taken, along with the patient, if emergency treatment ashore is needed (see Appendix 4 for details).

Training

Every day people die in their own homes, simply because their family or friends do not know what to do in an emergency, when every second counts – eg if someone stops breathing or starts to choke. Every person would benefit from training in at least basic first aid and CPR (cardio-pulmonary resuscitation), and a regular refresher course to ensure the knowledge is always up-to-date. While CPR may be a skill you will never have to use on board, the training prepares you psychologically for a myriad of small emergencies that will inevitably occur. CPR skills also teach you how to take a pulse rate, count respirations, and roughly estimate blood pressure. General courses are available almost everywhere in the world, offered by organisations such as St John Ambulance, the British and American Red Cross, and the American Heart Association.

Courses aimed specifically at sailors are the best choice for at least one member of crew as they not only teach basic first aid and CPR techniques, but also include particularly relevant items such as hypothermia. One-day courses are offered by the RYA and IYT. These courses are required for Coastal Yachtmaster Skippers and above, but are recommended for all crew members.

For sailors heading off on a lengthy offshore passage, more in-depth training should be considered. Training must include topics and procedures that are not normally covered by Red Cross Standard or Advanced First Aid. These programmes do a fine job of training 'first' aid providers who have immediate access to the emergency medical services system. It is short-term care designed to stabilise and transport a patient to a medical facility within a few minutes. The training does not pretend to address the problem of a patient 500 miles from land where a general cargo ship a day's distance away is the nearest medical facility. Aboard a boat far away from land, one person will have to play 'doctor', regardless of their level of training or certification. Long-term care and the problems associated with patient management in extreme environments and remote locations need to be considered. A medical course for yachtsmen needs to teach wound cleaning, straightening fractures and dislocations, emergency treatment for anaphylaxis, and other techniques usually performed by a doctor. Ongoing care of an injured or ill patient is also important, plus some basic pharmacology and diagnosis to distinguish between a true medical emergency and a problem that can wait for the next landfall.

Advanced medical training courses geared towards the private yachtsman are difficult to find. In the USA specialist companies offer wilderness medical courses which, though not designed for the sailor, are aimed at people who do not have immediate access to trained medical personnel. The disadvantage is that a yacht is likely to have more drugs and equipment than is likely to be available in the wilderness situation, plus other heavy items such as medical books. In the UK and many other parts of the world, the MCA (STCW 95) medical courses designed for commercial Skippers are also ideal for non-commercial yachtsmen. Courses designed for crew aboard large yachts, rather than for merchant navy officers, are the best choice, as they will emphasise the likely problems aboard a much smaller vessel. The disadvantage is that the MCA course assumes that the vessel carries the MCA Category 'A' medical kit. On the other hand, many of the items in the Category 'A' medical kit are going to be carried by the cruising yachtsman, and a study of the drugs list, for example, is only a very small part of the course.

The MCA course is in two parts, with practical and open book exams at the end leading to certification. The first part – Proficiency in Medical First Aid Aboard Ship – takes three days, and the second part – Proficiency in Medical Care Aboard Ship takes five days.

Medical reference books

Skills learned on a training course need to be practised to remain fresh, but aboard a yacht hopefully that practice will be rare. Therefore medical reference books are invaluable to refresh the memory. Of course, an onboard emergency should not be the first time the books are consulted. While regularly reading them from cover to cover might be desirable, realistically a knowledge of the layout of the books and where to find the necessary information is probably sufficient.

An emergency medical reference on CD-ROM is useful for drug information, but not as easy to use as a book for instant guidance in a crisis. There are a number of good marine and general medical reference books on the market. It is best to look at several of them and then choose one or two that best suit the planned type of sailing and the equipment aboard. The *Ship Captain's Medical Guide*, first published in 1868 and now in its 22nd edition, is the classic 'bible' of medical information for vessels without a doctor aboard and the textbook for MCA medical courses. As well as being available as a book, it can also be downloaded from the MCA website.

The *British National Formulary (BNF)* in the UK, and the *American Society of Health-System Pharmacists' (AHFS) Drug Information* in the USA are the 'bibles' for doctors, giving them all the information about every prescription drug available. While a medical professional needs the latest edition, an old copy begged from a friendly doctor will give an invaluable onboard reference for any prescription drugs.

Medical supplies and equipment

There is no end of advice in magazines, books and on the internet suggesting the perfect list of medical supplies to keep on board. The advice is generally excellent, but a profusion of choices is confusing for the non-medical sailor. There are many factors to consider when selecting the medical supplies to carry:

◎ Common ailments at sea: sunburn, skin infections and seasickness.
◎ Common onboard traumatic injuries: head, chest and hand injuries.
◎ Distance from shore that the yacht is going to travel.
◎ Endemic diseases in the cruising area.
◎ Medical problems associated with specific aquatic activities – eg scuba diving and snorkelling.
◎ Medical expertise of crew.
◎ Access to adequate medical facilities.
◎ Number of crew, age, sex and medical history.

'Home remedies'

Every yacht, like every home, needs a selection of 'home remedies' (ie non-prescription supplies) to deal with the everyday knocks, scrapes and illnesses. Hopefully, these are the only items that will be used aboard the yacht, but they are also the things that may well prevent needing to dig into the 'real' medical kit. The 'home remedies' supply should be kept separate so that the primary medical kit remains intact, organised and safe. Exactly which brand or how much to buy will depend upon where the yacht is going, personal preferences and crew numbers. Remember if the yacht is going 'foreign', not only may favourite everyday medicines be unavailable, but the instructions may well be in another language. Sign language is *not* the ideal way to communicate with a pharmacist, especially if the problem is in an intimate place! If you buy medicines while you are overseas, it is important that you purchase only from a reputable source. In certain developing countries, counterfeit or poor quality medicines might be supplied.

A list of 'home remedies' will include most of the items in your bathroom cabinet at home, plus those things you would take if going abroad on holiday. In addition, to have a complete 'home remedies' kit, you will need some items that you might not normally keep in stock at home (eg laxatives, athlete's foot cream, antihistamines, etc).

If young children are on the yacht, you may need further supplies (eg 'junior' versions of painkillers, etc).

It is very tempting to discard outer wrappings and repackage all medicines to save space, but this is very unwise as instructions for use and safety information may be mislaid. Even over-the-counter medicines may not be suitable for everyone. It is better to add packaging in the form of re-sealable plastic bags for each medical item, in order to help keep everything in perfect condition.

Personal medication

The medication that any crew member is currently taking must be carried aboard the yacht, and extra supplies should always be carried in case the boat is unable to return to port at the anticipated time. Before a long voyage, each crew member should review their own medical history with their personal physician or GP for possible additional medical supplies. It is important to take into consideration where the yacht will be going, the possible effects of seasickness, stress and different climates. Anyone susceptible to yeast infections would be well advised to carry a relevant course of medication if they are travel to tropical climes.

The Skipper must be made aware of the current medical status of every crew member, any known allergies, and all personal medication being carried. All crew should be informed of any medical conditions of other crew members – such as diabetes – which could be life-threatening in certain conditions.

The cruising yacht's medical kit

British-registered yachts used solely for pleasure (not chartered) do not have to carry any medical supplies, but if the yacht has any paid crew, then the vessel is required to carry specific medical stores. The current regulations are contained in the Merchant Shipping Notice (MSN) 1768 (M+F), which can be downloaded from the MCA website.

Category 'A'   No limitation on length of trips
Category 'B'   Less than 150nm from the nearest port with adequate medical facilities
Category 'C'   Very close to shore, plus liferafts and lifeboats

The Category 'A' and 'B' medical kits are a good starting point for any cruising yacht that does not have to comply with the regulations. The lists also make an ideal 'standard' to compare with other suggestions. See Appendix 4.

Dr Richard Clubb suggests a 'minimalist's medical kit' in an article for *Practical Boat Owner* magazine, and his suggestions (with a few additions) are shown in Table 6.1. This list is designed to reduce the number of items carried by not attempting to cover *every* conceivable eventuality – only those most likely to occur; where possible, the kit tries to ensure that items have a dual function. The assumption is made that at least one crew member has some medical training, but that there is no medical professional aboard. Looking back on our ten years of cruising, this list certainly reflects almost exactly our use of drugs and medical supplies over that period – apart from some extra items in the 'home remedies list'. The only addition to the list we would make is to add another broad-spectrum antibiotic such as ciprofloxacin, as one of our crew was allergic to penicillin.

When sailing close to home

A yacht that never ventures far from home may feel it is sufficient to carry crew medication plus a selection of home remedies, along with a simple first aid kit such as that recommended for British-registered vessels, which contains: triangular bandages; sterile bandages with unmedicated dressings – medium, large and extra large; safety pins; assorted elastic adhesive dressings medicated; sterile eye pad with attachment; sterile gauze swabs; disposable latex-free examination gloves; sterile eye wash.

All first aid items should be packed in a waterproof container, clearly labelled 'First Aid', and stored where it is accessible at all times by all crew members. Some of the 'home remedies', such as those items for cuts, should be packed in the first aid bag, but other items not needed so quickly are probably best stored separately in another waterproof container or locker.

Automatic external defibrillator (AED)

A normal heartbeat is triggered by electrical impulses, and a malfunction in this system causes the heart to beat erratically or quiver. This is called ventricular fibrillation. This happens in two-thirds of the cases of cardiac arrest. A heart in this state is unlikely to beat normally again, even with cardio-pulmonary resuscitation (CPR), and the only solution is to give the heart an electrical shock. The shock disrupts the twitching and allows the normal beat to restart. Special equipment is needed to administer this shock, which is called defibrillation. CPR extends the window of time in which defibrillation can be effective and provides a trickle of oxygenated blood to the brain and heart, and keeps these organs alive until defibrillation can shock the heart into a normal rhythm.

If CPR is started within four minutes of collapse, and defibrillation provided within ten minutes, a person's survival rate can be as high as 50 per cent. Without defibrillation, the chances of survival are pitifully low. Early defibrillation is so important and the equipment is so easy to use that many AED units are being put in municipal and corporate buildings, and public access areas. The equipment is coming down in price, and many large crewed yachts now carry defibrillators as part of their emergency first aid equipment.

Oxygen

Oxygen-giving equipment is required as part of the Category 'A' medical kit. It is used to treat nearly all causes of breathlessness including heart attack, anaphylactic shock, secondary drowning, smoke inhalation, etc. Unfortunately, an oxygen cylinder that is big enough to be useful is going to take up a lot of space on a small yacht. But oxygen is so important for dive-related injuries that it should always be carried aboard any yacht that carries diving equipment, and where dives are made directly from the boat or tender.

TABLE 6.1 CRUISING MEDICAL KIT
(To be packed in a robust waterproof container)

Essential items

Tablets
Broad-spectrum antibiotic (eg Amoxil)
Antiseasickness (cinnarizine, eg Stugeron)*
Painkillers, strong (dihydrocodeine – can double as anti-diarrhoeal
Painkillers, standard (eg aspirin, paracetamol)*
Prednisolone – for allergies and asthma attacks
Antacid (eg Zantac) – for gastritis and indigestion

Other medicines
Antiseasickness suppositories (eg Stemetil)
Antibiotic eye ointment (eg Fucithalmic)
Antibiotic eye/ear drops (eg Genticin)
Anaesthetic eye drops (eg Minims Amethocaine) – for scratched eye or to allow removal of foreign body
Anti-bacterial cream (eg Flamazine) – especially for burns

Instruments
Tweezers/forceps 6"
Syringe, sterile – for flooding eyes, flushing ears, etc
Scissors
Thermometer, clinical

Dressings
Hypo-allergenic paper tape (eg Micropore)
PVC insulating tape – to hold on dressings, etc in wet environment
Waterproof plasters, large box
Crepe bandages
Transparent waterproof wound dressing (eg Tegaderm)
Support bandages (eg Tubigrip)
Histoacryl – surgical 'superglue' to close simple skin cuts
Large gauze squares

Additional items

Tablets
Antihistamine (eg Triludan, Piriton)*
Anti-diarrhoeal (eg Imodium)*
Antacid (e,g, Gastrocote, Gaviscon, Asilone, Rennies)*
Anti-inflammatory (eg ibuprofen)*
Constipation remedy

Creams
Antiseptic
Anti-herpes (eg Zovirax)*
Anti-fungal (eg Canesten) – for yeast infections almost anywhere*
Anti-inflammatory (eg ibuprofen)*
Anti-inflammatory for skin (eg Betnovate, hydrocortisone)
Sunscreen
Insect repellent

Note: *Medicines marked with * are available over the counter without a prescription.*
See also Appendix 4

7 Fire and the Equipment to Fight It

Surrounded by water, fire might not sound much of a problem to a boat unless it is wooden. It is, however, a very real and constant threat, especially for any yacht with an engine and/or cooking facilities. A modern glassfibre yacht will burn very quickly and produce large volumes of toxic smoke that are equally as dangerous as the fire itself. A steel hull will also burn when temperatures get high enough, and there are plenty of flammable items that ignite at a low temperature on board every yacht that will help raise the temperature of a fire.

Fires and explosions are the principal causes of damage to yachts and of personal injury at sea, and petrol engines and bottled gas used for cooking and heating are frequently involved. The causes of the fire range from improper installations and inadequate ventilation, to careless handling of machinery, fuel, electrical equipment and gas appliances.

It is vitally important to deal with any fire on a yacht as quickly as possible, in its initial stages, as once a fire gets hold aboard a yacht, without back-up and extra equipment, it will be almost impossible to put out. Unless the yacht is alongside, immediate assistance is out of the question, and escape is at best hazardous in the tender or liferaft – and at worst impossible. Every yacht must be more than adequately provided with firefighting equipment. The RYA, MCA, USCG, etc firefighting equipment recommendations and requirements are minimums only and, wherever possible, equipment in excess of these numbers and types should be carried. Every Skipper must be fully conversant with the nature of fire and the principles of fire prevention and have a thorough knowledge of the practical methods of dealing with fire aboard a yacht. Any safety briefing he gives must include not only the position and stowage of extinguishers (manual and automatic), blankets and buckets, but also their operation. Every crew member must know:

◎ The potential fire hazards.
◎ The principles of fire prevention.
◎ What to do if fire breaks out.
◎ Where the firefighting equipment is stored.
◎ A basic knowledge of firefighting using the equipment available.

Tip: Write all the available information down for contacting emergency services (both home and abroad) and post it by the gangway where it can be found quickly by anyone who needs it.

The fundamentals of fire

Fire is the result of three elements, often called the fire triangle:

Heat	A flame, spark or hot surface.
Fuel	Any inflammable or combustible material, eg wood, paper, cooking gas, clothing, paint, oil, gasoline, etc.
Oxygen	A component of the air around us.

All three elements are needed to start and maintain a fire, combining to produce a mixture of heat, light, smoke and toxic gases.

If you keep the three elements (heat, fuel and oxygen) separated, then fire can be prevented. Remove one or more of these elements by starving, smothering or cooling the fire, and it will be extinguished. These are the basic principles of fire prevention and firefighting.

Examples of common causes of fire on a yacht
- Engine backfiring in air laden with combustible vapour.
- Hot exhaust pipe igniting adjacent to combustible materials.
- Spontaneous combustion of oily rags in a badly ventilated compartment.
- A spark caused by static electricity during refuelling.
- Short-circuiting and overloading of the electrical system.
- Smoking in bed.
- Welding or cutting during repairs or alterations.
- Bad practice in the galley.

Principles of fire prevention

By far the best method of dealing with fire aboard a yacht is to stop it happening in the first place, and the *Boat Safety Scheme Guide* (jointly administered by British Waterways and the Environment Agency: www.boatsafetyscheme.com) provides excellent checklists and information about safe boat design features to reduce the risks of fire.

Of the three elements of fire, little can be done to remove oxygen – obviously we need it to breathe – but fuel and heat can be controlled and, where possible, kept apart. This is largely good housekeeping and common sense. The following sections include some of the possible fire risks aboard a yacht and what to do about them.

Cleanliness and tidiness

A tidy boat is not just the sign of a tidy mind, but also of a *safe* boat:

- Do not keep inflammable material on board, such as galley rubbish or oily rags.
- Keep bilges, drip trays and the galley stove scrupulously clean of oil and grease.
- Keep the area around all heat sources clear, including any cooking or heating stoves, machinery and exhaust pipes.

◎ Paint and varnish are highly inflammable, so if possible store these ashore.
◎ Store painting and varnishing materials must be kept aboard in a proper metal-lined locker with adequate ventilation.
◎ Store any inflammable chemicals in accordance with the manufacturers' instructions.
◎ Check that all appliances are turned off when not in use.

 Tip: Close the valve on LPG cylinders before going to bed or leaving the boat unattended.

Naked flames and sparks

These are an obvious danger and yet they are still easily overlooked:

◎ Keep all naked flames such as matches and oil lamps under control, and ensure that they are properly extinguished after use.
◎ Control sparks by fitting spark arrestors to flues, exhausts and ventilators.
◎ Ban smoking aboard the yacht, or at least restrict it to on deck only.
◎ If you must smoke on board: use a metal ashtray; never smoke in bed.
◎ Cover batteries to reduce the likelihood of sparks caused by touching the terminals with a metallic object.
◎ Keep candles, matches, lighters and other sources of flame out of reach of children.

 Tips: Use only safety matches – vibration can ignite other types.

Dedicated cooker lighters are safer than matches.

The galley

Hot fat or oil igniting causes most galley fires:

◎ Stoves on sailing yachts should be designed for marine use and hung in gimbals.
◎ Even motor yachts should have fiddles to hold pots and pans securely when at sea.
◎ Fire-resistant materials or metal shields should protect woodwork near the stove.
◎ Gas cookers must have a flame-failure device to turn off the gas supply automatically if the flame is extinguished.
◎ Don't fit curtains to windows or ports above hob burners.
◎ If you must fry in deep, hot oil, wait until the yacht is tied up alongside.
◎ Never leave a hot hob unattended, especially when cooking with oil or fat.

Electrics

Electrical faults are a major cause of all fires, due to short-circuits or overloading. All electrical installation and maintenance should be carried out by a qualified marine electrician, who should also annually check and test the entire electrical installation and wiring aboard the yacht:

◎ Electrical equipment should be approved for marine use and all wiring be well insulated and adequately sized.
◎ Each circuit should be fused or fitted with non-self-resetting circuit breakers. Switches should be fitted above the bilges and must be spark-proof.

- Never undertake temporary repairs using makeshift materials, except in an emergency.
- Keep extension leads and multipoint adapters to a minimum.
- Ensure that all electrical leads are in perfect condition, and in safe places where they will not be damaged.
- Never replace an existing fuse with a larger one.
- Never overcharge batteries as these release excessive amounts of explosive hydrogen into the air.
- Ensure that battery spaces are well ventilated, and that no switches, relays or fuses are fitted in the locker.

Engines and fuel

The explosive hazards of oils are much less than those of petrol, but diesel fuel can be explosive under certain conditions of fume concentration, and of course the risk of fire is present whenever flammable fuels are carried.

The fire risk must be considered in the construction of all machinery spaces and fuel tanks, and every effort made to reduce the risk to a minimum. Ventilation and fire-resisting materials are very important and special consideration must be given to the hazard of overheated engines causing fires:

- The fuel system must be electrically earthed to prevent a spark from static electricity.
- Exhaust pipes should be water cooled or well lagged with supporting straps heat insulated.
- Engine components must be kept clean and in good condition.
- Shaft bearings must be lubricated frequently to avoid friction heat build-up.
- Drip trays must be large enough not to overflow in rough weather or when heeling in a sailboat.
- Regularly check that the engine room is properly ventilated.
- All fuel pipes, joints and fittings must be frequently inspected for leaks, and always kept tight.
- Approved gas-tight safety torches should always be used in machinery and other confined spaces, and everywhere when refuelling.

Tips: Carry spare fuel in approved containers and store them in fire-resistant drained lockers. Tie them into position to stop them falling over.

Never refill portable fuel tanks in the boat; take them ashore and wipe off any spillage before re-boarding.

Refuelling

The hull of a decked boat is a natural catchment for gas and vapour fumes when refuelling. The vapour from any fuel spilled into the bilges only needs one spark to ignite it, and that can all too easily be supplied by the yacht's own electrical system. The dangers can and must be minimised:

- Turn off all engines, motors, stoves, cookers, fans, heating devices, electrical equipment and LPG (liquefied petroleum gas) appliances before fuelling.
- Do not smoke or allow naked flames on or in the vicinity of a vessel while fuelling or afterwards – until you are sure the fumes have dispersed.

◎ Have a filled fire extinguisher handy.
◎ To reduce the risk of spills:
  – moor the boat securely;
  – never take fuel too fast or overfill;
  – leave room in tanks for fuel expansion.
◎ When finished, check the bilges for leakage and fuel odours, then ventilate until the fuel odour has gone.
◎ If fitted, run the engine compartment exhaust fan for five minutes before starting the engine.
◎ Before starting the engine, stove or cooker, use all natural means of ventilation to clear vapours.

Liquefied Petroleum Gas (LPG)

Only large yachts have the power supply to use electricity for cooking. Most smaller yachts use LPG, though alcohol (methylated spirits) or kerosene (paraffin) are alternatives. LPG cookers are easy to use, do not need priming, and fuel is widely available.

LPG is a mixture of light hydrocarbons which are gaseous at normal temperatures and pressures, and which liquefy readily at moderate pressures or reduced temperature. It is odourless and so, for safety reasons, a pungent compound, ethyl mercaptan, is added to make any leaks easily detectable. LPG occurs naturally in crude oil and natural gas production fields, and is also produced in the oil refining process.

The main component gases of LPG commonly used on yachts are butane and propane. Both gases are widely available in the UK, while butane is more common in Europe, and propane is the norm in the USA. Propane must never be filled into a butane cylinder because the setting of the pressure relief valve is different. Butane and propane cylinders do not have the same connections and their regulators are not interchangeable, but the gases may be safely interchanged if certain precautions are taken. Ideally, particularly for cruising boats, gas appliances should be approved to use both types of gas.

Tip: Check gas detectors each month by releasing a small amount of gas from an *unlit* gas cigarette lighter near the sensor.

LPG fire hazards

LPG and petrol or gasoline vapours have the same dangerous characteristics; both are heavier than air and both are potentially explosive. Escaped gas aboard a yacht is difficult to dispel by overhead ventilation, will sink in air, and will spread into spaces such as the cabin soles, engine and bilge areas. At a low level, the gas is easy to overlook, even in large quantities, despite its pungent odour.

The explosive limits of petrol, butane and propane vary between approximately 1.5 per cent and 10 per cent. What this means is that when there is less than 1.5 per cent of gas mixed with the air, an explosion cannot take place – nor can it occur when there is more than 10 per cent of gas mixed with air. If this explosive mix is exposed to a naked flame, such as lighting the stove, the resulting explosion is so powerful that it can potentially wreck a boat and maim or kill anyone nearby. An ignition of escaped gas has the added risk of flashback to the source of the leak. An LPG cylinder exposed to fire can be pressurised to the point where the pressure relief valve opens, causing a dangerous jet of burning gas. Cylinders can also explode in a hot fire and throw debris over a wide area.

Another hazard comes from faulty burners and insufficient ventilation leading to carbon monoxide poisoning. At very high concentrations, as LPG replaces the available oxygen it will act as an anaesthetic – and subsequently as an asphyxiate.

Safety Precautions

Stringent safety precautions must be observed with LPG installations. General rules for a safe system include the following:

◎ A trained and experienced person must do all work on gas installations and fittings, using suitable components for a boat.
◎ All appliances must be designed for butane/propane and use in a boat.
◎ Gas piping must be stainless steel or seamless copper.
◎ Flexible connections should only be used at the cylinder end or at a gimballed stove.
◎ Manufacturers' recommendations for operating, maintaining and servicing appliances must be followed.
◎ Include a regular annual system check in the yacht's maintenance programme.
◎ Do not allow children to play with gas burner taps or cylinders.
◎ Watch appliances while in use to check that the flame does not go out.
◎ Fit a pressure gauge to allow periodic checking for leaks.
◎ Never use a naked flame if a leak is suspected.
◎ Only leak-test with ammonia-free soapy water or leak detection fluid, which will bubble where a leak is present.
◎ Refit the plastic safety cap or plug on a disconnected cylinder.
◎ Even when 'empty', a cylinder may still contain vapour and must be treated as full; it must never be discarded or stored inside the vessel.
◎ With a gas detector to warn of leaks before a dangerous concentration is reached:
  – ensure the sensor is in the lowest part of the bilge, but above any normal water level;
  – ensure that it will be switched on before any other electrical equipment is used aboard.

All LPG gas cylinders, including spare, empty and those in use, should be:

◎ Located outside the accommodation.
◎ Securely fixed in a sealed locker that is fitted with a drain at the bottom, which leads overboard above the waterline.
◎ Turned off after every cooking or heating session – not just at the end of the day.
◎ Checked carefully for a leak after changing.
◎ Shut in an emergency.

When using the appliance:

◎ Light the match, lighter, etc before the valve is opened.
◎ Shut the cylinder valve before shutting the appliance valve to burn off any fuel in the line.
◎ Ensure the appliance valves are shut before the cylinder valve is turned on.

Special precautions with LPG in tropical and semi–tropical regions

It is extremely important to remember that LPG cylinders should never be filled to 100 per cent capacity. In a hot climate, the cylinder must not be filled to more than 70 per cent of its total capacity – compared to the usual 80 per cent in temperate climates. Many small cylinders do not contain a safety relief valve, so if heated when overfull, the liquefied gas in the cylinder could expand and burst with disastrous results. Extra care should be taken.

A gas leak

LPG systems should have a pressure gauge to allow for periodic checking for leaks. To check for a leak:

♦ Open the cut-off valve and cylinder.
♦ Shut all appliance valves.
♦ Read and note the pressure.
♦ Close the cylinder valve.
♦ Wait for ten minutes.
♦ Confirm the pressure has not changed. Any change indicates there is a leak.

If a leak is suspected, or you can actually smell gas:

♦ DO NOT PANIC.
♦ Open all doors, hatches, port holes, floorboards, etc to provide maximum ventilation.
♦ Stop all engines.
♦ Extinguish all naked flames, cigarettes, etc.
♦ Turn off all burner taps on cooking, heating and lighting appliances.
♦ Turn off ignition switches on all appliances.
♦ Do not operate any electric switches (except above).
♦ Do not use a mobile phone or touch any of its buttons.
♦ If near the shore or alongside:
  – tie up or anchor away from other vessels;
  – get everyone off the yacht and clear the immediate area;
  – inform the harbour or marina authorities;
  – if in doubt, call the fire brigade using a landline or mobile phone well away from the yacht.
♦ Do not use the LPG system until it has been checked and/or the leak rectified by a competent person.

Onboard warning devices

The risk of fire breaking out aboard a yacht can never be completely eliminated. But with prompt and correct action in the first few minutes, a fire can usually be readily extinguished. To fight a fire and win, early knowledge of its existence is as essential as the equipment to deal with it.

Every yacht should be fitted with a warning system to provide an alarm whenever smoke or gas, diesel or petrol fumes are present. The most disastrous fires on boats usually start with an explosion caused by fumes from fuel, bottled gas or battery hydrogen. A gas detector gives an audible alarm if combustible gas is present and will detect concentrations below the explosive level, giving time to fix a problem. The detector must always be turned on immediately on boarding the yacht, before the engine is started or any naked flame is lit.

Smoke detectors are cheap, widely available and very easy to fit, and have saved numerous lives both ashore and afloat. One should be fitted in every cabin and tested regularly to check that the battery is working. As domestic smoke detectors are not designed for the marine environment, it is advisable to replace them annually – a very small extra expense for the security this offers.

Large yachts generally have fire alarm systems, often connected to sprinkler or fog systems that require specialist servicing. Testing the alarm should form part of the regular firefighting practice.

 Tip: Domestic smoke detectors, available at DIY stores, are very cheap, and easy to fit on any boat. Replace them annually as they are not built for the marine environment.

Types of fire

Fires are categorised by fuel type, and each class of fire has a preferred method of extinguishment. The European system uses the classification and symbols shown in the box opposite.

Class F (UK)/Class K (USA) is a recent addition, and special fire extinguishers are designed specifically for this all too common and dangerous type of fire. Australia and New Zealand use the same fire classification system as Europe.

The US classification is similar, yet at the same time very different. Both systems use the first part of the alphabet for type, and even agree on the fuel for Type A and Type D. But unfortunately, Class B and Class C are different in the USA, and this could potentially be very dangerous. The US Class B is the same as EU Class B and Class C together, so great care must be taken not to confuse the two systems. Anyone cruising or chartering in a foreign country must check all fire extinguishers they have aboard their vessel very carefully, before they need to use them.

Firefighting equipment

A small boat, without an engine or cooking facilities, has only a small fire risk and the Skipper may feel a fire bucket is sufficient as firefighting equipment. Aboard a very large yacht there are likely to be fire buckets, fire extinguishers, fire pumps, fire hydrants, fire hoses, and even firefighting outfits plus a trained crew able to operate the equipment. A large yacht will also have fixed firefighting installations in both the accommodation and engine areas. The majority of yachts, with an engine and/or cooking facilities, rely on fire buckets, fire extinguishers and a fire blanket to fight a fire, though they may also have a fixed firefighting system if they have an engine room.

Fire bucket

A bucket is a very basic piece of equipment and there is usually more than one on every yacht. It has numerous uses – from tool carrier, to rain catcher, to bailer. With a lanyard fitted, it is also ideal for hauling up a bucket of sea water and dumping the contents on any Class A fire. Low tech it may be, but anyone can use it immediately and it is reliable (as long as the handle does not break!).

The EU system of fire classification		
EU type	**EU fuel**	**Symbol**
Class A	SOLIDS – wood, paper, upholstery, plastics, etc	
Class B	Flammable LIQUIDS – petrol, diesel, oil, etc	
Class C	Flammable GASES – propane, butane, LPG, etc	
Class D	Combustible METALS – aluminium, etc	
Class E	Fires involving ELECTRICAL EQUIPMENT	
Class F	Cooking OIL and FAT	

The US system of fire classification	
US type	**US fuel**
Class A	SOLIDS – wood, paper, upholstery, plastics, etc
Class B	All flammable LIQUIDS AND GASES
Class C	Fires involving ELECTRICAL EQUIPMENT
Class D	Combustible METALS – aluminium, etc
Class K	Cooking OIL and FAT

Fire extinguishers

Sea water and a bucket are perfect for putting out carbonaceous fires like wood, upholstery, etc, but aboard a yacht there may well be flammable liquids and gases involved and water is definitely not going to help. There are a number of different types of fire extinguisher available and they cover all types of fire. In the UK, fire extinguishers used to be colour coded to make the contents instantly identifiable. EU regulations now require all new portable fire extinguishers to be coloured red. UK fire extinguishers have complied, but maintained their colour code with a zone of colour. This colour indication appears on the front of the extinguisher above the operating instructions and will be clearly visible when it is correctly mounted. The class letter and symbol for each type of fire the extinguisher is designed to extinguish is also displayed. The different types of fire extinguisher are shown in the box below.

Different types of fire extinguisher			
Type	EU old colour or new 5 per cent band	Australia/NZ old colour or new band	Class of fire
Water	Red	Red	A
Dry powder	Blue	White	A, B, C, E
Foam	Cream	Blue	A, B
CO$_2$	Black	Black	B, E
Wet chemical	Yellow	Oatmeal/beige	A, F

In the USA, fire extinguishers are not required to be any particular colour. Emphasis is given to showing what sort of fire the extinguisher is suitable to fight. Older fire extinguishers are labelled with coloured geometrical shapes with letter designations. Newer fire extinguishers use a picture/labelling system to designate which types of fires they are to be used on. These pictograms are also used to show what not to use. For example, Type A extinguishers will show a pictogram of an electrical cord and outlet with a big slash through it. In other words, do not use it on an electrical fire.

Guide to extinguisher use		
Type	*Letter and shape*	Pictogram
Class A (Green)	**A** Ordinary Combustibles	
Class B (Red)	**B** Flammable Liquids	
Class C (Blue)	**C** Electrical Equipment	
Class D (Yellow)	**D** Combustible metals	**D** Combustible metals
Class K	**K** Combustible Cooking	

(Note: The American System does not feature Class E or F.)

Water fire extinguishers

Effective fire type: Class A fires ◎ Extinguishing method: Cooling

Water extinguishers are filled with water that is pressurised with a gas. These are the cheapest and most widely used fire extinguisher, and are excellent for use on accommodation fires involving woodwork and bedding. Water extinguishers can also be used to prevent re-ignition of a fire temporarily extinguished by another method.

Water in jet form must *never* be used on flammable liquids – it spreads the burning liquid and intensifies the fire. In addition, water must *never* be used on electrical fires because water is a conductor.

Foam spray fire extinguishers

Effective fire type: Class A and Class B fires ◎ Extinguishing method: Cooling/smothering

Foam spray fire extinguishers (AFFF – aqueous film forming foam) are more expensive than water ones, but more versatile. They are ideal for multi-risk situations where both combustible materials and flammable liquid risks are likely to be found. The blanketing effect of the foam spray gives rapid flame knockdown. The foam not only extinguishes flammable liquids, but also effectively seals the vapours, reducing the risk of re-ignition. The wetting and cooling characteristics of the foam solution also make them very effective on solid combustible materials, and offer wider extinguishing applications over water.

Foam spray extinguishers should not be used for fires involving electricity, gases or metal.

Multi-purpose dry powder/ABC dry chemical fire extinguishers

Effective fire type: Classes A, B, C and E fires ◎ Effective fire type (USA): Classes A, B and C fires ◎ Extinguishing method: Flame inhibition

Often termed the 'multi-purpose' extinguisher, this can be used on a wide range of fires – including gas fires. Standard dry powder/BC dry chemical fire extinguishers are also available, but these do not cover such a broad range. This type works by knocking down flame, and on burning solids the powder melts to form a skin. It does not cool, though, and any fire must be watched carefully for flare-up. They are safe to use on live electrical equipment, although the foam does not penetrate the spaces in equipment easily and the fire may re-ignite.

It is a good choice for below decks as it is not corrosive and does not give off fumes. On the other hand, this type can obscure vision in confined spaces, damage goods and machinery, and the foam is messy to clear up afterwards. It is not for use on chip or fat pan fires. See below for fires involving metal.

Dry powder special metal fire extinguishers

Effective fire type: Class D fires ◎ Extinguishing method: Smothering

This is a specialised powder fire extinguisher for use on metal fires such as sodium, lithium, manganese and aluminium when in the form of swarf or turnings.

CO_2 fire extinguishers

Effective fire type: Class B and Class E fires ◎ Effective fire type (USA): Class B and Class C fires ◎ Extinguishing method: Smothering

CO_2 extinguishers contain carbon dioxide, a non-flammable gas, stored as a compressed liquid. The liquid expands to a gas as it is expelled from the extinguisher, then cools the surrounding air and freezes the water vapour in the atmosphere, often causing ice to form around the horn and a white cloud to be seen. CO_2 is heavier than oxygen, so these extinguishers work by displacing or taking away oxygen from the surrounding area. This can be very dangerous in confined spaces, as the firefighter needs the oxygen to breathe. As the CO_2 is very cold when it emerges from the extinguishers, it cools to an extent, but the gas disperses quickly so there is a risk of re-ignition. Carbon dioxide is ideal for fires involving electrical apparatus, and will also extinguish Class B liquid fires. It is clean, non-contaminating, odourless and safe on clothing, equipment, food, etc.

Wet chemical fire extinguisher

Effective fire type: Class A and Class F fires ◎ *Effective fire type (USA): Class K fires* ◎ *Extinguishing method: Cooling/smothering*

This extinguisher is specially designed for kitchens and galleys where chip or fat pan fires are a high risk. It is extremely effective as the wet chemical, a potassium-based liquid, does not splash the grease, rapidly knocks the flames out, cools the burning oil, and chemically reacts to form a soap-like solution, sealing the surface and preventing re-ignition. It is also effective on combustible solids such as wood, paper, etc. Some extinguishers are also rated for Class B fires too. For any large yacht with a commercial-style galley this is invaluable, and far more versatile than a fire blanket.

Halon and halon substitutes

Halon was used in some handheld fire extinguishers and also in automatic fire extinguisher systems. It was the ideal all-round extinguisher, but unfortunately halon is a greenhouse gas and, with the exception of equipment deemed critical under the Regulations, all firefighting equipment in the EU containing halon had to be decommissioned before 31 December 2003. No substitute is available at present in the UK for non-automatic fire extinguishers, due to the high cost and large quantities needed of the alternatives. In the USA, there are alternatives manufactured – such as Halotron 1.

Fire extinguishers ratings

Fire extinguishers suitable for Classes A, B and F (Class K in the USA) are marked with a numerical rating indicating the maximum size of test fire that they can extinguish. The larger the number, the larger the test fire it can extinguish. In the case of Class A, a wooden crib 0.5m (approx 1½ft) wide x 0.56m (approx 1½ft) high x length is ignited, and the amount of burning crib that can be extinguished is measured. The rating figure is ten times the length in metres, eg 13A extinguishes a crib 1.3m (approx 4ft) long. Class B is related to fire surface area, and the rating figure to the quantity of flammable liquid that can be extinguished in a circular tray, eg 34B extinguishes 34 litres (approx 2 gallons) of fuel. For Class F fires, there are four benchmark tests using 5, 15, 25 and 75 litres (approx 1, 3, 5½ and 16½ gallons) of sunflower oil. The oil is heated to auto-ignition and allowed to pre-burn for two minutes. The fire is extinguished, and no re-ignition must occur within ten minutes of extinguishing the fire.

Fire extinguisher ratings are very important as they allow a quick comparison of different types of extinguishers. Unfortunately what they do not do is make it clear for the *layman*, what the various extinguishers can do. Most crew on a yacht will have little or no practical experience of using a fire extinguisher, and even a crew member who has taken part in a three-day basic firefighting course will in all probability have used only one or two different extinguishers. At best, the crew will be inexperienced and will probably need at least a few moments to get used to using an extinguisher. Unfortunately, small extinguishers do not have those few moments of grace – a dry powder 5A/34B extinguisher lasts only *eight seconds*!

TABLE 7.1 FIRE TYPES AND COMMON FIREFIGHTING EQUIPMENT						
	Class A	Class B	Class C	Class D	Class E	Class F
Fire bucket	👍					
Water extinguisher	👍					
Foam (AFFF) fire extinguisher	👍	👍				
Dry powder (multi-purpose) fire extinguisher	👍	👍	👍		👍	
Dry powder special metal fire extinguisher				👍		
CO_2 fire extinguisher		👍			👍	
Wet chemical fire extinguisher	👍					👍
Fire blanket						👍
Hose reel and fire pump	👍					

TABLE 7.2 US FIRE TYPES AND COMMON FIREFIGHTING EQUIPMENT					
	Class A (green	Class B (red)	Class C (blue)	Class D (yellow)	Class K
Fire bucket	👍				
Water extinguisher	👍				
Foam (AFFF) fire extinguisher	👍	👍			
Dry chemical (BC) fire extinguisher		👍	👍		
Dry chemical (ABC) fire extinguisher	👍	👍	👍		
Dry powder fire extinguisher				👍	
Co$_2$ fire extinguisher		👍	👍		
Wet chemical fire extinguisher					👍
Fire blanket					👍
Hose reel and fire pump	👍				

The figures in the box below, with information gathered from a manufacturer's internet site, give some idea of how long the contents of the most common size of fire extinguisher found on yachts might be expected to last. A big extinguisher may be unwieldy, heavy and difficult to stow, but it will give you a better chance of actually putting out the fire before the contents have run out.

Type	Weight	Capacity	Rating	Discharge time
Multi-purpose powder	1.5kg (3lbs)	1kg (2lbs)	5A/34B	8 seconds
Multi-purpose powder	3kg (6½lbs)	1.5kg (3lbs)	13A/89B	10 seconds
Multi-purpose powder	6.7kg (15lbs)	4kg (9lbs)	21A/113B	12 seconds
Foam (AFFF)	3.5kg (8lbs)	2lt (3½pts)	5A/55B	20 seconds
Foam (AFFF)	10.5kg (23lbs)	6lt (10pts)	13A/183B	30 seconds
CO_2	4.75kg (10lbs)	2kg (4lbs)	34B	12 seconds
Wet chemical	11.8kg(26lbs)	6lt (10pts)	13A/75F	43 seconds

Fire blankets

Fire blankets are an important fire protection item, especially in the galley. They are constructed from woven fire-resistant material and are available in several sizes. They extinguish by smothering the fire and can be used on small, contained fires instead of a fire extinguisher, as well as for fat fires in the galley. They are also ideal for wrapping a person whose clothes are on fire. They are light, small and require little or no maintenance. Compared with wet chemical extinguishers, the only alternative for galley fires, they are very cheap – though not as versatile. It is very important that the fire blanket is stored near or in the galley, but never above or behind the stove where it could be impossible to get at in an emergency. A fire blanket does require care in use, as the firefighter has to get very close to the flames to employ it. The blanket has no cooling effect on a fire, and to prevent re-ignition it must be left in place on a fat pan fire until the contents are cool.

Fixed firefighting systems

Opening an engine compartment to use a fire extinguisher when fire is suspected is very dangerous as the rush of fresh oxygen will fan the flames. It is far better to fight an engine room fire with a fixed extinguisher.

Engine room fires are one of the more common types of fire aboard a yacht. In a small, unmanned engine space, an automatic system, activated by a rise in temperature, can discharge and extinguish a fire long before the crew of the yacht can ever detect it and are able to use a portable fire extinguisher to deal with it.

Aboard larger yachts with big engine rooms where an engineer may be working, the fixed system relies initially on fire detection using one or more of the following: ✧ ionisation smoke detector ✧ particle smoke detector ✧ rate of temperature rise detector ✧ flame detector.

If an engine room fire is detected by one of the above devices, the alarms are sounded to alert the crew, who should proceed to muster station. At that point, if everyone is accounted for, the fixed firefighting system can be activated. If anyone is missing and suspected to be in the engine room, it will be necessary to recover that person before setting off the extinguishers.

The accommodation areas aboard larger yachts are generally protected by a pressurised water sprinkling system, or on newer yachts a water fogging system. These are frequently automatically triggered by a temperature rise and fire, as well as having a manual override system. Fogging systems deliver the water as mist, which is less detrimental to fixtures and fittings and also safer to use on a wide class of fires – including those involving electrical equipment.

What firefighting equipment is best?

A boat is an environment where almost all types of fire risk in a small space are omnipresent, and this risk of fire far exceeds that in the home environment. It might be ideal to have a variety of fire extinguishers, but on a small yacht this is probably impractical. Dry powder is a good all-round choice. Whatever type of fire extinguisher you choose, make sure it conforms to the appropriate British Standards (BSEN3 and BS7863). Look for the Kite mark or the special British Approvals for Fire Equipment (BAFE) mark. Australia and New Zealand have their own standards. In the USA, buy fire extinguishers that carry an independent testing laboratory label.

Where feasible, the number of fire extinguishers should exceed the basic recommendations and requirements – which are, at best, very basic. Bigger is definitely better, even if this also means *heavier*, though obviously it must still be manoeuvrable around the yacht. Extinguishers that have a controlled discharge are preferable as they allow some of the contents to be retained for use in the case of re-ignition of the fire. The location of extinguishers is very important; if the extinguisher cannot be found easily when it is needed, it is worthless. A fire extinguisher in each cabin, plus one near the galley and one in or near the cockpit, is an excellent idea. Add a fixed installation in the engine room, at least a couple of buckets with lanyards, plus a fire blanket, and most small to medium-sized yachts are well protected. Larger yachts will need to have much more extensive firefighting equipment, and any yacht with a large galley with commercial equipment should include a wet chemical fire extinguisher.

Escape routes

It is very important to consider how to escape from the yacht in the event of a fire down below. Small yachts, especially those without air conditioning, generally have plenty of hatches that offer an alternative to the main companionway. Designated emergency exits are common aboard larger yachts. It is important to ensure that all guests and crew aboard the yacht are aware of all escape routes and any alternative exits, and are shown how to open them.

 Tip: Plastic hatches can distort and jam in a fire, so keep an axe in a nearby and handy location.

Maintenance of firefighting equipment

Fire bucket Regularly check that the bucket is where it should be stowed and has not been removed or used for something else. Check the handle is secure and the lanyard is in good condition.

Fire extinguishers The marine environment is never kind to equipment made of metal, so it is very important to check all fire extinguishers regularly. At least monthly:

- Visually check that extinguishers have not been removed, used or damaged.
- If the safety seal has been broken or there is obvious damage or corrosion, the cylinder must be removed for further checking, replacement and/or charging.
- Refill or replace partly discharged extinguishers as soon as possible.
- Check that pressure gauges, where fitted, are in the operable range.
- Check CO_2 fire extinguishers by weighing them.

Every five years, cylinders should be discharged, tested and refilled. Hydrostatic pressure testing must be done at any time that an extinguisher shows evidence of corrosion or mechanical injury, and also at 5 or 12 years, depending upon the cylinder material, the contents and the regulating authority.

Tip: Fire extinguishers requiring discharge for testing or refuelling are perfect for demonstration and crew practice, allowing everyone an opportunity to handle an extinguisher.

Fire blanket Fire blankets require very little maintenance. Check regularly that the blanket is in the correct position. Once a year:

- Withdraw the blanket from its container and unfold.
- Check for damage or discolouration of the surface.
- Check the handle fixings.
- Discard it if there is any evidence of damage, or refold the blanket according to the instructions on the container and replace it.

This annual check should be combined with a crew fire drill to give everyone a chance to practise using a fire blanket.

Fixed firefighting systems Automatic fire extinguishers should be maintained in the same way as the equivalent portable fire extinguisher. Fixed systems aboard large yachts will need annual servicing by the supplier or his agent.

8 Emergency Situations

This chapter provides guidance and advice to help the Skipper and crew deal with emergencies aboard the yacht. In the event of an accident or emergency, the primary responsibilities of the Skipper are: *the safety of those entrusted to his care*; *the safety of the yacht*; *the protection of the marine environment*. All other considerations are secondary to these. If assistance is required, the Skipper should always assume that Murphy's Law is in force, which states: *if it can get worse, it will*. He should, therefore, take whatever action is necessary as soon as possible.

This chapter covers the following emergency situations:

- Collision
- Critical plant failure
- Firefighting
- Flooding

- Grounding
- Man overboard
- Heavy weather

Medical emergencies, rescue (including salvage) and abandoning ship are covered in separate chapters.

Collision

There are many harrowing tales of yachtsmen who were unaware of anything untoward until they suddenly saw the vast bow of a freighter towering above them, or felt the thud as they struck a submerged container, or came to a full stop as they hit a sleeping whale. Poor watchkeeping is the cause of the majority of collisions; but, despite taking all possible precautions, situations can arise when a collision, or near collision, becomes an act of God rather than a failure of man.

Flotsam and jetsam

Containers are an increasing hazard in the oceans of the world, every year, some reports claim, more than 10,000 fall overboard. Storms are often to blame, and with bigger ships and greater stack heights, individual incidents can see dozens and occasionally hundreds of containers lost or damaged as whole stacks collapse. Most sink right away. But a few, such as insulated refrigeration containers and those filled with boxes of light-weight items packed in foam, continue to float for a long time, often barely awash. In addition to containers, there are all sorts of other flotsam and jetsam floating in the sea including whole trees, cargo hatches, steel tanks, etc. These floating objects are found everywhere, carried by the ocean currents; and as they are unlit and often almost invisible, especially at night, they are an increasing hazard for small yachts. Collisions are fortunately rare, but they *do* happen; lookout vigilance is the only way to avoid a clash in which the yacht will undoubtedly come off the worst.

Lights, shapes and sound signals

The COLREGs include details of the lights, shapes and sound signals to be displayed during various accident and emergency situations. It is very important that these are displayed correctly and as soon as possible to prevent one accident leading to another.

Non-routine lights, shapes and sound signals

The following charts are a guide to some of the more unusual lights and shapes that a yacht might need to display during an accident or emergency.

Lights For details including position, power, arcs of visibility, see COLREGs Rule 20 to 30 and Annex 1.

Yacht less than 50m (164 ft) in length	Masthead		Side	Stern		All-round	
	Forward	Abaft		Stern	Towing		
	White	White	Red/Green	White	Yellow	White	Red
Towing (less than 200m (656ft))*	2		1	1	1		
Towing and RAM*	2		1	1	1	1	2
Being towed			1	1			
Not under command							2
NUC and making way			1	1			2
Restricted in ability to manoeuvre						1	2
RAM and making way	1		1	1		1	2
At anchor						1	
Aground						1	2

Note: *When towing in an emergency, these lights need not be displayed.

Shapes For details including position, shape and distance apart, see COLREGs Rule 20, 24 to 30 and Annex 1.

Vessel >12m (39ft)	Ball	Diamond
Being towed length >200m (656ft)		1
Not under command	2	
Restricted in ability to manoeuvre	2	1
At anchor	1	
Aground	3	

Sounds For full details including intervals, duration and technical details of sound signal appliances, see COLREGs Rules 32, 35 and Annex III.

Up to 100m (328ft) in length	Whistle	Bell	
		Rapid ring	Stroke
Not making way – power-driven	— —		
Under way – sailing	— – –		
Towing	— – –		
Being towed	— – – –		
Not under command	— – –		
NUC and making way	— – –		
Restricted in ability to manoeuvre	— – –		
At anchor*	– — –	5 sec	
Aground*	– — –	5 sec	3

Notes: — = prolonged blast – = short blast
*The sounding of the Morse letter by whistle is recommended but not compulsory.

Tip: Vessels that sight potentially dangerous floating objects must broadcast a SECURITE message to alert other shipping in the area.

Marine life

Sealife, especially dolphins and whales, are another hazard for a small vessel. Dolphins can and do collide with yachts, causing injury to both parties, but more often sighting them is a time of great joy aboard, as they usually happily play in the bow wave without harm to either party. As with ships, a large yacht, especially a high-speed vessel, can easily kill or maim a dolphin without much sign of damage to the vessel.

The sighting of a whale must be viewed as having the potential for a collision. Whales become more vulnerable in feeding, nursing, calving, and mating grounds where they spend more time on the surface, but encounters can take place anywhere. In the 1989–90 Whitbread race, the *Charles Jourdan* suffered a hole in its hull after a whale collision, and a sperm whale sunk the whaling ship *Essex* in 1820, an event that inspired the novel *Moby-Dick*. In whale and ship encounters the whale is the one to come off worse, but in yacht and whale mishaps it is the yacht that is likely to suffer the most. Obviously if sailing in an area where whales are common, crew must be extra vigilant and fast yachts should keep below 10 knots. If whales approach a vessel before the vessel can safely veer away, engines should be put into neutral until the whales move away.

Other vessels

There are very few instances of collisions occurring between big ships when watchkeepers are totally unaware of the presence of the other. There are, however, too many instances when the officer of the watch of a ship fails apparently to detect a yacht. One ship's officer told us: 'I know only too well how easily collisions can happen. I vividly recall steaming into the Persian Gulf serving as a junior officer aboard a huge tanker in 1969, and finding the mast and sails of a tiny Arab dhow impaled on our starboard

anchor. My ship was particularly well run with very conscientious watchkeepers, yet we were totally unaware that we had been involved in a collision in the middle of the night with such a small craft.'

Collision prevention is all about keeping a proper lookout and making the yacht highly visible. One of the revealing features of many yacht/ship collisions is the admission by the yacht that they were not necessarily keeping a perfect lookout. There are times when everyone fails to look around properly, especially away from the coast or a shipping lane, and it is all too easy at any time to forget to look astern for long periods. The temptation to leave the watch for 'just a few minutes' to plot a fix, heat up some soup, listen to the weather forecast or write up the log is all too great. Such visits can indeed be 'just a few minutes', but too often they are nearer 20 minutes than 3 minutes. A merchant ship doing 20 knots can appear from hull down on the horizon to being a collision hazard in less time than that, especially in reduced visibility.

Making the yacht highly visible is mostly about fitting a good radar reflector because most merchant ships rely more and more on using ARPA (Automated Radar Plotting Aid) to detect other shipping rather than a plentiful supply of real lookouts.

While collision avoidance using radio is not recommended in any way and can be positively dangerous, it can also be helpful to contact a ship early on in a crossing situation. The communication should be made on VHF channels 16 or 13. Using the All Ships button on a DSC radio can also be considered. It will alert the other ship to the presence of the yacht, and depending upon the future courses of both vessels, may save either having to manoeuvre unnecessarily.

A collision between two or more vessels under way is the most obvious scenario, but a collision can be caused in other ways – such as a yacht breaking free from her moorings and falling down on another yacht at anchor. It can also be the result of an illegal action – such as a yacht proceeding the wrong way down a shipping lane, causing other vessels to collide when they take evasive action.

Near collision

In the event of a near collision with another vessel, as well as taking avoiding action it is important to alert that vessel to the approaching disaster. White collision flares, designed to attract attention, should be kept close to the wheel of a yacht ready for immediate use. One flare is probably not enough. The other vessel's watchkeeper may only have seen it out of the corner of his eye and needs a better look. Murphy's Law says, *It is at that precise moment that the flare will choose to go out*, so a second or even third flare must be immediately to hand.

Tip: A signal lamp or powerful flashlight is a alternative to a white flare, and is especially effective when shone into white sails.

Deciding the yacht is the stand-on vessel and waiting in vain for the give-way vessel to make an alteration of course is no defence in law in the event of a collision. The COLREGs clearly state, in Rule 17b, that if the give-way vessel fails to take action, the stand-on vessel must do something to prevent a collision. It is very important that if the stand-on vessel decides it is time to take action, whatever he does must not conflict with any possible belated action by the give-way vessel. It is normally sensible to alter course substantially to starboard.

An actual collision

If a collision can possibly be avoided, the best action of a manoeuvrable yacht is probably to make a sharp 90° or 180° turn away from the oncoming ship. This may avoid or at least minimise the likely impact. If it is clear that a collision cannot be avoided, the best action for any two vessels in this situation is to hit bow on. This should cause the least damage. The watchkeeper must make all efforts to alert the crew, who prepare for impact by taking the 'brace position':

◎ Stand up and hold onto something solid at waist height (not the bulkhead).
◎ Bend your elbows and knees.
◎ Lift your heels off the deck.
◎ Face away from anything loose that could go flying in the impact.

In the event of being run down or colliding with a large ship, the impact may be so severe that the yacht breaks up and disintegrates immediately, precipitating the crew into the sea. It is important that everyone swims away from the larger vessel to stop them being sucked into the propeller. Once the offending ship is clear, and especially if the crew have been caught unawares and are not wearing lifejackets, everyone should swim back to the vicinity of the collision, where there will probably be sufficient floating wreckage of the yacht to cling on to. Rescue may not be imminent, as the crew of the large ship may neither have seen nor felt the collision despite the catastrophe it caused. The immediate search among the wreckage must be for distress signalling equipment to attract the attention of the departing vessel, followed by grabbing liferafts and lifejackets.

The Collision Flowchart (see page 119) details the actions to be taken in the event of a collision. If the collision disables the yacht, it is important that other vessels are alerted to the situation – especially in busy waters or reduced visibility. In the event of a collision involving another vessel, the Skipper must ensure he gets full details of the other party for insurance purposes and an accident report. This should include:

COLLISION FLOWCHART

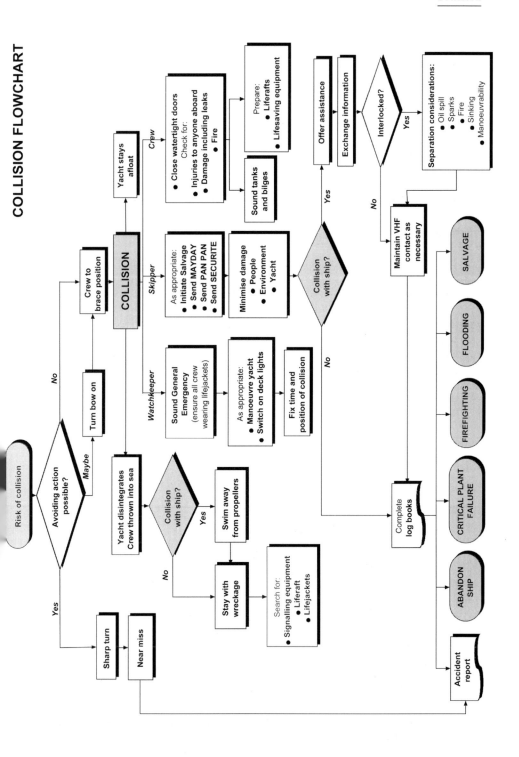

Risk of collision

Avoiding action possible?
- Yes → **Sharp turn** → **Near miss**
- No → **Crew to brace position**
- Maybe → **Turn bow on** → Crew to brace position

COLLISION

Skipper
As appropriate:
- Initiate Salvage
- Send MAYDAY
- Send PAN PAN
- Send SECURITE

Minimise damage
- People
- Environment
- Yacht

Crew
Yacht stays afloat
- Close watertight doors
- Check for:
  - Injuries to anyone aboard
  - Damage including leaks
  - Fire

Sound tanks and bilges

Prepare:
- Liferafts
- Lifesaving equipment

Watchkeeper
Sound General Emergency (ensure all crew wearing lifejackets)

As appropriate:
- Manoeuvre yacht
- Switch on deck lights

Fix time and position of collision

Collision with ship?
- Yes → **Offer assistance** → **Exchange information** → **Interlocked?**
  - Yes → **Separation considerations:**
    - Oil spill
    - Sparks
    - Fire
    - Sinking
    - Manoeuvrability
  - No → **Maintain VHF contact as necessary**
- No → **Complete log books**

Yacht disintegrates Crew thrown into sea

Collision with ship?
- Yes → **Swim away from propellers**
- No → **Stay with wreckage** → Search for:
  - Signalling equipment
  - Liferaft
  - Lifejackets

Complete log books

Accident report

- SALVAGE
- FLOODING
- FIREFIGHTING
- CRITICAL PLANT FAILURE
- ABANDON SHIP

◎ The vessel's details, including flag, name, call sign and port of registry.
◎ The owner's details.
◎ The port of departure and destination.

The Skipper will also need to request the same information from any other vessel(s) (this will be needed for insurance purposes).

When estimating the extent of damage, all areas of the yacht must be checked as problems can occur in places quite remote from the area of impact. Fastenings can be sheared, pipes fractured and the pumping system damaged. Sounding of tanks and bilges should be continued for some time until it is quite clear that there is no ingress of water. Even if the damage seems minor, the yacht should be hauled out of the water as soon as possible after any serious collision for a thorough check. All actions should be recorded carefully in the log book, as this may be required in the event of legal action or insurance claims. In addition, an accident report may need to be filed.

 Tip: Use any camera equipment on board to record events for use in later reports or insurance claims.

Critical plant failure

The failure of any major part or function of a yacht at sea can be critical to safety; and therefore it is important that all eventualities are considered, thought through, and practised before they happen. The Critical Plant Flowchart (see page 121) describes the actions to be taken in the event of a serious machinery failure.

Engine failure

There are many causes of engine failure, and most of them involve the fuel system. Fuel contamination can be caused by ingress of water mixing with the fuel, by bacterial growth inside fuel tanks, or by taking dirty fuel. Continually changing fuel filters or cleaning the fuel can overcome contamination. Without a fuel separator, paper coffee filters and even old rags have been used to strain fuel from a contaminated tank to a clean one.

Aboard a sailing yacht one of the biggest causes of engine failure is the wrapping of one of its own ropes around the propeller and over-straining the engine. Never start the engine without checking that all the lines are aboard the yacht. This is particularly important at night in rough weather when the end of a halyard can drop over the side unnoticed.

 Tip: When taking on fuel, only fill tanks after keeping a sample in a clean, clear, jam jar and checking it for contamination.

Steering failure

Loss or damage to the steering gear may result from from a variety of causes, including heavy weather, collision or poor maintenance. The inability to steer can imperil the yacht and all the crew must be familiar with the actions to be taken in the event of a steering breakdown. Without a rudder, a yacht is literally adrift. There will be little

CRITICAL PLANT FAILURE FLOWCHART

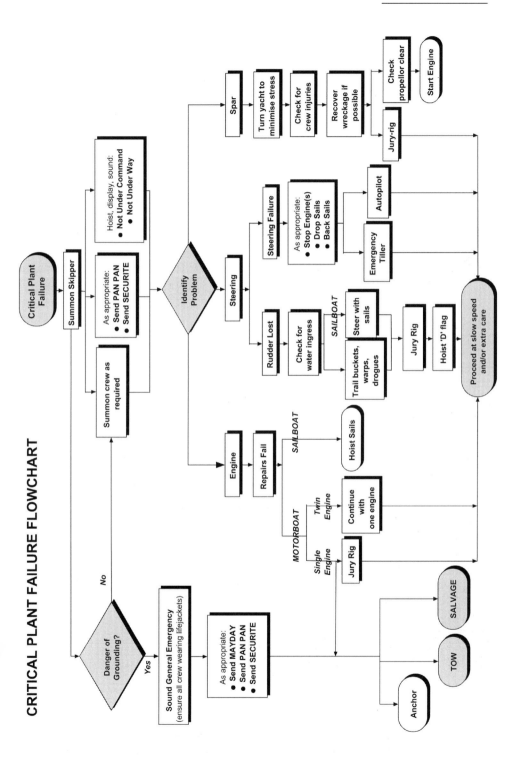

directional control until a jury rudder can be fixed, even aboard a boat under sail. The problem is compounded in strong wind with a steep sea when there is a high risk of knockdown. In the 1979 Fastnet Race, 14 boats suffered rudder failure and a few were knocked down or rolled as a result.

If a rudder is lost the first priority is to make sure the boat is not leaking. Aboard a sailboat it may be possible to steer the boat by trimming the sails, usually best on a moderate close reach. Trailing buckets, warps or improvised drogues astern will provide a better alternative. One technique is to set a warp, which might be a short heavy line or small sail, from a bridle and lead lines to a winch on each side of the yacht. The warp is trailed directly astern and the course is adjusted by winching in on one side to turn that way. A more effective method is to trail two small drogues, such as fenders, off each quarter, and turn by adjusting the line lengths. Buckets with a small hole cut in the bottom can be used, but unless they are very strong and a towing line can be attached through a drilled hole, they will not last long. The larger the yacht the greater the water resistance needed in the tow, and a tender half-filled with water may provide the desired steering effect.

Rudder failure far offshore means some sort of jury-rig must be created by using the imagination. A locker door makes an ideal rudder blade, a spinnaker pole the rudderstock, and careful lashing the created ensemble astern can give at least a temporary fix. The jury rudder will need to be weighed down with, for example, an anchor and chain shackled to the lower edge, to keep it from riding up in the water when under way. Chafe is a likely problem and must be checked for regularly. Few jury-rigs are really efficient, and it is important that the crippled boat is not driven too hard and that speed is kept down – even in good weather.

Steering failure is definitely annoying and can lead to further serious trouble. It may be that the wire cables have snapped or snagged or that there is a leak in the hydraulic steering system, but steering systems have a nasty habit of breaking down at the most inconvenient of times. Occasions where the yacht is overtaking another one or entering between breakwaters seem to be the favourite situations, according to MIAB reports. Testing steering gear before engaging it in a close quarters situation will at least reveal the problem with time for a cure or jury-rig. In the event of steering failure in a close quarters situation, it is important to first get all way off the yacht. Stop the engines or back or strike the sails. Notify vessels in the area by VHF and hoist day shapes or, at night, display NUC lights. An emergency tiller should be part of the inventory aboard all wheel-steered vessels, and with quick action it will usually avert most problems. If the autopilot is connected directly to the rudderstock, an ideal alternative steering is just a button or two away.

Tip: Ensure some thought has been given beforehand to the problem of steering failure.

Rigging and spar failure

The principal cause of rig failure is breakage caused by flaws, fatigue stress or wear of the metal linkage fittings. It is extremely important for the watchkeeper to be vigilant at all times on a passage for any sign of hairline cracks, loose locknuts, missing cotter pins, broken strands on standing rigging, bent or worn fittings, etc. At the first sign of a rigging weakness or a break, the yacht should be turned to take the stress off the weak area and repairs made. The greatest danger comes when a windward spreader or shroud breaks while the yacht is heeled to a fresh breeze. An immediate tack might save the situation, but it is highly likely that the mast will also break.

Any portion of the running gear that breaks can usually be repaired or replaced sufficiently well to get the yacht to port, but the loss of a spar is more serious. Broken booms have been splinted and repaired mid passage with a variety of materials. We have even sailed in a boat where the boom was splinted with a fire extinguisher whose top and bottom had been removed.

Dismasting

The loss of the mast is one of the most serious accidents that can happen to a sailboat, particularly in heavy weather. To rig a jury mast capable of carrying sufficient sail to keep her off a lee shore, or to complete her passage before stores are exhausted, may be impossible. The average sailing yacht has an engine as a back-up plant to facilitate reaching a safe haven, but often the range is restricted by fuel capacity. Loosing the mast is frightening, but seldom extremely dangerous if the correct action is taken. Injury to the crew is rare because the rig normally falls overboard to leeward.

In the event of a dismasting, all crew should be summoned to tackle the problem together. It is best to have a brief discussion on tactics before cutting a mast adrift, but time might not always be on the side of the beleaguered crew. In a heavy sea there is a danger of the mast pounding against the side of the boat and puncturing it. In these conditions the shrouds and backstays should be released or cut away with the yacht riding by the forestay to the wreckage, which will act as a sea anchor, until the weather moderates. Do not cut the mast away completely unless it is imperative to the safety of the hull, as the broken mast is going to be the best source of supplies and hardware needed to rig a jury replacement.

As soon as conditions permit, the wreckage of the mast should be brought alongside. The sails and everything else that can be removed should be, and then if possible the mast brought aboard. The more that can be saved the less expensive the repairs later, and the more there will be to fashion a jury-rig. Do not start the engine until after the propeller has been checked for any entanglement from the rigging.

Rigging a jury mast will depend upon the strength and ingenuity of the crew, and great care must be taken not to overburden the new mast in order to get the yacht home. Yachts without masts have arrived in port utilising the broken-off stub as a mast, others have used the boom as a mast and run downwind with a loose-footed sail fashioned from the remnants of the mainsail, or have utilised a storm sail carried on board. Yves Parlier, aboard *Aquitaine Innovations*, during the Vendée Globe 2000–1, managed to fuse his broken carbon-fibre mast back together using heat lamps to catalyse resin. He re-stepped the mast and continued on to France, arriving to a hero's welcome a month after everyone else.

Tip: Keep a dedicated pair of heavy-duty wire cutters close at hand, only to be used in the event of a spar failure.

Electric power failure

Alternators, batteries and generators all supply electric power aboard yachts. Large motor yachts frequently have an emergency generator, sailboats may have wind generators, and both are ideal back-ups. It never pays to be dependent on just one source of electrical output. If the loss of power comes at a critical point in a passage, it is essential that crew on watch quickly change from one source to another so as not to compromise the safe passage or become a danger to other vessels. Alternators generally stop producing electricity because belts are slack or a diode has failed, and both these are quick fixes and easy to repair. More serious situations are where the alternator has failed and the only effective repair is to replace it and send the failed unit ashore when harbour is reached. Batteries generally fail through poor maintenance, where fluids are often not topped up and batteries are left to cook on battery chargers. It is partly for this reason that many cruising boats are turning to gel batteries because they are maintenance free.

 Tip: Carry a spare alternator ready for immediate installation if planning an offshore passage.

Watermaker failure

A watermaker failure is not at all critical when daysailing or even when undertaking a short passage, but crossing an ocean when in the same yacht it can be a major problem. In a world where yachts are increasingly relying on watermaking machinery and installing less in the way of tankage, this could be a catastrophic failure. It is best to carry a back-up or at least a comprehensive spare parts inventory. A long passage should never solely rely on water produced from a single watermaker, and supplies must be safeguarded by alternative methods of producing water, including carrying sufficient in tanks to complete a passage or, if necessary, bottled water.

 Tip: Spare water can double as emergency supplies in the case of abandon ship. Use large plastic bottles, 80 per cent full of water (so they will float), and secure near the liferaft

Firefighting

Fire, its prevention, and the equipment to fight it, are discussed in chapter 7, but this chapter deals with fighting a fire aboard a yacht. Fires are rare but dangerous, and even a small fire can quickly get out of control if not dealt with correctly and promptly.

Class D fires involving combustible metal are generally beyond the firefighting capabilities of the crew aboard a yacht.

Principles of firefighting

To continue burning, fire requires all three elements of the fire triangle (oxygen, fuel and heat) to be present; if you remove one or more elements, the fire goes out. Fighting fire, therefore, is all about removing one side of the triangle. The most suitable method of firefighting depends upon the type of fire and may involve a combination of actions. The three primary methods are: 1 starvation of fuel; 2 smothering; and 3 cooling.

1 Starvation of fuel

This involves cutting off or limiting the fuel available by:

◎ Boundary starvation. This means removing flammable or combustible material from around the six sides of the fire area to form a fire break.
◎ Shutting off or stopping the supply of gas, oil or fuel.

2 Smothering

Smothering – or the exclusion of oxygen – can be achieved by:

◎ Covering the fire with a preventer or air excluder such as fire blanket, lid, foam or sand.
◎ Displacing oxygen with CO_2 or another inert gas.
◎ Enclosing the fire within a vapour – such as steam or a fine water spray.
◎ Switching off any re-circulating air conditioning system.
◎ Continue smothering until all heat has been dissipated otherwise re-ignition may occur.

3 Cooling

Cooling the combustible material until it ceases to burn is:

◎ Best achieved using water or solutions that are largely water.
◎ Most effective when the water has turned to steam and must only be used in that form on inflammable liquids.
◎ Used on the boundaries of a fire:
  – to reduce temperature inside;
  – to prevent the boundaries igniting;
  – to prevent the fire from spreading.
◎ Used as a secondary control to reduce temperature and prevent re-ignition.

Flame inhibition

Not all methods of extinguishing a fire relate to the fire triangle, and there is a fourth method, called *flame inhibition*. Dry powder and water fog achieve this by physically absorbing the energy in the flame.

Actions to be taken in an emergency

In any emergency, it is vital to take action in the proper order to deal effectively with the problem. Always remember a few moments of thought may prevent a lifetime of regret. In the event of a fire:

F	**Find**	detect using all senses
I	**Inform**	raise the alarm by all means available
R	**Restrict**	turn off fuel, isolate electrics, close doors, etc
E	**Extinguish**	or Escape and/or Evacuate

Find

Once a fire has started it will spread very rapidly if unchecked. The sooner a fire is tackled, the greater the chance of extinguishing it successfully. Therefore everyone aboard the yacht needs to be alert to the first signs of fire and the likely areas of high risk. A burning smell, loss of engine power or smoke trailing after the yacht may be a sign of fire and must be investigated immediately. The larger the yacht the more important it is that the watchkeeper's duties include a regular visit to all external and internal areas, paying attention particularly to unoccupied cabins, engine spaces, battery lockers, hazardous chemical storage, etc. If fire is suspected to be behind a closed door it is very important that the door is not opened. To do so would supply fresh oxygen, and this will not only permit continued combustion, but will also probably inflame the fire.

125

Inform

This is particularly important. It is very tempting to get on with fighting a fire, but invariably it is the failure to inform that allows an incident to become out of control. Once a fire has been discovered and before it is tackled, the alarm must be raised. The priority is to make everyone aware of the fire so assistance is available if needed and precautions can be taken to prevent the fire spreading.

By summoning everyone aboard the yacht it can easily be ascertained if anyone is missing, injured or trapped. The Skipper can then organise the firefighting effort, radio or telephone for help, and prepare the liferaft and lifesaving equipment.

If the vessel is alongside a dock, the fire brigade should be called and the appropriate local authorities notified of the situation. At sea, an urgency/PAN PAN call should be sent. If the fire is successfully extinguished the alert can be cancelled. If the fire cannot be controlled and the captain orders 'Abandon Ship', the alert can be upgraded to a MAYDAY. In the event of things getting out of control with no time to send a MAYDAY, the PAN PAN will ensure others have already been alerted to a possibly deteriorating situation.

If enough crew are available, the Skipper should send someone to begin the preparations to abandon ship. Even a very small fire can quickly escalate and get out of control, at which point there may not be time to get the liferaft or grab bag.

A fire in the engine room is very likely to involve an engine and/or generator failure and it is important that the Skipper takes this into account. At sea with plenty of open water around, this may merely be inconvenient. At night in busy, confined waters this could be as dangerous as the fire itself. Consideration must also be given to loss of electricity, especially the loss of lights at night.

Tip: Loss of electricity will affect navigation lights; lack of cabin lights will make moving around inside the yacht more difficult.

Restrict

Before deciding which extinguishing method will be best, the fire must be restricted or starved by:

◎ Throwing the burning object overboard – take great care, though, and never try this with a chip pan fire.
◎ Shutting fuel supply lines if it is a flammable liquid fire – oils, fuels, etc.
◎ Shutting cylinder valves if it is a gas fire – butane, propane, etc.
◎ Turning off switches and isolating power where electrical equipment is on fire.
◎ Reducing airflow:
  - turn off the air conditioning;
  - shut doors, vents, portholes and hatches;
  - turn off the engine room fans and block ventilation;
  - reduce speed if under way;
  - turn the yacht, so that the wind blows the fire in the direction of least vulnerability or least flammability.

 Tip: An oven glove from the galley is ideal for shutting off hot valves, moving a burning object, etc.

Extinguish

To successfully extinguish a fire:

◎ Determine what class or classes of fire are involved.
◎ Decide on the appropriate method of attack – starvation, smothering, cooling, flame inhibition.
◎ Select the firefighting equipment.
◎ Fight the fire.

If the fire is very small, barely a smoulder, all that may be required after alerting someone else to the fire is to smother it with anything to hand. Fire blankets are ideal, but use anything else suitable that can be quickly grabbed such as a cushion, towel, sand, etc.

The table of fire types and suitable firefighting equipment in chapter 7 (Tables 7.1 and 7.2) and the Firefighting Flowchart in this chapter (page 129) may help to organise your thoughts. Circumstances surrounding any particular fire will always be different, and it is impossible to make hard and fast rules specifying do this or do that. It is necessary to consider all the facts of a particular case to make the right decision for that fire. It is important, though, to remember that a fire on a yacht may not fall neatly into just one fire class when considering the best extinguishing method.

When fighting an engine room fire it is very important not to open a ventilation hatch. Operating a fixed extinguisher inside the engine room may be the best fire attack; in the absence of a fixed system, a gas extinguisher should be used, ideally through a fire port, or a small opening in the engine compartment.

When moving around in a fire zone great care must be taken:

◎ Before opening any door or hatch, carefully feel the door, sides and handle with the *back of your hand* to prevent:
  - damaging the palm of your hand;
  - fingers involuntarily gripping a handle or projection that has electricity flowing through it.

◎ Keep as low as possible:
 – hot expanding gases rise, cooler air is drawn in at the bottom;
 – smoke builds up from the deckhead down.

Using a fire blanket

Quickly smothering a small fire with a fire blanket is an excellent idea. It can be used on most types of fire, both solids and liquid. It is particularly good for small fires in clothing and chip pan fires provided the blanket completely covers the fire.

To use on a chip pan fire:

◎ Fold back the top edge over your hands to protect them.
◎ Hold your hands up with your arms widespread, to allow the blanket to protect the body and face from radiant heat and flames as you approach.
◎ Advance and drape over the fire, stretching towards the back to avoid dipping the blanket into the liquid.
◎ Do not throw the blanket down as this may cause a flare-up as air is forced into the container.
◎ Cover the pan completely.
◎ Turn off the heat (if not already done) and leave until it is quite cool.
◎ *Do not* remove the blanket prematurely, as there is a high risk of re-ignition.

To use a fire blanket on a person with burning clothes:

◎ Lay the victim on the floor.
◎ Pat out the flames.
◎ *Do not* leave the casualty rolled in the blanket, as this may trap heat from the smouldering clothes next to the skin.

Using a fire extinguisher

Most small fires aboard a yacht are dealt with using a fire extinguisher. Especially below deck, this is probably the quickest thing to grab in an emergency. It is extremely important to use the correct fire extinguishers for the class of fire involved, as it is all too easy to make a bad situation far, far worse. Modern fire extinguishers look alike and have similar methods of operation whether they contain water, foam or powder. The main difference is generally the style of the nozzle.

Before using any fire extinguisher, the instruction label must be read and the extinguisher checked to ensure it is the right type for the classes of fire involved.

There is a simple acronym to remember when operating most fire extinguishers – PASS, which stands for **P**ull, **A**im, **S**queeze and **S**weep.

◎ **Pull** the pin at the top of the cylinder. Some units require the releasing of a lock latch or pressing a puncture lever.
◎ **Aim** the nozzle at the base of the fire.
◎ **Squeeze** or press the handle.
◎ **Sweep** the contents from side to side at the base of the fire until it goes out.

Tip: After you have put out the fire, shut off the extinguisher and then watch carefully in case it rekindles. If possible, have a back-up extinguisher ready.

FIREFIGHTING FLOWCHART

FIND
Fire detected

ALERT
- By voice – Shouting FIRE until acknowledged
- Sound General Emergency
- Fire alarm – break glass box

Crew to muster stations
Check for missing, injured, trapped persons

At night: Switch on deck lights

At sea

Send PAN PAN
by Inmarsat A, B, C, Mini M
VHF/MF/HF/DSC

In port

- **Call Fire Brigade**
- **Call Harbour/Marina Authority**
  by VHF, landline, mobile or satellite phone

Prepare liferaft and lifesaving equipment

At anchor

Alongside

Send guests ashore

Engine room fire? — No

Yes

Prepare for engine and/or generator failure

RESTRICT
Turn off ac/ventilation, shut doors, vents, portholes, hatches, etc.
Reduce speed, turn yacht to blow fire in best direction

EXTINGUISHABLE — *No*

Yes

Class A SOLIDS wood, upholstery	**Class B** LIQUIDS petrol, diesel, oil	**Class C** GASES propane, butane	**Class E** ELECTRICAL EQUIPMENT	**Class F** COOKING OIL and FAT
Throw burning object overboard	**Shut off fuel supply lines**	**Shut cylinder valves**	**Turn off switches**	**Turn off stove**
Fire bucket **Fire extinguisher** • Water • Foam • Dry powder • Wet chemical **Hose reel and fire pump**	**Fire extinguisher** • Foam • Dry powder • Carbon dioxide	**Fire extinguisher** • Dry chemical	**Fire extinguisher** • Dry powder • Carbon dioxide	**Fire blanket** **Wet chemical extinguisher**

Re-ignition?

Yes

Fire extinguished?

Yes

No

ABANDON SHIP

No

Cancel alerts
Check stability

As appropriate complete:
Log books
Accident report

Replace used fire extinguishers

Using a water fire extinguisher: Class A fires

◎ Keep it low to avoid heat and steam.
◎ Point the jet at the base of the flames.
◎ Sweep quickly to break the water into droplets to enhance the cooling effect.
◎ Move around the fire if possible to get all sides of it.
◎ Once the fire is knocked down, use the full force of the jet to help the water penetrate and break up the fuel.
◎ DANGER:
    – *Do* NOT use on Classes B, C, D, E or F fires such as burning fat, oil or electrical appliances.

Using a foam (AFFF) fire extinguisher: Classes A and B fires

◎ For Class A solids fires:
    – Point the jet at the base of the flames.
    – Keep it moving across the area until the fire is out.
◎ For Class B liquid fires:
    – Do not aim the jet straight into the liquid.
    – Point the jet on a nearby surface above the burning liquid.
    – If the liquid is in a container, point the jet at the inside edge.
    – Allow the foam to build up and flow across the liquid.
◎ DANGER:
    – Do NOT use on chip pan fires.

Using a dry powder/chemical fire extinguisher: Classes A, B, C and E fires; and Classes A, B and C fires (USA)

◎ Point the jet discharge horn/nozzle at the base of the flames.
◎ Use a rapid sweeping motion to drive the fire to the far edge until all the flames are out.
◎ DANGER:
    – This type does not cool well, so there is a risk of re-ignition.
    – This type does not penetrate electrical equipment, so effectively there is a risk of re-ignition.

Using a CO_2 fire extinguisher: Classes B and E Fires; and Classes B and C Fires (USA)

◎ Aim the discharge horn/nozzle at the base of the flames.
◎ Keep moving across the area of the flames.
◎ Do not hold the horn – it gets so cold that it can cause a burn.
◎ The time of discharge is very limited, so be quick,
◎ DANGER:
    – CO_2 fumes are very dangerous in confined spaces.
    – Ventilate the area as soon as the fire has been extinguished.
    – Do NOT use on chip pan fires.
    – This type does not cool well, so there is a risk of re-ignition.

Using a wet chemical fire extinguisher: Classes A and F fires; and Classes A and K fires (USA)

◎ Keep well back, using the long nozzle at arm's length.
◎ Aim at the base of the fire, but on no account dip the nozzle into the liquid.
◎ Gentle spraying prevents splashing the burning liquid onto the user.
◎ This type is safe if it is accidentally sprayed onto electrical appliances.

◎ DANGER:
  – There is the risk of electrocution of the operator if the long extended wand is in direct contact with a high voltage source.
  – There is a very violent reaction if the wand's tip is submerged into the burning liquid and the extinguisher discharge initiated.

 Fire extinguishers last a much shorter period than may be imagined. Be sure to use the contents correctly in the short time allowed.

Fighting a fire with water

Water is an extremely effective method of fighting interior fires involving bedding and furnishings and is the most readily available resource on a yacht. A fire extinguisher may be the quickest thing to grab and use, but a fire bucket filled with salt water is an ideal back-up.

It is very important to apply sufficient water into the heart of the fire to extract the heat. The resultant expansion that takes place as the water turns into steam means that the steam vapour has to press its way out of the heart of the fire; this helps to smother the fire by displacing the oxygen. Dense items such as bedding or wood may be difficult to penetrate properly and must be well saturated to ensure that the heart of the fire is out. Re-ignition – even *hours* later – is always a risk with any fire.

However, water does have some disadvantages:

◎ Large quantities of water may precipitate a free surface effect, causing a yacht to wallow or heel – local fire brigades unused to boats may not realise this.
◎ Water and electricity *do not* mix – pouring water on live electrical equipment risks electrical shock.
◎ Sea water is death to electrical equipment.
◎ Solid jets or buckets of water on burning oil (or fat) will only spread the fire as the oil will simply float further afield.
◎ Water applied to a liquid fire above the boiling point of water will immediately flash into steam at a 1700:1 expansion ratio, and throw the burning liquid into the air.

 Water in spray or fog form has a wider range of uses than ordinary water. It can even extinguish an oil fire if it has not been burning too long, and does not spread the fire.

Preventing re-ignition and afterwards

Once the fire has been extinguished there is still a great danger of re-ignition and this may continue for hours, not just minutes. This can be caused by vapour contacting hot surfaces and by smouldering material, so there must be efficient cooling both in and around the seat of a fire after it has been extinguished. Examine all fire-affected debris carefully to ensure that the fire is really out.

Having successfully extinguished the fire, the Skipper may need to:

◎ Cancel all alerts as soon as possible.
◎ Check the stability of the vessel if a great deal of water has been used.

131

◎ Arrange towage or salvage.
◎ Complete the ship's log.
◎ Complete a damage report and contact insurers if appropriate.
◎ Replace or refill all used fire extinguishers and fire blankets imediately.

Evacuate or escape

Only a large yacht will have firefighting outfits, including breathing apparatus plus the high pressure fire pump, hoses and fittings, capable of dealing with anything more than a small fire. Even aboard a large yacht, fire can get out of control, especially if it is the result of an explosion. A fire that spreads quickly or is well seated before it is discovered may be impossible to fight, and the Skipper must be prepared at all times to call a halt to firefighting and get everyone safely off the yacht. To give the maximum time to organise abandoning the yacht, shut every possible door to slow the progress of the fire. If crew can be spared, pour water on all the boundaries (chapter 11 deals with abandoning ship.)

Flooding

Flooding can be the result of either internal or external factors. Internal failures that can result in water ingress include: leaking seacocks; problems with the fresh or salt water system; or the stern gland. The main causes of external damage to the boat that can allow water to enter the hull are: collision; grounding; or heavy weather.

Minor flooding

Most internal failures certainly begin as a minor incident and, if noticed quickly, can usually be repaired or patched easily. The trouble comes if no one identifies the problem until the water starts to rise above the floorboards or the power supply fails due to water causing a short circuit. Alarm systems in the bilges are an excellent early warning system but can, and do, fail. Your eyes are the surest way to detect a problem, and good watchkeeping must include a regular check of the engine space and bilges to ensure any sudden excess of water is spotted at once.

Minor leaks may be caused by driving hard in rough weather and will result in water ingress through chain plates, mast partners, deck joins or the stern gland. Slowing down will ease the strain and probably alleviate most of the leaks. Any cracks or leaking seams will need to be plugged – ideally, with caulking cotton and seam compound.

Major flooding

Whatever the cause, serious flooding needs immediate action by the watchkeeper. The Flooding Flowchart (page 133) details actions to be taken in the event of serious flooding. On a larger yacht, soundings of bilges and tanks are very important to:

◎ Establish the extent of flooding.
◎ Indicate the approximate rate of water ingress.
◎ Calculate the current effects of flooding on stability and stress.
◎ Discover the probability of stemming or removing the water with the pumps available.

Locating and repairing internal damage

Most internal damage that causes flooding is the result of a failure of a fixture or fitting. It may be as simple as a broken hose clamp or as potentially disastrous as a sea

FLOODING FLOWCHART

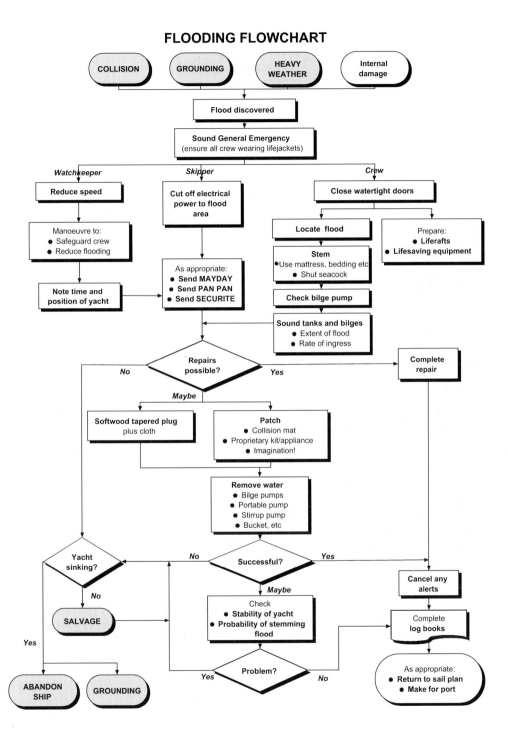

chest failure. External damage is usually easy to identify and will therefore permit the crew to tackle it quickly; internal problems generally need detective work to locate.

To quickly locate the source of flooding, first taste the water to see if it is fresh or salt; this will help eliminate many potential areas immediately. Through-hull fittings are the cause of most leaks. If a pipe or hose has come loose or broken, shut the seacocks at once. If there is no seacock or the seacock is the problem, the best solution may be to use a plug in the through-hull orifice. If a through-hull fitting did not cause the flooding, a thorough check should be made of: the toilets; water tanks; domestic hot and cold water piping; the grey water tank; the saltwater taps where fitted.

Repairing external damage

Any rupture, break or hole in the yacht's outer hull, particularly below the waterline, will allow water to enter the boat. The first priority, as with any damage, is always to stem the flow of water. Pumping can carry on simultaneously, but never in place of closing the hole. If flooding continues uncontrolled, the vessel will sink. Even the biggest onboard pump will ultimately lose the battle with a 5cm (13in) hole. When the underwater hull is pierced there are only two possible courses of action:

◎ To plug the hole or opening.
◎ To establish and maintain flood boundaries to prevent the progress of the flooding.

A yacht can sink just as easily from a series of small and insignificant-looking holes as it can from one large dramatic opening. The natural tendency is to attack the obvious damage first, leaving small cracks, but this can waste valuable time pursuing the impossible when it would be better to seal off an entire area, concentrate on making the rest of the yacht watertight, and make for harbour as quickly as possible. Really large holes in an underwater hull can seldom be repaired while the boat is still in the water.

Every effort should be made to lift any hole out of the water if possible – holes near the waterline may be raised out of the seas on a sailboat by tacking the yacht or moving the crew to the appropriate side. A hole in the bow may be lifted out of the water by moving weight aft and sailing downwind to stop waves from being swept in.

All holes in the hull should be plugged or patched completely as soon as possible, but even a partial fix can substantially reduce the danger of sinking. While obviously the first attack should be holes below the waterline, those at or just above must not be forgotten. As the yacht rolls or loses buoyancy, these higher holes can become submerged and allow water to enter at a level that is dangerously above the ship's centre of gravity.

Plugging the hole

The simplest method of stopping up a fairly small hole is to insert some kind of plug, so an assortment of softwood tapered plugs should be included in every flood prevention kit carried aboard every yacht, no matter how small or large. A plug alone will seldom stop a hole, but wrapped in some sort of lightweight cloth it will not only fill in the gaps better, but also help keep the plug in place as the soft wood swells. Often, plugs must be used in groups to fill an irregular hole.

Plugs are best inserted from inside the yacht as they hold better and can be adjusted more easily if necessary. If it is impossible to get to the hole from the inside and the plug is inserted from outside the hull, fit the inboard ends of the plugs with screw eyes.

Tip: A line running from each screw eye and secured to a solid part of the yacht will help keep the plug in place.

Patching the hole

The greatest difficult in repairing underwater holes in a yacht is usually the inaccessibility of the damage. Unfortunately, there can be a liner, furniture or a tank in the way. If this is the situation, drastic action may be required using a crow bar and a sharp axe to get to the hole and save the boat. Clearly, something has to be done to stem the flow of water immediately.

Sealing the hole from outside, by stretching a piece of canvas, a sail or a mattress with lines attached to the corners over the damaged area, sounds sensible and straightforward. It may be the only choice if it is impossible to get at the damage from inside. Unfortunately, it will not work on a concave section, and even in a good location getting canvas stretched over a hole in anything but calm conditions is likely to be very difficult. The idea is to draw the collision mat over the side of the hull until it covers the damaged area, whereupon the pressure of the water holds it in place. Getting the mat into position will be easier if its bottom is weighted, perhaps with a hand lead or anchor and the mat worked slowly backwards from the bow. The leak may not be stopped completely, but it may buy precious time to fashion a better repair.

Patching, like plugging, is best done from inside the yacht and is simplest if the necessary equipment is on board the boat in the first place. There are various different devices and patching kits on the market, ranging from underwater epoxy to an umbrella device or collision mats. It is important that instructions are carefully studied before any attempt is made to remove any temporary plug to use the repair equipment.

A patch can also be made from any suitable material on the yacht that can cover the hole and be held into place – for example, a locker lid pressed against a towel pushed into a hole and held in place with a wedged boathook.

Removing the water

With flooding controlled, if not stopped, the water inside the yacht should be removed if possible. Even if water continues to enter the yacht, using the bilge pump, buckets and any other method of removing water may buy the necessary time to get the yacht to the nearest harbour, even if the leak cannot be completely sealed.

Watertight doors

In the event of a flood, the ability to close a watertight door if the damage cannot be repaired may mean the difference between the safe return to port and taking to the liferaft. Shutting a watertight door must never be left too late if the yacht is to be saved. If a door was closed before the damage occurred, it is essential that you are very careful before re-opening the door. It might well be holding back water from a flooded compartment.

Shoring

Once leaks have been controlled following external damage such as a collision, any weakened or damaged structures and patches or pads covering fractures will need to be strengthened by shoring. Any available spars or planking can be used – such as dinghy oars or thwarts, a spinnaker pole, bunk leeboards, etc. The shoring should be put on a pad rather than directly onto the hull or deckhead in order to spread the load and be wedged in place. The shoring will need to be inspected very regularly for signs of loosening.

Grounding

If a yacht is grounded intentionally, she is said to be beached. If she is grounded accidentally, she is said to be stranded (see chart page 138).

Beaching

A yacht is usually beached as a very last resort because she has been damaged and the flooding is so rapid that pumping and bailing by crew is failing to keep up with the ingress of water. If there is sufficient time, the action of beaching and the method of approach should be made with a view to eventually re-floating, but if the danger of foundering is imminent, there will be little time to waste other than considering anything but the immediate future.

With the decision to beach made, the selection of a shoreline clear of rocks and other obstructions is important. The greatest danger is that of broaching-to where seas could quickly pound the yacht to pieces. The aim is to ground the entire vessel in one movement, so if there is a choice, choose a beach that shelves gradually rather than steeply. The best approach is to lower the sails or stop the engine, stream a sea anchor over the bow to hold the yacht head to sea, and drift stern first towards the beach. When close inshore, the main anchor should be dropped and about 8m (26ft) of cable allowed to run before being stopped and snubbed. In this way, the yacht should stay bow-on to any advancing breakers and move very slowly astern, dragging her anchor. Beaching in this way is probably the best option, to assist with later re-floating, although there is an increased risk of damage to the rudder and propeller.

Stranding

A vessel that has been stranded may be in contact with the ground on any part of her hull. Other shoals or rocks nearby, adverse tidal streams and weather and damage to the yacht may all cause complications for re-floating attempts. Taking the ground may be a sudden event, causing the boat to stop abruptly and with everyone aboard being thrown forward, or it may be a slow occurrence caused by the tide removing all the water under a yacht at anchor. The response to stranding will depend upon the circumstances.

Backing off

A light touching, where the hull damage appears to be minimal, can be prevented from becoming a full-blown stranding by quick action and correct procedure. If the bottom is hard and the yacht is moving slowly, a series of bumps may give enough early warning of an imminent stranding to enable the helmsman to get back afloat. If the bottom is soft, the first indication of a problem may be lack of steerage. While damage is less likely from a soft bottom, getting clear can be more difficult as the ground will hold the hull.

On a large sailing yacht, altering course instantly towards the deeper water while striving to heel the boat to diminish her draught may get the vessel off. The various methods of getting off the ground all follow the principle of increasing the angle of heel in order to raise the keel off the bottom. This may be hardening or backing the sails or by using the main boom as a lever for weights to increase the angle of heel. On a small boat, sending crew forward so their weight depresses the bow may give enough lift to free the aft end of the keel and allow the boat to sail off. Tuning on the engine may give the necessary power to pull the yacht clear.

When using an engine, the temptation to go full astern must be resisted. First, a quick check must be made for any lines, such as the dinghy painter, that could wrap around the propeller. A slow and careful backing off must be attempted using the engine in reverse – the prop wash may throw sand and mud towards the bow, grounding the yacht more firmly. The temperature gauges must be monitored carefully, and any rise will indicate that the raw water intake has sucked up dirt and debris that could clog or damage an engine's cooling system. Engines must be shut down immediately if there is a rapid rise in temperature. If available, assistance from another vessel pulling the yacht off might be a better option. Aboard a small yacht, and depending on circumstances, a crew member could try going over the side and pushing the boat sideways in both directions. This may free the boat more quickly and easily than backing with the engine.

On coral or sea grass, backing off can cause tremendous damage and invoke stiff penalties and fines.

 Tip: When stranded, it may be better to simply wait for the tide to rise, or call for professional towing assistance.

Stuck

If immediate action fails to get the yacht clear and the tide is falling or the grounding was hard, it is very important that no one panics and the Skipper must not take hasty action before giving thought to all the consequences. Backing off will not be a good idea if the hull has been compromised. So immediate action must begin with the watch-keeper summoning the Skipper, though in most cases the captain will have felt the grounding and probably have reached the watchkeeper before any call can be made. This being the case:

◎ Stop the engine or drop the sails.
◎ Sound a General Emergency.
◎ Ensure that the crew are wearing their lifejackets.
◎ Close any watertight doors.
◎ Switch on deck lighting at night.
◎ Display the signals appropriate for a vessel aground.
◎ Check for damage to the yacht, including possible leakages.
◎ Take soundings of tanks and bilges.

GROUNDING FLOWCHART

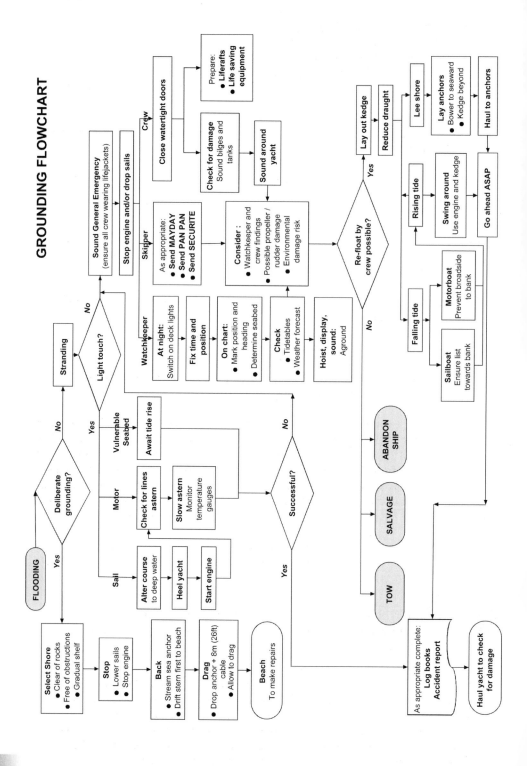

◎ If appropriate, initiate a salvage plan.
◎ Prepare liferafts and lifesaving equipment.
◎ Note the yacht's position and update it as necessary.
◎ Send a distress call/MAYDAY if appropriate.
◎ Send an urgency call/PAN PAN or SECURITE message, as appropriate, to alert vessels in the vicinity.

With the immediate actions necessary in hand, it is time to assess the situation calmly and decide on the best strategy:

◎ Note the time, and lay down your exact position on the sea chart, indicating the heading.
◎ Take soundings around the yacht, noting the exact time of each one.
◎ Determine the nature of the seabed.
◎ Determine the direction of deep water.
◎ Check the tide table for HW and LW times and range.
◎ Check the weather forecast, wind and current, direction and force.
◎ Calculate the trim and stability of the yacht.
◎ Consider the potential effect on the situation of heavy weather, current or tide.
◎ Consider re-float attempts in view of:
  – any damage to the hull;
  – possible damage to the propeller and rudder;
  – an increased risk of oil spill;
◎ Minimise further damage to personnel, the environment and other vessels.
◎ Continually enter all actions in the log book.

With all the information gathered, a plan of attack should begin with the laying out of a kedge anchor to help heave off the yacht and stop it being driven further aground. If the yacht has suffered hull damage, she is probably better staying grounded until repairs have been made. With no holes and a rising tide, both time and heaving on the kedge will probably re-float the yacht. Any method of reducing the draught, such as removing tenders and people, should be taken. As the tide rises, judicious use of the engine and kedge should be made to swing the yacht around, so that engines can be used ahead as soon as possible.

On a falling tide, it is important to use the soundings to ensure a sailboat will list towards a bank. Swinging the boom towards the bank or applying weight on that side, such as the anchor chain, can accomplish this.

 Tip: Aboard a motor yacht, ground tackle must be used to stop her turning broadside to the bank, which might prevent the use of engines for re-floating.

Stranding on an exposed lee shore may be dangerous, especially if the bottom is hard and there is a sea running, so every effort should be made to haul the yacht off with the kedge. If this fails, the bower anchor should be laid out to seaward with all the chain and the kedge set beyond, fastened to the bower chain about 10m (33ft) from the bower anchor. As soon as there is any chance of breaking the yacht free, the bower chain should be hauled in and the yacht will be taken out towards the bower anchor. In fair conditions, the anchor can be weighed and the yacht can sail or motor on to pick up the kedge. If the weather does not co-operate it may be better to save time by simply buoying the anchor chain, for recovery later, and slipping it before moving out to the kedge. At worst, this is the loss of an anchor and chain to save the yacht.

Towing a stranded yacht clear must be carried out with great care, and checks must be made to see that any fittings used to secure lines are substantial and through-bolted. Jerking the vessel free is extremely dangerous, since the towing line could break and the resulting whiplash can cause severe injuries (see chapter 9 for more details on towing).

Heavy weather

Any yacht sailing some distance from port or shore will eventually meet unfavourable winds and seas. The conditions may be a near-gale, gale or, worse still, a tropical revolving storm. The arrival of bad weather can be defined as when wind and sea state dictate a change in the Skipper's passage plan, and this will vary from boat to boat and from voyage to voyage.

No boat should ever put to sea without an up-to-date weather forecast, but even the best forecaster gets it wrong sometimes. The further from land the yacht sails, the harder it is to get regular forecasts, unless the boat is fitted with satellite communications equipment. With adequate knowledge, a sailor can and must use the changes in the sky plus readings obtained from the barometer to corroborate the forecast, and thus gain a much more accurate prediction of the likely weather in his area.

Avoiding bad weather

Good planning can help to avoid some bad weather, but not *every* storm – especially if the yacht is undertaking a long passage. Obviously the most basic avoidance technique is not to set sail if the weather forecast is predicting unfavourable conditions for the yacht. Similarly, the forecast that is acceptable to the Skipper of a 30m (98ft) sailboat, with a full crew of experienced sailors, will not necessarily be suitable for a 10m (33ft) yacht with just a couple plus two small children aboard. When planning an ocean passage it is inevitable that bad weather will be met at some point, but it is still not sensible to set sail with a poor forecast.

Preparations for heavy weather

When a weather report or a change in the sky or barometer indicates that bad weather is imminent, the watchkeeper should immediately inform the Skipper and crew.

The greatest weakness in any emergency is never the yacht or its equipment, but the crew who sail in it. So it is the Skipper's job to ensure that the crew's condition and morale remain as high as possible. He must make every effort to occupy all the crew in the immediate preparations that begin aboard the yacht, as well as keeping them fully informed about the expected conditions, any strengths and weaknesses of the boat, and the passage plan. Calmly communicating and involving everyone reduces fear and stress, not only for the crew but for the Skipper too. It is very important that the Skipper reminds the male members of the crew of the dangers of urinating over the side in rough weather – the last thing that is needed is a man overboard in heavy weather.

The Heavy Weather Flowchart (page 141) details the actions to be taken at the onset of deteriorating weather.

While the crew make the storm preparations, the Skipper must consider his options, bearing in mind the yacht's present position, including any possible ports of refuge; the

HEAVY WEATHER FLOWCHART

HEAVY WEATHER PREDICTED

Summon crew
- Inform
- Allocate jobs

On deck
- Secure gear, anchor, lockers, lazarettes, etc
- Remove all loose gear
- Rig safety lines
- Make emergency gear accessible
- Prepare drogue and sea anchor

On a sailboat
- Deep reef sails
- Prepare storm sails
- Lash weather cloths
- Fix companionboards

Below deck
- Secure all movable objects, lockers, watertight doors, ports, hatches, deadlights, storm covers, etc
- Set up lee cloths
- Prepare damage control items
- Prepare snacks, sandwiches, hot drinks in Thermos flasks

Engineering
- Check all pumps working
- Pump out bilges and heads
- Shut non-essential seacocks
- Check engine including oil and coolant
- Check steering system and emergency gear
- Fully charge batteries

Navigation and watchkeeping
- Adjust course and speed as required
- Fix yacht's position regularly
- Monitor all weather broadcasts
- Every 30 mins record barometer reading, wind, sea state and cloud cover
- Prepare white collision flares and signalling light

Skipper
- Transmit SECURITE message if appropriate
- Consider setting up radio schedule with nearby yachts
- Check possible ports of refuge

All crew
- Consider antiseasickness medication
- Use heavy weather gear, lifejackets, and safety harnesses on deck
- Consider eating hot meal

Select course

Run for shelter

Port entry possible?
- Yes → **Enter port of refuge**
- No → **Head offshore**

Head offshore

Yes – Sailboat
- Heave-to
- Lie a' hull

Maintain course

Conditions deteriorate?
- No
- Yes

Run downwind

Yes – All yachts (including sailboats)
- Spread oil
- Run with drogue
- Lie to sea anchor

WAIT OUT STORM

yacht's size and characteristics; the strengths and weaknesses of the crew; and any information about the approaching weather, including the probable track.

Running for shelter

Seeking shelter inside a well-protected harbour is ideal, especially for a motor yacht, but the Skipper must be quite sure he can safely get the vessel there. Therefore before making for any refuge it is very important to check the entrance and approaches on a chart, in a pilot book, and with the tides checked. Running wildly before a storm is very dangerous, especially close to a lee shore where a strong wind is blowing towards the land. If you then add wind against the tide, the land can become a deadly enemy. Smaller sailing boats will have a very hard job beating off a lee shore in an onshore gale with the added discomfort of confused seas.

Carrying on

If a port of refuge is impossible, the Skipper must consider the merits of standing out to sea with plenty of room and allowing a storm to pass, or perhaps maintaining his course with suitable adjustments for the changing conditions. It is very important that the yacht should keep as far offshore as necessary to avoid danger, choosing a course that avoids tide races, shipping routes and shallow water. Even the smallest seagoing yacht is quite capable of surviving the worst that the weather can do, provided she is in a seaworthy condition, properly equipped and correctly handled. A well-founded yacht will certainly be able to take much more punishment than her crew will be capable of handling, therefore the crew must be considered carefully in any decision taken. There is no single 'best tactic' for heavy weather survival – only the best for that particular combination of weather, yacht and crew.

Navigation in heavy weather must not be forgotten, and with GPS the yacht's position can be regularly plotted on the relevant chart. Leeway and surface drift induced by the wind may be as much as 2 knots and needs to be monitored carefully to ensure that the yacht is not standing into danger. A good lookout is very important, especially in heavy rain.

If the weather deteriorates and the boat begins to roll or pitch badly, the galley stove should not be used. The likelihood of starting a fire, scalding or burning one of the crew is increased and will certainly make a bad day much, much worse.

Over time all fuel tanks accumulate sediment and water, and in rough seas this dormant water and dirt may be kicked up and taken into the system, which could cause an engine to stop. The problem is exacerbated in fuel tanks whose level is low. In preference, use fuel from full tanks or day tanks first.

Tip: In heavy weather, keep white flares and a powerful signalling light to hand in case there is a risk of collision.

Heavy weather aboard a sailing yacht

As bad weather approaches, the Skipper must decide what course he can best make, bearing in mind his desired destination. It is very important to ensure that the boat is never over-powered and that any sail change is made early and safely with the crew wearing safety harnesses and lifelines. The main objective when sailing in heavy weather is to keep the boat balanced while making reasonable and safe way.

To balance the rig, it is best to use a reduced or storm headsail and mainsail rather than just running on a foresail alone. This has the other advantage of helping the rig to

absorb the shock of high seas and the jarring motion. Storm sails, made of heavier material than normal sails, are better able to cope with strong winds. Regardless of which sails are in use, they, plus the sheets and deck hardware, will come under enormous strains. Flogging and chafing can happen in minutes in a storm and must be watched for very carefully.

Extra care must be taken in heavy weather with all the sailing equipment around the yacht. It is important to keep plenty of turns on winches, check that leads are correct so there will be no overrides, and that fingers are clear at all times. Winch failure is always a possibility in high winds, so this must be considered. Make sure all winch handles are always removed when not in use. Blocks can also fail under load, and if this should happen the line will sweep anything in its path as it straightens out. Greater thought should be given as to where to sit or stand in heavy weather.

Sailing in a storm requires constant vigilance and can be very hard work. In severe conditions, downwind sailing is the favoured approach by many. The greatest danger comes from speed. Not enough, and steerage will be lost in the troughs, just when it is most needed to counter the next crest astern. Too much, and the boat risks surfing down a sea into an exceptional trough and into the face of the wave ahead, causing the yacht to somersault stern over bow (pitchpole). Wave lengths about 1.25 times the waterline length of the yacht are the most likely to cause loss of steering and broaching. Sailing tactics in heavy weather are a specialised subject, and there are some excellent books available, the classic being *Heavy Weather Sailing* by K Adlard Coles (published by Adlard Coles Nautical).

As wind and sea state increase, conditions may become too severe to make any headway in the planned direction. This is the time to slow or stop the boat by heaving-to, lying a'hull, or using a drogue or sea anchor.

Heaving-to

Theoretically, heaving-to consists of luffing up, with the seas on one bow, backing the jib to weather and lashing the helm slightly to leeward to stop the boat from sailing and so hold her in position. In practice, the yacht will make considerable leeway and also drift under current or tide, so plenty of sea room for this manoeuvre is essential. As the yacht may be lying almost beam-on to the weather, it is highly likely that she will have to be steered and the sails watched for flogging.

 Tip: Practise heaving-to in calmer conditions before trying to do so in a storm, as it all depends upon balance and each yacht reacts differently.

Lying a'hull

In even more severe conditions it may be necessary to lie a'hull – that is, allow the yacht to take up her own natural position under bare poles. Lashing the helm to lee may help to prevent the boat from gathering way and reduce leeway. This is a good tactic for a multihull, as there is a possibility of the vessel being rolled over on the crest of a wave and receiving a severe knockdown or even capsizing in extreme conditions.

Heaving-to or lying a'hull is probably not the best idea when waves reach or exceed the yacht's beam width in height. Having some control is a better option. obtained by running with a drogue or riding out the storm with a proper sea anchor.

Running with a drogue

A traditional storm tactic with sufficient room to leeward is to run downwind under bare poles, while streaming long warps over the stern to hold the boat steady and reduce her speed. Warps are generally insufficient alone to act as a brake and anything that will sink – such as a bundled-up mattress – should also be attached. A jury-rigged device cannot expect to have adequate or consistent performance under severe weather conditions, and a purpose-made drogue, as discussed in chapter 2, offers consistent performance and stability and proven durability to last out a storm and allow the boat to run safely. It is essential to keep the yacht stern-on to any following seas, with the speed slow enough so that the boat does not surf, and fast enough so the waves do not impact the boat at full strength and cause it to broach.

 Tip: It is essential that the Skipper knows how to use a drogue correctly. Read the instructions when the item is bought and review them before using.

Lying-to a sea anchor

This is the classic method of riding out a storm, but it is out of favour with many off-shore sailors. There are a number of successful sea anchors of parachute design on the market now that have proved themselves in heavy weather (see chapter 2 for more information about choosing a sea anchor). A sea anchor has the merit of permitting the yacht to make the least leeway of any other storm tactic and this may be very important near a lee shore. Modern yachts with a great deal of windage forward ride better to a sea anchor if a riding sail is used to hold the stern downwind. A sea anchor relies upon the stretch of a long nylon rode for yielding to the seas, not standing up to them. At least 100m (328ft) or ten times the boat length, must be streamed. To deploy the sea anchor:

◎ Secure items on board, lower sails, etc.
◎ Head into the wind.
◎ Toss the trip line and sea anchor into the water over the weather bow, followed by the rode.
◎ Allow the yacht to drift back, paying out the required scope.

◎ Make the rode fast and then secure the trip line with slack.
◎ Protect the rode from chafing in the fairlead.
◎ Secure the rudder amidships.
◎ Secure the boat and get some rest.

In an emergency, a jury sea anchor can be made by lashing together any spare gear that will give sufficient resistance to the water – such as dinghy oars, floorboards, hatch-covers, etc – to which a line can be attached.

Tip: If conditions are severe enough, consider using the inflatable dinghy as a sea anchor.

Heavy weather aboard a motor yacht

The crew of a motor yacht must endeavour to maintain steerage in rough weather so that the boat always remains under control. It is essential to keep the vessel end-on to the seas, either bow-on or running before them. Unlike a sailboat, a motor yacht cannot be left to her own devices because she is not so strong, and because she does not have a deep, heavy keel to keep her upright. In the event of a capsize she would probably remain upside down.

Trial and error with experience may be the only option when deciding on the best course in heavy weather. The helmsman aboard a displacement yacht would probably be best heading into the seas at a speed sufficient to maintain steerage way, while a planing boat might be better with the sea dead astern. On meeting a very large vertical wave, the throttle should be opened wide so that the best possible control is maintained and the boat forced over the wave rather than allowed to be thrown backwards. The greatest difficulty aboard a motorboat comes with nightfall, when the ability to see the waves and anticipate behaviour is lost.

If the sea breaks too heavily for holding up to weather, it will be necessary to choose a suitable moment and turn stern-on to the sea. The yacht should then be steered downwind, but the great danger here is too much speed. To reduce speed, the bight of two long warps lowered over the side and made fast on either side of the transom may be sufficient. If necessary, engines may need to be run astern or a drogue towed.

Using a drogue

A drogue towed astern while a vessel is under power will stabilise steering and prevent her sheering off course in a heavy following sea. The pull at the stern from the drogue acts as a fulcrum to facilitate normal steering; and because it is reacting against the thrust of the propellers, the faster the boat travels, the greater the pull and the greater the stabilising effect. Unlike a sailboat running under bare poles with a drogue, a motor yacht must run at full speed to gain the maximum stabilising effect. This demands a strongly constructed drogue with a sturdy polypropylene rope to attach it to the boat.

The ideal amount of drogue rode to pay out is about one and a half times the wave length, so when a wave is approaching the boat's stern, the drogue is pulling at the next wave. In a very short steep sea the drogue will need to be dropped back a couple more waves. With so much strain on the drogue, the rode must be attached to a very strong point on board the yacht, well protected from chafing and run through an enclosed fairlead to stop it jumping out.

Tip: Tripping lines should be run through a separate fairlead to prevent tangling.

Using a sea anchor

A sea anchor on a powerboat will reduce drift if the yacht is disabled for any reason or the crew need to rest. It can also be used to keep the boat at any angle to the wind. If the sea anchor is employed over the bow, the yacht is kept head-to-wind, but by leading a second rope to another point on the yacht, the angle of the hull to the wind can be altered. This can be useful when the wind and sea are not running in the same direction.

Oil to quell the sea

The old saying 'spread oil on troubled waters' is quite true. A very small quantity of oil, properly applied, may prevent much damage to a yacht caused by breaking seas in deep water. The oil reduces the crest-forming tendencies of waves, but has no effect on the swell.

Low viscosity animal, vegetable or fish oils are best, though engine lubricating oil can be used if nothing else is available. In cold weather the oil is better warmed to improve its flow; however, any oils that congeal at low temperatures (eg coconut oil) should be avoided as the cold water will stop them working properly. Oil should be distributed in any way that allows a very small quantity, about $4\frac{1}{2}$ litres (1 gallon) or so an hour, to spread. Use, for example:

- ◎ In weighted canvas bags, such as sailbags, packed with rags or old clothes, then filled with oil, sealed, punctured with a sail needle and trailed over the side.
- ◎ In a $4\frac{1}{2}$ or 9 litres (1 or 2 gallon) container of oil, punctured in the base, wrapped in rags to prevent too rapid a flow and placed in the galley sink with water running so that the oil runs out via the drain.
- • In a $4\frac{1}{2}$ or 9 litres (1 or 2 gallon) container of oil as above, but placed in the toilet and the oil allowed to flow out by activating the flush system at regular short intervals.

The best position for the bags will depend upon the yacht's storm tactics. When not making way, the oil should be distributed to the weather side. When moving through the water, the oil should be spread from up forward near the bows, to provide protection from quartering seas. In this crisis situation, do not worry about MARPOL regulations – saving lives is more important than incurring fines for pollution.

Extreme conditions – tropical revolving storm

Tropical revolving storms (TRS) are intense depressions around which winds of hurricane force blow, inclining slightly towards the centre, in an anticlockwise direction in the northern hemisphere and clockwise in the southern hemisphere. Formed in low latitudes, they occur mainly in late summer and early autumn. Depending upon the area, they are called hurricanes, typhoons, cyclones or a willy-willy. High and confused seas can cause considerable damage to even large ships, and for small vessels the results are devastating. The greatest danger is in restricted water without room to manoeuvre.

The size and extent of a TRS varies from storm to storm. Force 8 winds are likely inside 200 miles from the centre, increasing to Force 10 inside 100 miles – and sometimes up to Force 12 inside 75 miles. Gusts over 150 knots have been reported. At the centre, in the eye, there is a temporary lull of wind, but the sea state remains very confused, while just outside the eye hurricane-force winds, torrential rain and driven spray all reduce visibility to almost nil.

Weather satellites now identify and track TRS so that their position, intensity and likely movements can be regularly broadcast. In the TRS season it is very important to monitor all weather services for storm warnings and keep an eye on the barometer for an unusually steep and regular fall in pressure. Unfortunately, TRS do not always follow a predictable path and it is essential to take early avoiding action if notification is received of a possible TRS in the vicinity of the yacht or her future sailing area.

Evading a TRS

It is vital to avoid passing within 50 miles of the centre of a TRS and preferable to keep outside 200 miles. A TRS can be split across the centre along the line of the path into two semi-circles: the dangerous semi-circle and the navigable semi-circle. The poleward semi-circle is the dangerous side where the wind is strongest and a yacht here will tend to be blown into the centre. The aim is to sail away from a TRS and the tactic will depend upon where the yacht is in the world. For example, in the northern hemisphere, if the wind steadily veers, the yacht is in a dangerous semi-circle. In this scenario:

◎ If under power, proceed with all available speed, keeping the wind 10°–45° off the starboard bow, altering direction as necessary.
◎ If under sail only, heave-to on the starboard tack, hauling round to starboard as the wind veers.

If the wind remains steady in direction or backs, in the northern hemisphere the yacht is in the path of the storm or the navigable semi-circle:

◎ If under power, proceed with all available speed, keeping the wind well on the starboard quarter, altering direction as necessary.
◎ If under sail, run with the wind well on the starboard quarter, altering direction as necessary.

Unfortunately, this neat solution to TRS tactics is not quite perfect, particularly if the yacht is nearly in the path of the storm, because the wind does not always behave according to the rules.

Tip: If there is insufficient room to run, because of land or other navigational hazards, and safe shelter is impossible, a yacht, regardless of its power, should heave-to with the wind on the starboard bow in the northern hemisphere and do the opposite in the southern hemisphere.

A TRS in harbour

Riding out a storm, especially where the centre of the disturbance passes within 50 miles, is very hazardous – even in the best-protected harbour. This is especially true if there are other vessels nearby, and inevitably in any recommended spot there will be. If at all possible, the best advice is to get out of the path of the TRS as quickly as you can. If a harbour is seen as the best or only choice, certain precautions must be taken. These include:

◎ Stripping everything that can be moved off the decks of the yacht and taken below including: loose gear; sails; running rigging; weather cloths.
◎ Preparing fenders to use in case anything falls down on the yacht.
◎ At moorings or at anchor, every anchor available should be set and buoyed.
◎ Alongside a dock, the yacht must be pulled off the dock with lines to piles or by using anchors
◎ All mooring lines, ropes, rodes, etc used to make a vessel fast must be doubled if possible, and well protected from chafe.
◎ If alongside, putting out as much extra fendering as possible using old car tyres, mattresses, etc.
◎ Engine, if available, must be made ready to use to hold your position.

 Tip: Be sure to anchor clear of other vessels in a TRS; generally, the greatest danger is not from the weather, but from other vessels breaking free and falling down on the yacht.

Man overboard

Man overboard (MOB) is an increasing problem, and each year the figures show that the number of rescues by the authorities following a person falling from the side of a yacht is increasing. It is a well-established fact that many of the male bodies recovered from the sea, having fallen over the side, are found to have their trouser flies undone. So to avoid becoming a statistic, don't relieve yourself over the side – use a bucket and chuck it!

If, despite all precautions, a MOB situation does occur, the most important thing to remember is – DO NOT PANIC. The victim faces a number of dangers including panic, injury caused by or during the fall and, in most waters, hypothermia.

Stage 1: Immediate actions

The first thing to do when someone falls overboard is to mark the position and provide the victim with support. When there is more than one crew member left aboard the yacht, the first crew member to see the casualty must:

◎ Shout 'Man overboard port [or starboard] side' and point to the position in the water.
◎ Keep watching the casualty and pointing at him until he has been recovered.

Even if the MOB situation leaves only one person aboard, they must still shout as the casualty may hear the cry 'man overboard'. Hopefully this will inspire him with confidence and reassure him that the accident has been spotted. If you are alone on board, do not go below, as it is easy to become disoriented and lose sight of the casualty. Pointing with an outstretched arm is the most effective way of maintaining visual contact if other crew are performing the actual rescue. The next available crew member at the scene should:

◎ Locate the nearest lifebuoy and throw it overboard towards the person, to aid them and/or to mark their position.
◎ Release marker and orange smoke buoys and all MOB recovery equipment.

The watchkeeper should:

◎ Take immediate avoiding action so as not to run over the person in the water:
   – throttle back the engine and put it into neutral;
   – disengage the autopilot, if necessary, and turn towards the casualty.
◎ Hit the MOB button on the GPS and chart plotter.
◎ Sound the MOB signal on the whistle (three long blasts).
◎ Summon the Skipper.
◎ Sound a General Emergency to get all the crew on deck.

The current position, course and heading must be noted before making any alterations of the course. The MOB button on the GPS will automatically log the position where the person fell overboard, but it will take no account of any tide that may affect the casualty over time.

At night, white or red parachute flares should be ignited to illuminate the area. This may help to identify the casualty by picking up the retro reflective tape on clothing; it will also inspire the person in the water and alert nearby shipping.

A MAYDAY message should be sent and the distress alert button on the DSC pressed. If the casualty is recovered, the MAYDAY can be cancelled, but if things do not go according to plan, it is good to know that all nearby vessels and the emergency services have been alerted and may be on their way to assist as early as possible.

Stage 2: Going to the recovery site

Returning to the victim as quickly as possible is vitally important, but how this is done will depend upon numerous factors on the day – including the weather, type of yacht, and how quickly the crew react.

Sailing

MOB training on a sailboat for examination purposes is done under sail to ensure the Skipper is comfortable in the event of engine failure. There are numerous methods taught, involving either gybing or tacking the yacht, and much will depend upon the sail configuration, point of sail and number of crew aboard. But in the event of a real MOB, it is important to realise that the engine is usually the best option for speed and manoeuvrability. With all the possibilities of approach it is important that the Skipper can make a quick decision and, to this end, it is perhaps best to concentrate crew training on just a couple of methods that are suitable regardless of weather conditions. Two methods should cover most situations and weather conditions:

◎ **Quick Stop with Engine**
   – tack the boat immediately into a hove-to position;
   – bear away slowly and roll the headsail;
   – check for any lines in the water and start the engine;
   – turn downwind and pass abeam of the casualty in the water;
   – gybe round;
   – motor slowly head-to-wind to the casualty.

QUICK STOP METHOD

1 Man overboard.

2 Tack into heave-to position as soon as possible. Do not adjust sails.

3 Check for ropes over side. Roll headsail, make preparation.

4 Motorsail to downwind position (control the gybe).

5 Motor slowly head-to-wind towards MOB.

6 Pick up on either side, making contact near shrouds away from propeller).

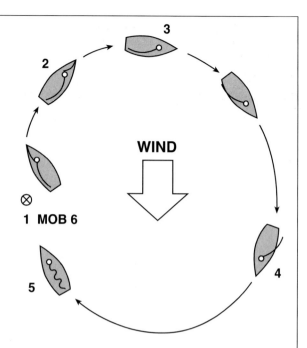

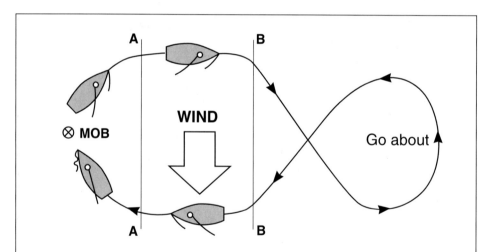

The reach-tack-reach method – with or without engine

1 Put the yacht on a beam reach, noting the course steered and the time.

2 As soon as the crew is ready, tack.

3 Come back on a reciprocal course for the same length of time.

4 Steer to about two boat lengths' leeward of the casualty.

5 Luff up head-to-wind beside the casualty.

On some sail plans, such as running under a spinnaker or with preventers rigged, getting the boat back to the MOB may be a slow process, even with a large and competent crew.

Tip: Accurate navigation will be needed in a MOB situation, as it is unlikely that the victim will be in sight the whole time.

Motoring

In calm weather and where the casualty is in plain sight, simplicity is best:

◎ Stop the boat.
◎ Turn the yacht short around, through 180°; if fitted, use the thrusters to assist.

In all other instances, such as poor visibility, heavy weather, rough seas or if the casualty is no longer in sight, the 'Williamson Turn' is the best way to get a boat back on a reciprocal course and take it back along its own wake:

Williamson Turn

1 Note the course.

2 Put the helm hard over to starboard (right full rudder) and add about 60° to the course.

3 Put the helm hard over to port (left full rudder) when the compass is on the new heading.

4 When the yacht has turned through approximately 240° and the compass reads the reciprocal course (ie course + 180°). Centre the wheel.

5 The yacht will now be motoring back down the original track even if the weather makes it impossible to see the old wake.

6 Reduce speed; the casualty should be somewhere straight ahead of you.

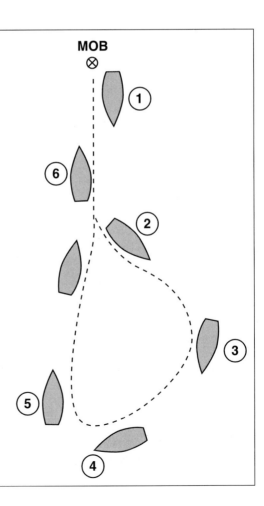

| **Tip:** | The actual amount of turn on each heading varies from boat to boat, and can only be ascertained by practising beforehand. |

Stage 3: Preparing for recovery

It is very important not to waste time while getting back to the victim; use it to get prepared. If alone on the yacht, think through what needs to be done, and in what order you need to do it, once you are alongside the casualty. The aim is to get the casualty out of the water as quickly as possible:

◎ Prepare a heaving line. A buoyant line is best, with a couple of knots in the throwing end for weight.
◎ Rig ladders, nets, etc to assist recovery.
◎ Prepare purpose-made recovery equipment.
◎ Prepare the rescue boat if available.
◎ Ensure that everyone assisting with getting the casualty aboard is wearing a lifejacket and, if possible, a lifeline – *another* man overboard will not help!
◎ Decide which side of the boat will be best to use for the recovery, taking into account:
   – the physical conditions – wind, sea state and tide;
   – the yacht – her layout and rescue equipment.

Stage 4: Coming alongside the casualty

If you lack boat-handling confidence, stand off a little and throw a line (taking care not to get it around the propeller). In strong wind, bring the stern into the wind and use the engines astern. Any large waves will cause the victim and yacht to go up and down, and not crash into one another. On a twin-screw boat, control the final approach by only using the engine *away* from the casualty.

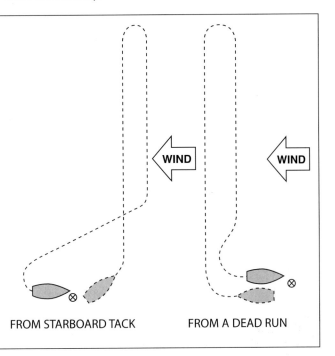

Coming alongside the casualty

When coming alongside the casualty, it is important to get the elements to help you – not hinder you. So use the wind or tide, whichever is stronger, to drift down onto the casualty. As a general rule, finish up to windward with the casualty close by on the leeward side of the yacht to prevent drifting off before recovery can be made.

FROM STARBOARD TACK   FROM A DEAD RUN

 Tip: Cease all engine activity when alongside the casualty; the propeller must not be turning.

Stage 5: Home and dry

Contact should be made with the casualty as soon as possible. On the final approach, one crew member should go forward with the heaving line or purpose-made recovery gear and throw it to the victim as the yacht comes to a halt. Do not throw it too early; it takes a long time to recoil a rope for a second attempt. With a line on the victim, it is easier to get him right alongside, but getting the casualty out of the water is always difficult. Wet people are far heavier than dry ones! It is best to avoid the stern where the propeller is close and pitching is likely to be most apparent.

◎ If the casualty is able to help himself, use:
  – the swim platform if available;
  – a boarding ladder rigged amidships.
◎ To assist the casualty, consider putting a swimmer wearing a lifejacket and attached by a line to the boat, into the water.
◎ An exhausted victim will need to be lifted on board using:
  – brute strength;
  – any available yacht gear – main halyard, davits, crane, anchor windlass;
  – specialist equipment – Jon-buoy recovery raft, life sling, etc.
◎ An unconscious victim should be taken out of the water in the horizontal position.

◎ At any time, but especially in rough weather, use a rubber dinghy or liferaft:
  – attach it securely to the yacht;
  – consider partly deflating the dinghy to make boarding it from the water easier;
  – once the victim is in the raft or dinghy, he can be transferred more safely to the yacht.

With the casualty aboard, the MAYDAY can be cancelled, unless immediate medical assistance is required. In many MOB situations, the victim is likely to be suffering from exhaustion, hypothermia or near-drowning, so first aid for these conditions should be implemented immediately.

Ensure that a casualty suffering from even the smallest degree of hypothermia or drowning is seen as soon as possible by a doctor.

Missing person

If the missing person cannot be found immediately when the yacht has reached the estimated position where the accident occurred, the boat should continue past the location until it is quite certain that the vessel has travelled far enough. Do not panic as if you cannot see the victim as drift can be considerable – especially if the yacht was slow in returning. Though both yacht and victim will make leeway, there may be a difference. A search must now be organised and a MAYDAY sent or updated.

Tip: When searching for a casualty, make each leg an equal length either side of the estimated position, with tracks no more than double the range at which the victim can be spotted, taking into account wave height and visibility.

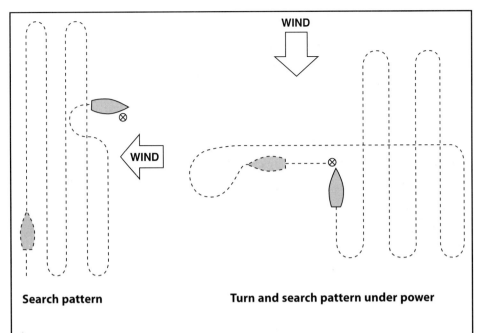

WIND

WIND

Search pattern

Turn and search pattern under power

Under sail, the yacht should beat to a location dead to windward of the victim's esti-mated position. Under power, the vessel can continue on a direct reciprocal course. Once the Skipper is sure that the yacht is past the victim, the vessel should work back towards the victim using a back and forth parallel search pattern.

In the water: self-help

The greatest threat to the survival of an MOB victim, in most waters, is cold. In waters with a temperature of around 16°C (61°F), the ability of the victim to assist in his rescue is greatly diminished after just 15 minutes in the water. It is important for the casualty to try to remember the following tips:

◎ Don't panic – try to remain calm.
◎ Look for the lifebuoy, or anything else thrown from the yacht and grab it.
◎ Do not try to swim too far to get a lifebuoy – this wastes energy.
◎ Do not attempt to swim to the boat – let them come to you.
◎ Turn to face away from the waves to keep your mouth and nose clear of spray.
◎ Exercise or swimming does not generate warmth – it just loses more body heat.
◎ Use HELP (Heat Escape Lessening Posture) to minimise the heat loss from your body (see page 192).
◎ Tighten the fastenings of your protective clothing at the neck, wrist and ankles to stop cold water entering.

MOB: time unknown

If someone on board is missing and is presumed to have fallen overboard, the Skipper must be summoned immediately and the General Emergency sounded to gather all the crew. A search must then be made of the yacht to make absolutely certain that the miss-ing person is not on board. The Skipper must then consider any facts that may be important, including:

◎ Observations about the missing person – such as when and where they were last seen, their personality, etc.
◎ Sea conditions, including the water temperature and sea state.
◎ The course at the time of the accident.
◎ Course changes since that time.
◎ Visibility before and at the time of the accident.
◎ Wind and current, direction and force.
◎ Speed before and at the time of the accident – according to the log reading.
◎ Bearings and distances to other ships.

The Skipper should then:

◎ Send a MAYDAY.
◎ Decide whether to turn the boat or not:
  – this decision is solely the responsibility of the Skipper;
  – even if a long time has elapsed since the missing person has fallen overboard, the slightest possibility that the missing person is still alive is reason enough to turn round and search.
◎ If the decision is made to turn the boat:
  – fix and synchronise the time on board;
  – transfer your position to a clean chart and keep continuous track.

Personal survival

Skippers should always worry about crew if working on deck in rough weather, and therefore insist on harnesses being worn and safety lines rigged. They should also consider equipping crew with small personal locator beacons. On activation, these small palm-sized units transmit the digitally encoded distress on 406 MHz and also transmit the homing signal on 121.5 MHz, making it easier to locate a crew member should he indeed be swept over the side. The units are designed to be worn on a belt loop and they float if they are accidentally dropped overboard.

Early warning

While safety devices such as personal EPIRBs are useful for finding the location of someone at sea, the response time in recognising, verifying and initiating a rescue reduces the chances of survival. The costs of a search and rescue are tremendous, as is the additional personal risk to those who participate in such hazardous attempts.

A combination of electronic technology and software programming has produced devices that constantly monitor all persons aboard the yacht and immediately raise the alarm the moment anyone falls or is knocked overboard. Each person aboard wears an individually coded transmitter, which constantly sends a signal to the central receiver console on board, which is continuously monitoring these signals. The moment that any one of the signals is not received, the device immediately raises the alarm, identifying the person or persons lost and giving the time, bearing and distance to aid recovery. An interface with the onboard GPS pinpoints the precise location where a person went overboard, and it can also link with an autopilot and be programmed to release a danbuoy or initiate an EPIRB distress call.

Training

Practice makes perfect, and that is never truer than in an MOB incident. All well-executed recoveries result from adept crew who had practised before they encountered the real-life situation. Professional captains have a legal obligation to drill crew in MOB procedures, but everyone who sails needs to practise. Couples who sail together need to consider how the weakest of the pair would be able to cope in an MOB situation. And new crew, especially novice sailors, need experience in the particular handling characteristics of the yacht and the use of its equipment.

Tip: Use an inflatable fender tied to a plastic bucket to simulate a casualty in the water, and practise MOB drills regularly in all weather and sea states.

9 URGENCY: PAN PAN

When an emergency arises it is important that the Skipper takes charge as soon as possible. Ideally, with a large crew, the Skipper will be in control and organising matters rather than actually doing the work. With a small crew, of course, the Skipper will not have that luxury, but it is still important that he delegates as much as possible to gain time to keep an overall picture of the situation. If the situation deteriorates he must take any action necessary to maintain the safety of life. He should be guided at all times by his primary responsibilities, which are for the safety of those entrusted to his care, the safety of the yacht, and the protection of the marine environment. All other considerations are secondary to these.

An urgent situation

While trying to cure the problem, alerting others must take a very high priority; if possible, an early and immediate attempt should be made to the rescue services and nearby vessels, to alert them to the situation. A vessel or crew with a serious problem, but not yet in a distress situation, should send an urgency PAN PAN message rather than a distress MAYDAY by radiotelephone. It is sometimes difficult to decide whether to send a MAYDAY or PAN PAN, but MAYDAY messages may only be sent by vessels in distress and the definition of 'distress' is 'grave and imminent danger that requires immediate assistance'. PAN PAN should be used for 'urgent messages'. Examples of urgency include a boat taking on water, but not yet sinking; serious, but not life-threatening injury to a crew member; or a fire still under control. An urgent situation can always be upgraded later to a distress situation, or subsequently cancelled if the problem is solved to enable the yacht to continue, or return to port under her own power. Meanwhile, help can be on its way, or standing by ready to assist as required.

DSC alert

An important element of GMDSS aboard any yacht is radio equipment fitted with a digital selective calling (DSC) controller. With GMDSS now fully implemented on commercial vessels over 300GT and an increasing number of other vessels, it is altering the likelihood that some of the traditional radiotelephone emergency signals will be as effective, especially deep sea and away from coast radio stations.

 Tip: Every new radio fitted aboard a yacht should be GMDSS-compliant and have a DSC controller.

The DSC controller will, at the touch of a button, broadcast a distress message indicating the name and position of the vessel in distress, together with the nature of that distress. That message continues to be sent every four minutes, until such time as some other DSC station acknowledges the distress. A VHF DSC alert must be followed up with emergency radio procedures on VHF channel 16 to alert any potential helpers who have only non-DSC equipment.

A PAN PAN can be sent using a radio fitted with a DSC controller by selecting 'All Ship Calls', then 'Urgency'. Once the alert has been sent, the radio will automatically switch to the correct frequency, ready for the verbal message. It is important that the verbal PAN PAN includes the position of the yacht as this is not transmitted in an automatic urgency call. An urgency message follows the same format as a MAYDAY, except that the words MAYDAY are replaced by:

PAN PAN (3 times), ALL SHIPS (3 times)

Emergency terrestrial radio frequencies

An automatic DSC distress, urgency or safety alert will be sent on one or more of the following frequencies dedicated exclusively for that purpose:

VHF	Channel 70	HF	4207.5 kHz
			6312.0 kHz
MF	2187.5 kHz		8414.5 kHz
			12577.0 kHz
			16804.5 kHz

The alert should indicate on which frequency the follow-up message will be transmitted. The available frequencies are:

	Radiotelephone	Radio telex
VHF	Channel 16	
MF	2182 kHz	2174.5 kHz
	4125 kHz	4177.5 kHz
	6215 kHz	6268.0 kHz
HF	8291 kHz	8376.5 kHz
	12290 kHz	12520.0 kHz
	16420 kHz	16695.0 kHz

159

Sailboats that lose the use of their aerials following a dismasting should resort to using handheld VHF units.

Medical advice by radio

Medical advice is available from any nearby ship with a doctor aboard and from a number of ports in all parts of the world. The ITU List of *Radio Determination and Special Service Stations* lists commercial and government radio stations that provide a free medical message service to ships. These messages are normally delivered only to hospitals or other facilities with which SAR authorities or the communications facilities have made a prior arrangement. It is always best to find a common language to prevent any misunderstandings, but if this is impossible the medical section of the International Code of Signals can be used to aid communications.

To obtain radio medical advice, the Skipper should first contact the rescue services by VHF channel 16, VHF DSC, MF DSC or Inmarsat. Urgent calls may be broadcast as follows:

PAN PAN, PAN PAN, PAN PAN

All Stations, All Stations, All Stations (*or individual Coastguard/coast station*)

This is .... *x 3*

Call sign ....

In position ....

I require medical advice

Over

The Skipper should have the following prepared:

◎ Brief details of the casualty's illness or injury.
◎ Type of vessel.
◎ Next port of call or nearest at which the casualty can be landed.
◎ Confirmation of position.
◎ List of drugs and medical equipment on board for treatment.
◎ Pencil and paper ready to make notes of the advice given.
◎ Ideally, a recorder to tape the exchange to help clarify any notes taken.

The radio medical staffs are specially trained, and should be aware of the problems and limitations of treatment at sea. Depending on the circumstances and the advice of the doctor, the SAR authorities may assist in arranging evacuation by helicopter or ship.

In Europe

European legislation requires member states to provide radio medical advice when an individual suffers either illness or an accident at sea. This medical advice is available free of charge and is intended to supplement the first aid training of the crew and any written guidance that is available, such as the *Ship Captain's Medical Guide*. In the UK, a PAN PAN call requesting medical advice will be directed to a working frequency, brief details taken, and then put through to a doctor. This will be one of the two designated radio medical advice centres in Portsmouth or Aberdeen.

By satellite

Yachts with satellite telephone and facsimile can make direct contact ashore from almost anywhere in the world:

+32   Medical advice
+38   Emergency patient evacuation

Commercial enterprises

There are various companies offering a 24-hour medical hotline with emergency care physicians qualified in remote diagnosis and in directing non-medically skilled people to provide aid. These services are generally subscription based and aimed at large yachts or merchant ships.

The best known medical advisory service is Centro Internazionale Radio-Medico (CIRM) with headquarters in Rome, Italy. They have doctors available 24 hours a day and provide free medical advice by radio to ships around the world.

In the future, telemedicine using digital imaging and satellite communications will undoubtedly revolutionise the handling of medical problems far from shore.

Medical evacuation

Most yachts do not have trained medical personnel on board or the equipment to deal with a serious condition. Add a small unstable platform, and in the event of someone aboard being badly hurt or gravely ill, medical evacuation may be the only answer. The first priority will be to obtain medical advice by radio, and following this advice, the decision may be taken to attempt an evacuation. Transferring a crew member off a yacht at sea is difficult – whether directly to a large ship with a doctor on board or despatching by helicopter ashore – and it is especially hard if the weather conditions are adverse. The decision about whether it is safe to conduct a medical evacuation will remain with the person in command of the rescue facility tasked with conducting the evacuation.

Medivac by helicopter

Never call for a helicopter unless the casualty is seriously ill or injured, and never use the service for a trivial matter or because it is more convenient. Helicopter evacuation is expensive, and crews often put their lives at risk to recover people at sea. The search and rescue authorities (SAR) will make the arrangements for any evacuation and will keep in touch with the yacht.

Once helicopter evacuation has been decided upon, as much medical information as possible will be required, particularly about the patient's mobility. The SAR authorities must also be kept informed about any changes in the condition of the patient. The details of helicopter rescue, included preparation of the yacht and methods of getting crew off are included in chapter 12. However, there are special preparations for a medical evacuation that need to be completed before the helicopter arrives:

◎ Prepare a waterproof package to go with the patient. This should include:
  - passport or other identification documents;
  - medical insurance details;
  - details of all medication administered prior to evacuation;
  - any other medical information.
◎ If possible, ensure that the patient is wearing a lifejacket.
◎ Instruct the crew about what to expect when the helicopter arrives and their probable tasks.

A helicopter evacuation takes time to arrange, especially if it will be operating at the extremes of its range. Arrangements may have to be made for a refuelling stop, or an aircraft escort for safety reasons. Do not keep calling to ask where the helicopter is.

Once the helicopter arrives it is very important always to obey all instructions given by the helicopter crew. Remember that the aircrew are the experts – they know best how to do their job quickly and safely.

'Ship-to-ship' transfer

Moving the casualty to a ship, or transferring a doctor from a ship to the yacht, may be the best option in a medical emergency – and the *only* one available in the middle of the ocean, out of helicopter range.

A ship will probably need to be diverted to meet the yacht and, like helicopter medivac operations, this is expensive. Most commercial ships run to very tight schedules and an extra day at sea caused by a medical evacuation will cost a great deal of money – an average daily commercial charter rate for a ship is $50,000 and that does not include fuel and other expenses.

In most cases, it will take time to bring the ship and yacht together even if they are nearby. A large ship under way at sea may require 30 minutes or more to bring her engines to stand-by, several miles to take off headway, and it will become difficult to manoeuvre close to a yacht, which is very small in comparison. Most transfers will use a small boat from the ship as this is far safer than attempting to bring the yacht alongside the ship.

Tip: If the patient is being evacuated by ship, he and the crew will need to be prepared in the same way as for a helicopter evacuation.

Towage

There are many stories of Skippers in trouble who end up being financially penalised for merely allowing their boat to be towed. The root of the problem is a lack of understanding of the difference between towage and salvage. Knowledge is the key to dealing successfully with any problem, and it is certainly true if the yacht needs outside help.

Salvage is not to be feared and rewards to the salvor are not necessarily out of order, particularly as the alternative would probably be the total loss of the yacht and maybe

– far worse – loss of life. Add wreck removal, possible hazardous waste containment expenses, and fines – plus charges for endangering other boats or property – and the insurance company may be very happy to pay just a percentage of the yacht's value.

The rules surrounding towing and salvage fill many volumes of maritime law and span centuries of seafaring history and tradition. This section contains a brief introduction to a very complex issue.

 Tip: Always negotiate towage fees in advance – do not leave it until the yacht reaches a safe haven.

Towing definition

Towing is essentially a service offered in the absence of peril. Examples could include soft grounding, engine breakdown in open water, etc where *there is no immediate danger to*: other vessels; the marine environment; the yacht herself; the people aboard the yacht.

Towing implies only one vessel and one line used for the tow, and that the yacht's Skipper is not in a situation that necessitates accepting the first tow that arrives if the price seems out of line.

The tow

The Skipper must never make any assumptions about a 'tow', and it is imperative that prior to handing over a line to any tow vessel he should ask: 'Is this a tow or a salvage?'

In UK waters, towing is offered freely by the RNLI in an emergency and there are a couple of towing organisations offering a contract or pay-as-you-need service. In the USA, where there is no voluntary service like the RNLI, membership of a towing service is common.

Aboard the towed yacht

The Skipper must discuss the tow with his crew and ensure that everything is prepared before the tow begins. The towed yacht should:

◎ Agree a price if a commercial vessel such as a fishing boat is helping.
◎ Prepare a bridle in advance.
◎ Advise the towing vessel of any hazards, such as ropes or sails in the water, especially if she plans to come alongside.
◎ Consider attaching the towline to the yacht's bower anchor, as the weight will give some spring to the tow:
   – let out the anchor and a length of chain;
   – secure the chain on board very firmly to prevent more being pulled out or it jumping out of the fairlead.
◎ Choose a method of communicating instructions once the yachts are under way, such as selecting an inter-ship channel on the VHF.
◎ Agree hand signals to use in an emergency.
◎ Secure the towline to the planned points.
◎ Avoid using knots or loops that cannot be released under load.
◎ Protect the tow rope from chafe where necessary, using rags, canvas, etc.
◎ Use a bridle in preference to a single rope.
◎ Steer the yacht to prevent yawing.
◎ Display appropriate signals by day, night and in reduced visibility.
◎ Have a small drogue streamed astern in the event of a lost rudder.

Aboard the towing boat

This section offers guidance to a yacht acting as a tug for another yacht. While a professional towing organisation will probably dictate the method of towing, with a yacht not designed to tow it is important for both Skippers to discuss everything before beginning. The biggest problem for a yacht is the probable impossibility of attaching a towline anywhere but near the stern, causing loss of manoeuvrability. The towing yacht should:

◎ Choose a method of communicating instructions once the yachts are under way, such as selecting an intership channel on the VHF.
◎ Agree hand signals to use in an emergency.
◎ Use a heaving line to pass the tow rope. Alternatively, in severe weather, float the line down.
◎ Use a bridle rigged between cleats on the stern quarters.
◎ Make fast so that it is possible to release the towline under load in an emergency. Alternatively, have an axe, knife, etc ready to cut the line.
◎ Protect the tow rope from chafe where necessary using rags, canvas, etc.
◎ Ensure that everyone is clear on both yachts before getting under way in case the line parts.
◎ Avoid starting to tow until the towed yacht signals its agreement to begin.
◎ If possible, display appropriate signals by day, night and in reduced visibility.
◎ Begin the operation slowly and gradually increase speed to get both yachts under way.
◎ If the towed yacht is lying abeam to sea, start the tow across the swell and then turn once when under way.
◎ Avoid towing too fast, especially if the towed vessel is much smaller.
◎ Avoid making any sudden alterations of course, especially if the tow cannot steer.

◎ Give plenty of notice of any planned course or speed change.

◎ In poor weather add something heavy such as a small anchor to the middle of the towline; adjust the length of the towline so both yachts are in step, moving up and down the waves at the same time.

When towing in an emergency, the lights required by the COLREGs need not be displayed, but every effort should be made to indicate the relationship between the two yachts and the towline should be illuminated. In confined waters, where manoeuvring will be necessary, towing alongside allows the best control. If possible, bring the tow close inshore or to a safe anchorage and arrange for smaller and more manoeuvrable boats to help to get the disabled yacht safely into harbour. A RIB with a powerful engine is a very good choice. If you secure the dinghy on the outboard quarter, steering will be nearly as good as the yacht under her own power.

10 Emergency: MAYDAY

Recognised distress signals

Annex IV of the International Regulations for Preventing Collisions at Sea, 1972, gives a list of the recognised distress signals. These are quoted here, with the permission of the International Maritime Organisation (IMO).

Recognised distress signals

(Annex IV of the International Regulations for Preventing Collisions at Sea, 1972)

1 The following signals, used or exhibited either together or separately, indicate distress and need of assistance:

   (a) a gun or other explosive device fired at intervals of about a minute;

   (b) a continuous sounding of any fog-signalling apparatus;

   (c) rockets or shells, throwing red stars, fired one at a time at short intervals;

   (d) a signal made by radiotelegraphy or by any other signalling method consisting of the group • • • − − − • • • (SOS) in the Morse Code;

   (e) a signal sent by radiotelephony consisting of the spoken word 'MAYDAY';

   (f) the International Code Signal of distress indicated by N.C.;

   (g) a signal consisting of a square flag having above or below it a ball, or anything resembling a ball;

   (h) flames on the vessel (as from a burning tar barrel, oil barrel, etc);

   (i) a rocket parachute flare or a hand flare showing a red light;

   (j) a smoke signal giving off orange-coloured smoke;

   (k) slowly and repeatedly raising and lowering arms outstretched to each side;

   (l) the radiotelegraph alarm signal;

   (m) the radiotelephone alarm signal; signals transmitted by emergency position-indicating radio beacons;

   (n) approved signals transmitted by radio communication systems, including survival craft radar transponders.

2 The use or exhibition of any of the foregoing signals except for the purpose of indicating distress and need of assistance and the use of other signals which may be confused with any of the above signals is prohibited.

3 Attention is drawn to the relevant sections of the International Code of Signals, the Merchant Ship Search and Rescue Manual and the following signals:

   (a) a piece of orange-coloured canvas with either a black square and circle or other appropriate symbol (for identification from the air);

   (b) a dye marker.

The majority of the signals in Annex IV are self-explanatory – as of course they should be. A visual representation of some of the signals is shown on pages 7 and 8. A photocopy should be made of this and added to the On Board Training Manual.

Tip: Consider pinning up the MAYDAY VHF procedure on the back of the door of the heads, so everyone who comes aboard the yacht has a chance to learn it!

Some of the signals would be difficult or impossible to produce aboard a yacht, especially a small one. Firearms, for example, are seldom carried aboard a British yacht, nor is radiotelegraph equipment. Flames on the distressed yacht would also be almost impossible to create safely, especially making them large enough for other people to realise it is a distress signal and not the barbecue playing up, for example! A pyrotechnic, especially a red flare at night or an orange smoke flare in the daytime, would be far more effective than flames. While red stars are included in the distress signals, these are not nearly as efficient as a SOLAS-specified parachute flare which, because of its brightness and longer aerial time, is far more likely to be spotted. An indefinite succession of blasts on your fog-signalling equipment, as with flames, could easily be misunderstood. But the rules offer an easy alternative employment for the equipment; use the apparatus to keep repeating the Morse signal SOS (• • • − − − • • •). Other signals, such as flying the code flags N and C, raising and lowering the arms or flying a square flag and a ball, will only be of any use if there is anyone near enough to see them.

Radiotelephone

If possible, radiotelephone, which includes VHF, HF and MF, or Inmarsat, should be used to make the initial distress alert. This enables a direct exchange of information between casualty and rescuer. If a PAN PAN message was sent, it must then be upgraded to a MAYDAY. An example of the MAYDAY procedure for GMDSS-enabled VHF is given on page 169. Every yacht with radiotelephone equipment should display

a similar card for each radio, prominently near the installation, carrying details pertaining to the particular yacht, her name, her call sign and her equipment. These cards should enable even a novice to make a MAYDAY call, and ensure that in an emergency no elementary mistakes are made – such as failing to turn on the equipment or using low power on a VHF. The format for a MAYDAY message is internationally recognised; it ensures all the important information is transmitted, as well as providing a familiar format to help a potential rescuer (for whom English may be a foreign language) to understand what they hear. There are basic spoken radio procedural words that persons involved in the search and rescue may use, and these must be understood by the Skipper. The most common words are detailed below. (For a more detailed listing, refer to the International Code of Signals.)

If the yacht is fitted with SSB radio equipment, which includes a two-tone radiotelegraph alarm signal, it should be used before the distress call on 2182 kHz. Although large ships are no longer obligated to listen for this, many still do and the alarm may attract the attention of a person on watch on another vessel.

Procedural words spoken by radio	
AFFIRMATIVE	What has been transmitted is correct
BREAK	Used to separate portions of a message or one message from another
FIGURES	Spoken just before numbers are given in a message
I SPELL	Used just before a phonetic spelling, such as a proper name
NEGATIVE	Means 'no'
OUT	Indicates the end of a transmission when no reply is expected or required
PRU-DONCE	Restricted working may be resumed for urgent traffic on the distress channel or frequency, but caution (prudence) should be used
ROGER	Means 'I have received your transmission satisfactorily'
SEELONCE	Repeated three times, it means 'cease all transmissions immediately'
SEELONCE DISTRESS	Issued by any station close to the incident who believes it essential to impose radio silence on the distress channel or frequency being used.
SEELONCE FEENEE	Used by the station controlling the distress traffic to indicate 'silence is lifted and that the normal working on the frequency may resume
SEELONCE MAYDAY	Issued by the station controlling distress traffic to impose radio silence on the distress channel or frequency being used
THIS IS	Said before the station name or call sign that immediately follows
WAIT	Means 'I must pause for a few seconds; stand by for further transmission'

Satellite radio alerting

Inmarsat is at present the world leader in satellite communication. The distress alert by Inmarsat is totally automatic and sent by priority connection to a Maritime Rescue Co-ordination Centre (MRCC). Once a connection is made, the message should be spoken or typed as appropriate.

A satellite alert is a point-to-point system. This will not immediately notify any nearby vessel; it is similar to dialling the emergency services from a house telephone – the next-door neighbours are not made aware of a problem at the same time. The alert will be re-broadcast to vessels carrying GMDSS equipment by the MRCC.

MAYDAY VHF Procedure

M/Y Happy Days
November Hotel Golf Whisky 8
MMSI 366924365

IF THE VESSEL OR A PERSON IS IN GRAVE AND IMMINENT DANGER AND IMMEDIATE ASSISTANCE IS REQUIRED:

VHF (GMDSS)

♦ Check VHF is on. If not, depress green button on handset.
♦ Remove handset from wall unit.
♦ Lift plastic lid, on wall unit, covering orange button.
♦ PRESS AND HOLD THE ORANGE 'DISTRESS' BUTTON FOR 5 SECONDS.
♦ Wait and listen.

On receipt of an acknowledgement or after 15 seconds:

♦ Press red 'CH 16' button.
♦ If 'LOW' is displayed on screen, press 'HI/LO' button.
♦ PRESS TRANSMIT BUTTON, and say slowly and clearly:
    MAYDAY, MAYDAY, MAYDAY
    This is Happy Days, Happy Days, Happy Days.
    Mayday Happy Days, November Hotel Golf Whisky Eight.
    MMSI 366924365
♦ My position is .... (latitude and longitude using GPS)
    IF YOU DON'T KNOW, DON'T GUESS!
♦ I am .... (sinking, on fire, etc)
♦ I require immediate assistance
♦ I have .... (number of persons on board, any other information – drifting, flares fired, etc)
♦ Over
♦ RELEASE THE TRANSMIT BUTTON and listen for an acknowledgement.
♦ KEEP LISTENING ON CH 16 FOR INSTRUCTIONS

If an acknowledgement is not received, then repeat the distress call process from the beginning. Consider repeating the call on a different channel.

This is an example of a Mayday VHF procedure appertaining to a particular radio. Everything printed in grey should be altered to reflect the equipment and details aboard your yacht, and any extra instruction, relevant to your particular equipment, should be included, to enable a novice to make a successful MAYDAY transmission.

When contact has been made by radio (including Inmarsat) it is important not to cause confusion by also activating a distress beacon, unless that original contact is lost, or the rescue authority request it. In the event of total electrical failure, dismasting, abandoning ship or some other problem preventing the radio working, the EPIRB should be activated and any of the other signals in Annex IV that seem appropriate to attract attention should be used.

Mobile phones

A mobile phone is not a recognised method of sending a distress signal. Currently, a cellular phone is designed for land use and coverage at sea is only likely in certain areas when close to shore. A satellite mobile phone has much wider coverage, although exactly what that is will depend upon the service provider. A mobile phone has a major disadvantage compared with VHF: it can only contact one person at a time. Of course, if a mobile phone is the only means of making a distress call, it should be used. To make a call from a cellular phone in an emergency:

◎ In the UK, dial 999 or 112 and ask for the Coastguard.
◎ In the USA, dial 911 or the Coast Guard directly.
◎ In Australia, dial 000 or 112.
◎ Anywhere in the world with GSM coverage, dial 112:
  – this is automatically converted to that country's particular emergency number;
  – you can do this even from a mobile phone without a SIM card;
  – you can do this without having to enter a security-protection key/PIN number.

Tip: Make sure a mobile satellite phone has a selection of numbers pre-programmed for emergency use. The MRCC in Falmouth would certainly be a good choice – as the case history below shows.

Case history
In November 2002, the MRCC in Falmouth co-ordinated the rescue of a yachtsman from the sea, thousands of miles away, using a mobile satellite telephone from inside a liferaft. Thomas Jordan and his crew had been sailing his 12m (38ft) yacht *Blue* when it hit a rock in the Malacca Straits. VHF calls to local coastguards and rescue services went unanswered. The yacht was sinking quickly when Mr Jordan and his crew took to the raft carrying with him his EPIRB and mobile satellite phone. From within his liferaft he was able to speak personally with the duty watch at Falmouth, and they in turn were able to alert the Malay authorities to the yachtsman's plight. Even before the EPIRB signal had been received and processed, the hapless couple were plucked from disaster by a fishing boat, which subsequently transferred them to a police launch sent to intercept them.

EPIRB

When a yacht is in contact by radiotelephone with either a Rescue Co-ordination Centre or another vessel, the crew will know that help is on its way. The next best method of communicating distress if no other vessel is in sight is to set off an EPIRB. Unfortunately, there is no means of telling for sure when, or even if, help is actually on its way. In theory, if the unit functions properly, within five minutes of activating an Inmarsat E EPIRB, or a 406 MHz EPIRB with GPS, the Maritime Rescue Co-ordination Centre (MRCC) should have the details. Without GPS, it may take up to two hours to gain attention, and a 121.5/243 MHz beacon message may never be received. Without any means of directly contacting the world at large, the chances of help shrink in direct relationship to how far offshore the yacht is and whether anyone ashore will set in motion a search.

Once an EPIRB is activated, it should not be switched off until you are directed to do so by the rescuing authorities. It must not, under any circumstance, be turned off and on, perhaps in the hope of preserving the batteries; this will only confuse the rescue authorities and may make the final homing using the 121.5 MHz signal impossible.

 Tip: Any civil aircraft flying over the area, though far too high to see a yacht, liferaft or notice a flare, could be receiving the 121.5 MHz signal (they are required to listen out on this frequency) and may be notifying an MCC or aeronautical RCC.

Case history

In March 2003, a German man was sailing singlehanded from north of Lanzarote to Tenerife when some 80nm from Tenerife and 60nm from Gran Canaria he discovered a severe leak. Unable to get rid of the water with either an electric or manual pump, he took to his liferaft and switched on his Inmarsat E-plus beacon at 8:43 UTC.

The recently installed Inmarsat E+ equipment at Bremen RCC received a distress alert via the Inmarsat satellite. Simultaneously, the distress was received by the MRCC in Falmouth. The rescue was conducted by the MRSC Las Palmas, who tasked a rescue helicopter and rescue boat at 9:45 UTC. At 11:10 UTC, the SAR helicopter picked up the sailor, less than two and a half hours after his first alarm.

Pyrotechnics

If no radiotelephone equipment is available and it is possible there may be other vessels in the area, even if they cannot be seen, flares should be used. Two parachute flares fired, one after the other, about three minutes apart, are a good idea. The first flare may catch someone's eye; the second will give them a direction. Do not waste any more flares until it is known that help is nearby.

Once used, a flare is gone for good, so it is important not to waste them. Unless the yacht has a very large supply it is best to wait, after the initial attempt, until a ship or aircraft is actually sighted. If the crew have had to retreat to the liferaft, then only use flares when a ship is as close as it is likely to get, because a liferaft is a very small object to spot from a large ship.

Pyrotechnics are dangerous; they must be used properly. They can give someone a nasty burn, have killed people, and can easily make a hole in a liferaft. Always read the instructions written on the pyrotechnic before using it, to refresh the memory. In the event of a signal failing to operate, keep it in the firing position for at least 30 seconds. If it has still not worked after this time, remove the end caps and place it in a bucket of water or throw it over the side; water will penetrate and render the signal harmless.

Tip: Many training schools run special courses during which participants fire pyrotechnics; there is no substitute for hands-on training.

Rocket parachute flares

A red parachute rocket should be used first to attract attention. A SOLAS-specified rocket contains a single red flare suspended on a parachute and will reach an altitude of at least 300m (984ft). This can be very dangerous to aircraft and helicopters and can cause serious damage. *Do not fire a parachute flare when aircraft or helicopters are in the immediate area.*

Under normal conditions, rocket parachute flares should be fired vertically. If a strong wind is blowing, they should be angled at about 15° away from the direction of the wind. If pointed into the wind, the rocket will tend to seek the wind and be deflected at a greater angle. This will reduce the maximum altitude and hence its range of visibility, plus there is a risk of them blowing back aboard. If there is low cloud, fire rockets about 45° downwind so that the flare burns under the cloud. Although there is little recoil, the sudden 'whoosh' as the rocket is fired can be disconcerting, so it is important to hold the flare canister firmly.

Handheld flares

When help is in sight in conditions of poor visibility, high winds or darkness, use the red handheld flares to pinpoint your position. In daylight with good visibility and a light wind, an orange buoyant smoke flare will be more distinctive. Both orange smoke and red handheld flares should be held firmly, as close to the bottom as possible, at arm's length and downwind. Although a flare can easily be held in a non-gloved hand, use a wet cloth around the user's hand, if available. In a liferaft, hold a flare over the leeward side to prevent any hot ash burning the liferaft.

Buoyant smoke signal

An orange buoyant smoke signal is a very effective distress signal during daylight hours, especially when viewed from above. It shows up well in bright sun, but tends to blow parallel to the waves in high winds. Throw buoyant smoke signals into the water to leeward.

 Tip: Do not look directly at any flare at night, as it may damage your night vision.

Other distress signals

Close to shore and anywhere where there are other vessels, any of the recognised distress signals listed on page 166 can be used to attract attention if no radiotelephone equipment is available. The first choice will probably be pyrotechnics, and if a SART is available it should certainly be turned on. Much will depend upon the circumstances including the availability of equipment and the position of the yacht.

Distances

Possible distances that a distress alert may be received, assuming equipment of the highest quality and good conditions, are:

- ◎ *EPIRB 121.5 MHz homing signal: line of sight*
- ◎ *Pyrotechnics (SOLAS)*:
  - – Red parachute: *44km (28 miles)*
  - – Red handheld: *8km (5 miles)*
  - – Orange handheld smoke: *5km (3 miles)*
  - – Orange buoyant smoke: *10km (6 miles)*
- ◎ *Radar reflector*: depends greatly on type and position
- ◎ *SART: 16km (10 miles)*
- ◎ *Signal mirror: 16km (10 miles)*
- ◎ *Signalling torch: 35km (22 miles)*
- ◎ *VHF*:
  - – Handheld: *8km (5 miles)*
  - – Fixed installations: *Line of sight plus 10%*

These distances will be much greater when received by specialised search and rescue aircraft, but may be reduced if the equipment used for signalling is not of the best quality, or in bad weather when poor visibility can be a problem.

Who might arrive?

Sailors should have some knowledge of search and rescue (SAR) capabilities and procedures for the sea areas through which they are passing. Unfortunately, it is not always easy to get hold of this information for every area of the world.

The flowchart on page 175 shows the immediate action taken by any RCC on receipt of a distress alert.

United Kingdom

In the UK, information about SAR assistance is given in the *Annual Summary of Admiralty Notices to Mariners*.

HM Coastguard, a division of the MCA, is the authority responsible for initiating and co-ordinating all civil maritime SAR measures for vessels in their region. This area is bounded by latitudes 45° and 61° North, by 30° West and by the adjacent European Search and Rescue Regions. The area is subdivided into five maritime Search and Rescue Regions (SRR), each containing at least one Maritime Rescue Co-ordination Centre (MRCC), with additional Sub-Centres (MRSC), which all maintain a constant manned communications watch. The MRCC Falmouth acts as the primary contact for rescue control centres outside Europe, the link for Inmarsat alerts and all EPIRB alerts, on 406, 121.5 and 243 MHz.

If a vessel in distress is within this UK area, help may be expected from any or all of the following:

◎ Other vessels in the area.
◎ HM Coastguard SAR helicopters based at strategic locations around the coast.
◎ MCA Emergency Towing Vessel (ETVs) based in the Northern Isles, Minches, the Dover Straits and the South Western Approaches.
◎ The Royal Air Force operating Nimrod Maritime Patrol fixed-wing aircraft and dedicated SAR Sea King helicopters at six locations around the UK coast.
◎ The Royal Navy SAR Sea King helicopters from two Royal Navy air stations, plus Royal Navy ships and aircraft, including non-SAR helicopters.
◎ The Royal National Lifeboat Institution (RNLI), a private organisation supported entirely by voluntary contributions, which maintains all-weather, intermediate and inshore lifeboats, operating up to 50 miles offshore around the coast of the UK, the Republic of Ireland, the Isle of Man and the Channel Islands.
◎ The Automated Mutual-Assistance Vessel Research System (AMVER) Centre in New York, which will establish and control commercial vessels that may be in the area.
◎ Auxiliary Coastguard Response Teams.

The USA

The US Coast Guard is the authority responsible for initiating and co-ordinating all civil maritime SAR for vessels in their region. This huge area includes the Caribbean and a large part of the northern Pacific Ocean. The area is subdivided into ten RCCs and one Sub-Centre (RSC San Juan). Each of these 11 rescue centres receives distress alerts directly. The USCG undertakes the majority of the SAR operations themselves, though they do receive help from the US Navy, US Air Force and AMVER when they request help. Close to the coast, the USCG is augmented by the USCG Auxiliary.

DISTRESS ALERT FLOWCHART

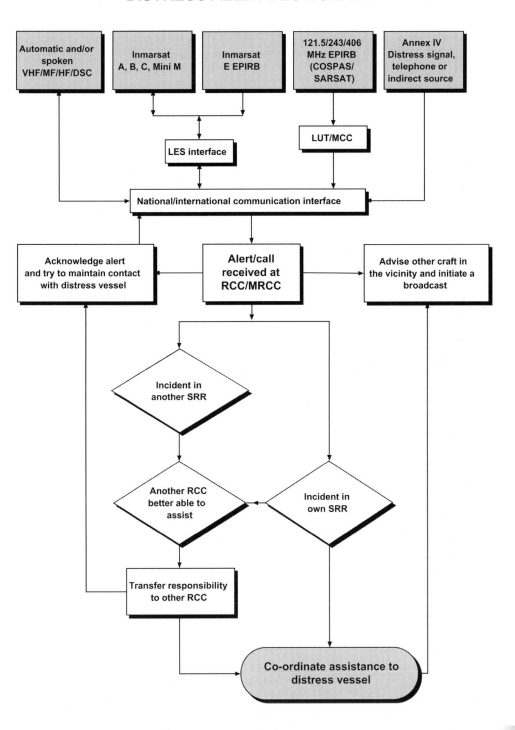

Australia

In and around Australia, SAR is provided by AusSAR, the national search and rescue organisation, which is part of the Australian Maritime Safety Authority (AMSA). AusSAR operates a 24-hour Rescue Coordination Centre (RCC) in Canberra and is responsible for the national co-ordination of both maritime and aviation search and rescue. The RCC will co-ordinate a search and rescue with assistance from appropriate organisations, such as the defence forces, trained aviation organisations (Civil SAR Units), emergency medical helicopters, state police services, state emergency services, the Australian Communications Authority (ACA), airlines, the general aviation industry, volunteer marine rescue groups, the Bureau of Meteorology, the shipping industry and fishing co-operatives.

Other countries

Information about SAR assistance in other countries in the world is detailed in Radio Lists issued by the UK Hydrographic Office and in publications issued by the individual countries.

Assistance by SAR aircraft

SAR aircraft may be used to assist a yacht in distress. They can drop liferafts and equipment, and helicopters may lower trained personnel or evacuate survivors. The Aircraft Rescue Flowchart on page 177 can be used in this situation.

Fixed-wing aircraft

Fixed-wing aircraft have a much greater range than helicopters and may be the first to reach a distressed craft. They may:

◎ Drop equipment.
◎ Direct rescue facilities.
◎ Confirm the distress.
◎ Remain on the scene to:
  – serve as a radio and radar beacon;
  – show lights;
  – drop flares;
  – provide radio signals for DF and similar homing for other rescuers;
  – provide reassurance.

Depending on what the aircraft is searching for, different search patterns are used. Off the coasts of the UK, SAR Nimrod MR2 aircraft in the search area fly between 100m and 1500m (300ft and 5000ft), or below cloud, day or night. A yacht is relatively easy to find, but a liferaft, especially in rough seas, may be difficult to spot. The crew of the yacht should make every effort to alert overhead aircraft to their presence, to stop the aircraft moving away to search another area. To indicate that survivors have been sighted, the aircrew will:

◎ Flash a signal lamp or searchlight.
◎ Fire two, preferably green, flares a few seconds apart.
◎ Fly over with the plane's landing lights on.
◎ Fly over, rocking the wings.

AIRCRAFT RESCUE FLOWCHART

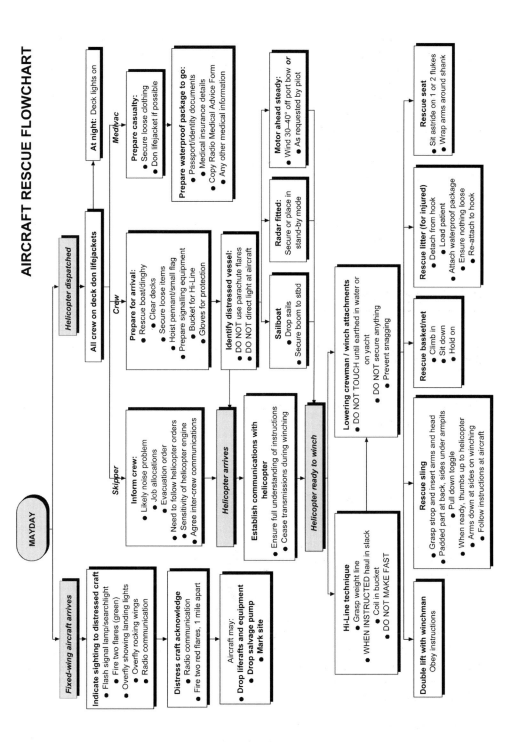

MAYDAY

Helicopter dispatched

At night: Deck lights on

All crew on deck don lifejackets

Medivac

Prepare casualty:
- Secure loose clothing
- Don lifejacket if possible

Prepare waterproof package to go:
- Passport/identity documents
- Medical insurance details
- Copy Radio Medical Advice Form
- Any other medical information

Crew

Prepare for arrival:
- Rescue boat/dinghy
- Clear decks
- Secure loose items
- Hoist pennant/small flag
- Prepare signalling equipment
- Bucket for Hi-Line
- Gloves for protection

Identify distressed vessel:
- DO NOT use parachute flares
- DO NOT direct light at aircraft

Motor ahead steady:
- Wind 30–40° off port bow *or*
- As requested by pilot

Radar fitted: Secure or place in stand-by mode

Sailboat
- Drop sails
- Secure boom to stbd

Rescue seat
- Sit astride on 1 or 2 flukes
- Wrap arms around shank

Rescue litter (for injured)
- Detach from hook
- Load patient
- Attach waterproof package
- Ensure nothing loose
- Re-attach to hook

Skipper

Inform crew:
- Likely noise problem
- Job allocations
- Evacuation order
- Need to follow helicopter orders
- Sensitivity of helicopter engine
- Agree inter-crew communications

Helicopter arrives

Establish communications with helicopter
- Ensure full understanding of instructions
- Cease transmissions during winching

Helicopter ready to winch

Lowering crewman / winch attachments
- DO NOT TOUCH until earthed in water or on yacht
- DO NOT secure anything
- Prevent snagging

Rescue basket/net
- Climb in
- Sit down
- Hold on

Rescue sling
- Grasp strop and insert arms and head
- Padded part at back, sides under armpits
- Pull down toggle
- When ready, thumbs up to helicopter
- Arms down at sides on winching
- Follow instructions at aircraft

Fixed-wing aircraft arrives

Indicate sighting to distressed craft
- Flash signal lamp/searchlight
- Fire two flares (green)
- Overfly showing landing lights
- Overfly rocking wings
- Radio communication

Distress craft acknowledge
- Radio communication
- Fire two red flares, 1 mile apart

Aircraft may:
- **Drop liferafts and equipment**
- **Drop salvage pump**
- **Mark site**

Hi-Line technique
- Grasp weight line
- WHEN INSTRUCTED haul in slack
- Coil in bucket
- DO NOT MAKE FAST

Double lift with winchman
Obey instructions

◎ Attempt radio communication, if they have the equipment, using:
  - VHF channel 16;
  - 2182 or 4125 kHz, MF distress and calling frequencies;
  - AM VHF if the yacht looks as if it may have air band VHF (eg if there is a helicopter landing pad aboard the yacht).
◎ Relay by radio from the RCC ashore if possible.

To acknowledge the aircraft signal, the Skipper should:

◎ Try communicating by radio as above.
◎ Use pyrotechnics, being very careful not to aim directly at the aircraft:
  - fire one red flare;
  - fire another red flare after one minute, to allow the aircraft to line up on the bearing;
  - fire a third flare if the aircraft appears to be badly off course.

The aircraft will be able to confirm with the RCC:

◎ Position and condition of the distressed craft and her crew.
◎ Weather and sea conditions.
◎ Type and location of nearby surface craft.
◎ Supplies and survival equipment required.
◎ Action or assistance given and future actions required.
◎ Any risks involved in the rescue.

The aircraft should remain at the scene until relieved, forced to return to base, or the rescue has been completed.

Droppable SAR apparatus

Special droppable liferafts and equipment may be supplied to craft in distress. They will usually be dropped about 100m (328ft) upwind of the position of the vessel with a 200m (656ft) buoyant trail line, so as to let the trail line float downwind to the survivors. An individual liferaft, or liferafts linked in pairs by a buoyant rope, can be dropped. Each container or package should:

◎ Be clearly printed in English and one or more other languages.
◎ Have self-explanatory symbols.
◎ Have colour-coded streamers:
  - red – for first aid equipment and medical supplies;
  - blue – food and water;
  - yellow – blankets and protective clothes;
  - black – miscellaneous equipment such as stoves, axes, compasses, cooking utensils.

Depending upon the distress requirements, time before the rescue can be effected, sea conditions, location of the distress, etc, other equipment may be dropped, such as:

◎ Salvage pumps to assist the yacht.
◎ Buoyant radio beacons and transceivers.
◎ Dye and smoke markers and flame floats to mark the site.
◎ Parachute flares for illumination.

Sea planes and amphibians

Under favourable conditions seaplanes and amphibians may be used for rescue operations, particularly in inland seas, large lakes, bays and coastal areas.

Helicopters

A helicopter may be used to supply equipment and rescue or evacuate people. Normally limited to a maximum operating distance from base of 300nm, a helicopter can be used for rescues at greater distances with air-to-air refuelling. SAR helicopters can rescue between 1 and 30 people, depending upon the type of craft it is.

Except in the exceptional circumstances where a yacht is equipped with a proper helicopter landing pad, rescue will be carried out by winching. If the yacht has a mast, the helicopter will be unable to hover very close. However, winching is fraught with dangers, especially in bad weather. It can be hazardous to the persons being hoisted, the helicopter and others on the distressed vessel, and all instructions from the helicopter crew must be obeyed quickly and precisely.

Prior to arrival of the helicopter

Before the helicopter arrives, the yacht crew must begin preparations:

◎ Ensure that everyone on deck is wearing a lifejacket.
◎ At night, switch on the deck lights.
◎ Issue a portable VHF/UHF for inter-crew communications.
◎ Prepare the rescue boat or dinghy in case of MOB.
◎ Clear the decks as much as possible.
◎ Secure all loose objects on deck, including sails.
◎ Place a large bucket ready to collect loose line from Hi-Line technique.
◎ Hoist a pennant or small flag to show the wind direction.
◎ Prepare the casualty if this is a medivac rescue (see chapter 9):
  – put a lifejacket on them if possible, depending on their injuries;
  – secure any loose clothing or blankets;
  – securely attach their medical information to them.
◎ Prepare equipment to help the helicopter recognise the distressed yacht:
  – orange smoke flares by day;
  – red flares and/or a signalling lamp by night.

"IF POSSIBLE, KEEP THE VESSEL AS STEADY AS YOU CAN"

◎ Skippers should:
  – inform the crew about problems of noise when the helicopter is on site;
  – agree the hand signals to be used if voice communication is impossible;
  – allocate crew jobs during the rescue;
  – arrange the order of evacuation if more than one crew is being rescued;
  – emphasise the possibility of causing the helicopter to crash if even *one* small piece of paper is ingested into the engine;
  – insist that all crew follow the helicopter crew's instructions implicitly no matter what they have learned elsewhere;
  – ensure that any crew likely to be helping to grab helicopter lines, etc wear gloves to prevent rope burn.

As the helicopter gets close:

◎ Establish communications with the helicopter via VHF channel 16 or the RCC ashore.
◎ Be prepared to give the following information:
  – position, course and speed of the yacht;
  – local weather conditions including: wind direction and speed; sea state.
◎ Make sure that the pilot's instructions are fully understood as it may be impossible to hear the radio when the helicopter is overhead.
◎ Identify the distress yacht to the helicopter using the prepared flares or the signalling lamp.
◎ DO NOT fire a parachute flare.
◎ DO NOT direct any light towards the helicopter.
◎ Secure the radar or place it in stand-by mode.
◎ Drop the sails and secure the boom to starboard, away from transfer area.
◎ Aboard a sailboat without a motor, deploy the sea anchor, if available, to reduce drift.
◎ Motor steadily with the wind 30–40° off the port bow.

By choice, the helicopter pilot will approach the yacht from the stern on the port side so that the pilot sitting on the starboard side can see the vessel. To assist the operation, if possible the yacht should motor at a constant speed with the wind 30–40° off the port bow. The helicopter can then hover almost dead into the relative wind. It will be very noisy, and the rotor downwash will whip up spray and blow unsecured items overboard.

 Tip: If being rescued from a liferaft, be prepared for a severe buffeting.

Helicopter overhead

It cannot be repeated often enough that all crew must follow the instructions of the helicopter crew *even if they differ from what they have learned in the past or what is written here*. The helicopter crew are fully trained personnel and are expert in rescue operations, or otherwise they would not be undertaking the mission. During the winching:

◎ DO NOT touch the winchman, stretcher or winch hook until it has been earthed.
◎ DO NOT secure any lines passed down; simply hold them until the winchman arrives.
◎ Ensure that nothing snags on anything.
◎ DO NOT transmit on the radio while winching is in progress.

Hi-Line technique

Transfer to and from a yacht to a helicopter will usually involve using a Hi-Line, especially in sailboats with masts still standing, in bad weather, or in a confined winching area. The Hi-Line, a weighted line attached to the aircraft's hook by a weak link, acts as an umbilical from the helicopter to the yacht. First of all:

◎ The weighted line must be lowered or trailed to the yacht.
◎ The line must be grasped by a crew member on the yacht.
◎ ONLY WHEN INSTRUCTED BY THE HELICOPTER CREW, the yacht crew must haul in the slack line (wearing gloves).
◎ THE LINE MUST NOT BE MADE FAST AT ANY TIME.
◎ As the helicopter pays out the line and descends to one side, the yacht crew must take up the slack, coiling it neatly in a bucket and ready to run.

The helicopter will then lower a crewman or a lifting harness while the yacht crew should assist by hauling in the 'umbilical' to bring the winch hook on board.

◎ DO NOT touch the hook until the static discharge line has made contact with the yacht or the water.
◎ During winching up, pay out the line, maintaining sufficient force to stop a swing, but retain the end.
◎ On the final lift, gently toss the end of the line over the side of the yacht.

During the rescue operation a helicopter normally uses a special device for hoisting or lowering persons, and these are described below.

Rescue sling

This is the most common method for evacuating uninjured persons. SAR helicopters in the UK use a double lift, where a winchman is lowered with a strop for the evacuee. When there are several survivors to be rescued, the winchman may take two strops with him. In this case, when he reaches the liferaft, the winchman will detach himself from the winch-hook and feed the survivors up to the helicopter two at a time.

A potentially hypothermic evacuee may be winched with two strops. One is placed under the armpits, the other behind the knees, to allow winching in a horizontal position to minimise further injury.

If a single strop is supplied without a winchman, it must be used as follows:

◎ Grasp the strop and put both arms and head through the loop.
◎ Ensure the wide padded part is as high as possible across the back, with the two sides coming under the armpits and up in front of the face.

- Pull the toggle down as far as possible.
- When ready to be lifted, look up at the helicopter, put one arm out and give a clear 'thumbs up'.
- Put both arms down beside the body.
- When you have been winched up alongside the helicopter, do nothing until instructed by the helicopter crew.

Other winch attachments

As an alternative to a rescue sling, one of the following may be attached to the end of the winch cable:

- A rescue basket – climb into this, sit down, and hold on.
- A rescue net – this is a conically shaped cage, open on one side; climb in, sit down, and hold on.
- A rescue litter – this is designed for hoisting someone who is injured. The litter should be unhooked from the winch cable while the patient is loaded.
- A rescue seat – this can be used to hoist two persons at once. It looks like a three-pronged anchor with flat flukes or seats. Sit astride one or two of the seats and wrap your arms around the shank.

Rescue by ship

Bringing a yacht or liferaft alongside a much larger ship is fraught with dangers and problems, and different drift rates can crush the yacht or her crew. The safest method for a ship to rescue the crew from a distressed yacht or a liferaft is for the ship to stand off and use her lifeboat, liferaft or rescue boat. The yacht's crew must all wear life-jackets before any rescue begins. Once the distressed crew are safely aboard the ship's boats, they can be transferred to the ship by:

- Hoisting the rescue boat aboard.
- Using scrambling nets and ladders rigged over the side.
- Using a boarding station.
- Canvas slings, bosun's chairs, cargo nets or hooks secured to a survivor's lifejacket.

Search and rescue obligations

There are two sides to the rescue coin: rescuer and rescued. It is certainly better to be in the position of saviour! Under longstanding traditions of the sea and various provisions of international law, such as SOLAS Chapter V Regulation 33, it is the duty of the Skipper of any vessel at sea to assist others in distress whenever they can safely do so. Upon receiving a distress signal of any kind, the yacht must proceed with all speed to assist, unless or until specifically relieved by the co-ordinating MRCC.

Distress and MAYDAY Relay

A watchkeeper who receives a distress message by radio should write down all the information broadcast and immediately summon the Skipper. The Skipper should then wait for a short time for the nearest shore station or some larger vessel to acknowledge this. If nothing is heard, the Skipper should respond and offer assistance if possible.

Every effort should be made to transmit the distress information to the SAR authorities using a MAYDAY Relay message, making it quite clear which vessel is in distress. A MAYDAY Relay should also be used when the yacht sights a non-radio distress signal, such as those in Annex IV of the COLREGs: pyrotechnics, flags, shapes, etc.

DSC distress or urgency

A DSC alert will sound an alarm that is different from a routine alert alarm. The watchkeeper must immediately select the appropriate voice channel or frequency on the radio and write down all distress information received. The Skipper should then be called, and a short time left to elapse to allow a coast station to acknowledge the distress. If no other contact is heard, the Skipper should acknowledge the alert by radio or, if unable to contact the distressed vessel by voice, by DSC. The distress information should then be relayed ashore by any means.

 Tip: If you are not involved in the distress, search or rescue, maintain radio silence.

If the alert is received on HF, the distress may be halfway around the world. Listen on the associated frequencies for five minutes, but do not acknowledge unless there is no reply or relay by a Coast Station (CS) or Rescue Coordination Centre (RCC). If nothing is heard, transmit the distress as a relay to the Coast Station and inform the RCC.

Assisting a distressed vessel

No matter what size your yacht or how large the distressed vessel, the yacht may be the nearest help and must provide any assistance possible. In the case of the distress involving a person in the water, such as MOB from another vessel, a swimmer in trouble, etc, the MOB procedures in chapter 8 should be followed. There are various actions the Skipper must take if he is participating in assisting a distressed craft.

Initial actions

Having acknowledged the distress, the Skipper must if possible gather the following information from the craft: ✧ position of distress ✧ distressed craft's identity, call sign and name ✧ number of persons aboard ✧ nature of the distress or casualty ✧ type of assistance required ✧ number of victims, if any ✧ distressed craft's course and speed ✧ type of craft ✧ any other pertinent information that might assist the rescue.

The Skipper should maintain communications with the distressed craft and a listening watch on all distress frequencies available, while attempting to advise the SAR system of the situation. If possible, the distressed craft should be informed that the yacht is coming to help and given the following information about the rescue yacht: ✧ identity, call sign and name ✧ position ✧ speed and ETA to the distressed craft's position ✧ distressed craft's true bearing and distance from the rescue yacht.

All means available should be used to continuously monitor the position of the distressed craft, such as radar plotting, chart plot, GPS, etc. The information should be passed on to the SMC (Search and Rescue Mission Coordinator) ashore or the ship or coast radio station co-ordinating the distress traffic.

Proceeding to the distress area

As the yacht sails towards the distressed craft, the Skipper should:

◎ If appropriate, establish communications with other vessels in the area and any SAR units involved.
◎ Plot the position, courses and speeds of other assisting vessels to estimate their ETA.
◎ Maintain active radar plots on all vessels in the general vicinity.
◎ Monitor radar using 6 or 12nm range, looking for a survival craft transponder (SART) signal.
◎ Put extra crew on watch to look out for all visual signals from the distressed vessel or survival craft, including pyrotechnics, signal mirrors, etc.
◎ Assess the distress situation to prepare for operations once on the scene.

The crew must prepare equipment ready for use at the scene, including:

◎ Lifesaving and rescue equipment: binoculars; boarding ladder; boat hook; buoyant lifelines; copy of the International Code of Signals; firefighting equipment; lifebuoys; lifejackets; liferaft; line-throwing apparatus; MOB equipment; portable pumps and bailers; portable VHF radios; rescue boat or dinghy; survival suits for crew; other supplies and survival equipment as required.
◎ Signalling equipment: flashlights; loud hailer; pyrotechnics; searchlights; signalling lamps.
◎ Preparations for medical assistance: blankets; clothing; first aid kit; stretcher; water and food.
◎ Miscellaneous: cameras; fenders; mooring lines.

Developing a rescue plan

When two or more craft are involved in a rescue, one person at the incident must be designated the On-Scene Coordinator (OSC) to control and direct the others. This is normally the person in charge of the first facility to arrive at the scene, though the SMC may arrange for a more qualified relief. The SMC will normally prepare a rescue plan, but sometimes the OSC may have to develop it himself or adjust the plan as necessary based on the situation in consultation with the SMC. Factors to consider include:

◎ Risk to SAR personnel.
◎ Number, location and position of survivors.
◎ Condition of survivors and any medical considerations.
◎ Current meteorological conditions and forecasts.
◎ Current sea conditions and future predications.
◎ Time of day.
◎ Survival equipment available.
◎ Type of rescue craft.

The Skipper must bear in mind that in a distress incident even uninjured persons may be in a poor mental state and unable to help themselves – or they may even hinder the rescue. It is also important to consider the limitations of a yacht, particularly a small one sailing shorthanded, when it comes to assisting a distressed vessel. In the event that a large number of survivors are involved, water, food, accommodation and stability may be a problem.

11 Taking to the Liferaft

It is always better to remain with the yacht until it is almost certain she is going to sink. A yacht is bigger than any liferaft she carries, and is therefore better able to withstand the battering effect of the sea and to provide shelter for people. The yacht is also far easier for rescuers to find – being larger, higher in the water, and generally produces a stronger signal on radar. The liferaft should be thought of as the final and ultimate retreat, not the first choice when things go wrong. Never abandon ship until the last possible moment; help may arrive bringing a pump to deal with flooding or to help fight a fire, for example. Crew may be able to transfer to another vessel or helicopter without ever inflating the raft, or getting their feet wet.

There have been too many cases of crew taking to the liferaft only to be lost, while the ship they left behind remained afloat; additionally, a yacht is more easily detectable by the SAR units, who can find spotting rafts difficult. Without additional equipment, the maximum distance a liferaft is likely to be sighted is about 8km (5 miles). These distances will be considerably reduced in bad weather or poor visibility. In some situations, an out of control fire, for example, it may be prudent to take to the liferafts initially with a possible return to the mother ship later.

Preparing to abandon ship

If it is clear that the accident or emergency situation is not going to be resolved, or that there is even a slight possibility that the situation may escalate and become out of control, the Skipper must prepare to 'abandon ship'. In an ideal world, with a large crew, the various jobs related to this can be carried out while part of the crew continues to try to save the yacht.

Avoiding hypothermia and drowning

The two major threats for people abandoning ship are hypothermia and drowning, and the most common cause of death following a shipwreck is exposure. People become too cold to help themselves in the water and drown. Even without getting wet, crew aboard a survival craft can still die from the effects of cold. The epic survival stories have nearly all taken place in tropical waters.

If it should be necessary to enter the water on abandoning the yacht, the initial 'cold shock' may prove disabling, or even fatal, so it is particularly important to insulate the greatest heat-loss areas: head, neck, armpits, sides of chest and groin. Extra clothing (wool and polypropylene), with as many layers as possible, will markedly reduce the shock effect. A waterproof outer layer, such as an immersion suit, could prevent it entirely; if this is unavailable, put on foul weather gear, fastening tightly at the wrists and ankles (with duct tape if necessary), and cover the extremities with socks, shoes, gloves and hat. The extra clothing will prolong survival time by reducing loss of body heat. It will not weigh a person down – in fact, just the opposite is true! When the person enters the water, the air trapped between the extra layers of clothing will help the lifejacket keep them afloat. Even if crew do board the survival craft without getting wet, the extra clothing will help to save their lives while awaiting rescue. *Cold*, not lack of food and water, is the greatest killer following abandonment. If possible, pack spare clothes in a dry bag in case the crew have to swim; this bag can also be used as a substitute flotation device.

The final item to put on is a lifejacket, unless crew are wearing buoyant immersion suits. Without a lifejacket, even a good swimmer will have difficulty in staying afloat in cold water because of the disabling effects of cold, shock and cramp. With a lifejacket, people in the water can float effortlessly or swim, regardless of how much clothing they are wearing; and if they are unconscious, the jacket should keep their mouth out of the water. Survival time will depend upon water temperature and how much clothing is worn. The following table is a guide to probable survival time if well dressed with a lifejacket, but without special protective clothing:

Water temperature	Expected survival time
Less than 0°C (<32ºF)	Less than 45 minutes
0° to 4° C (32.5° to 40ºF)	Less than 90 minutes
4° to 10° C (40° to 50ºF)	Less than 3 hours
10° to 16° C (50° to 60ºF)	Less than 6 hours
16º to 21º C (60° to 70ºF)	Less than 12 hours
Over 21º C (70ºF)	3 hours to indefinitely

Case history

On Sunday 22 December 1963, a fire started aboard the passenger liner *Lakonia* while cruising in the Atlantic. Soon the fire became out of control and the lifeboats were launched. Among the confused passengers was a woman claiming to be a nurse. She moved among the passengers, instructing each and every one she could reach to remove as much of their clothing as possible before jumping into the sea; and once in the water, to begin moving as vigorously as possible to generate warmth in their bodies. There is little doubt that this misinformation, given by this misguided woman, contributed to the many deaths from exposure that occurred among the passengers.

Preparing the liferaft

NEVER LAUNCH A LIFERAFT UNTIL THE 'ABANDON SHIP' ORDER IS GIVEN BY THE SKIPPER, but the liferaft must be made ready. There are too many stories of even professional crews launching a liferaft and tying it alongside to await orders, only to have it swept away before anyone boarded it.

Depending on where a liferaft is stowed normally, it may be necessary to release the securing arrangements and move the raft to the launch position. A liferaft is not designed to be inflated on deck – the actual inflation can be dangerous to those around as the canister explodes, as well as the risk of jamming or piercing the raft on parts of the yacht. The ideal position to board a liferaft is from the lowest deck, amidships on the leeward side, though in a calm sea the stern may be suitable where a yacht has a swimming platform. The painter must be made fast to a strong point such as a mooring cleat, but definitely not to the lifelines, which could easily break under a strain.

Case history

During the disastrous 1998 Sydney–Hobart Race, the yacht *Naiad* inflated her two liferafts and tethered them to the yacht on the leeward side. A large wave struck the *Naiad* and the liferafts quickly vanished. Liferafts have pockets on the bottom that are designed to quickly fill with water and restrain the raft from moving freely through the water. When tied to a moving yacht the liferaft will naturally resist being pulled through the water. Immense strain is placed upon the tether or its anchor point, and one of these will eventually fail.

Tip: If time permits, launch any dinghies, surf boards, canoes or anything else that floats and tie them alongside ready to use or later attach to the liferaft.

Grab bags

First get the grab bag, and then the extras, in one place – ideally near the liferaft launching area. This is where the Last Minute Grabs List (see page 88) is invaluable as a memory aid for collecting various articles – such as binoculars, EPIRB, food and water, medical kit, portable VHF, etc. Make sure every item has a long lanyard attached to it.

If time permits, everyone should take antiseasickness tablets with plenty of water. A liferaft can affect the strongest stomach, and most medication is only effective before seasickness sets in. Encourage everyone to drink as much water as possible before leaving the yacht, as this will increase the level of body fluids and help to overcome any tendency to retain urine when in the very public confines of a crowded raft.

Abandoning the yacht

Only the Skipper should give the 'abandon ship' order by word of mouth. No matter what the vessel, this is a spoken instruction to prevent any possibility of confusion. In the event of the Skipper being incapacitated, the next most senior member of the crew takes the role of Skipper and should give the order.

Once the 'abandon ship' order has been given, but before the liferaft has been actually launched, the Skipper should:

◎ Ensure that the engine has stopped and the propellers are secured.
◎ Stop overboard discharges, especially those in the way of liferaft and tender launch areas.
◎ Make a note of the position of the yacht to take to the liferaft.
◎ Make a final MAYDAY call to announce the abandonment.
◎ Check that everyone is ready with lifejackets correctly fitted, and thermal suits if applicable.

187

Some yachts have been reboarded again after abandonment during fire, etc. To aid the survivability of the yacht, three additional tasks are recommended, where time permits and if applicable: ✧ shut all watertight doors ✧ close all fuel valves ✧ leave the emergency fire pump running with hoses rigged to flow outboard.

Launching the liferaft

Once the order is given to abandon ship, the liferaft must be launched (see flowchart opposite).

◎ Read any instructions on the liferaft.
◎ Check that the painter is secured to a strong point on the yacht.
◎ Check that all the fastenings are undone.
◎ Make sure that the water in the launching area is clear of people or obstructions.
◎ Throw the raft over the side.
◎ Pull the painter to its full extent. This may be as short as 7m (22ft) or as long as 60m (200ft); SOLAS suggests 15m (50ft).
◎ Jerk the painter to fire the CO_2 bottle to inflate the liferaft.
◎ Do not allow the liferaft to drift any distance from the yacht, or it may be impossible to pull back.

A SOLAS-specified liferaft should be fully inflated in one minute at an ambient temperature of between 18° and 20°C (64°F and 68°F). This will take longer at lower temperatures.

Tip: When inflating the liferaft, there will be excess gas, which will vent from overflow valves; this is a good sign that the liferaft is fully inflated.

Boarding the liferaft

If possible, everyone should board the liferaft without entering the water. Body heat loss in water is 20 times that which would occur in the same temperature conditions on land, neglecting the wind chill factor. The biggest problem with unloaded liferafts, apart from being separated from the yacht, is that they are prone to tipping over, especially before the ballast bags are full of sea water. It is important to get someone heavy on board as soon as possible. To board the raft, first pull it close alongside, taking care to protect it from chafing on the side of the yacht and damaging the fabric. Once the liferaft is fully inflated, but not *before* as it could prevent proper inflation, start to load the raft.

The order in which people, the grab bag and 'extra grabs' are transferred to the liferaft will depend on circumstances and crew numbers. Leave any injured survivors until last, as other crew may land on them and make the injuries worse. Crew should climb aboard the raft using overside ladders or ropes, if it is impossible to simply step down. Do not let anyone jump onto the liferaft as this could harm them, the raft canopy, or other people already inside. Equipment should be passed down carefully, throwing the lanyard first to be fastened to the liferaft, and then the item itself can be passed down. Some equipment, such as water in 80 per cent full containers, can be left to float tied onto the outside of the raft.

ABANDON SHIP FLOWCHART

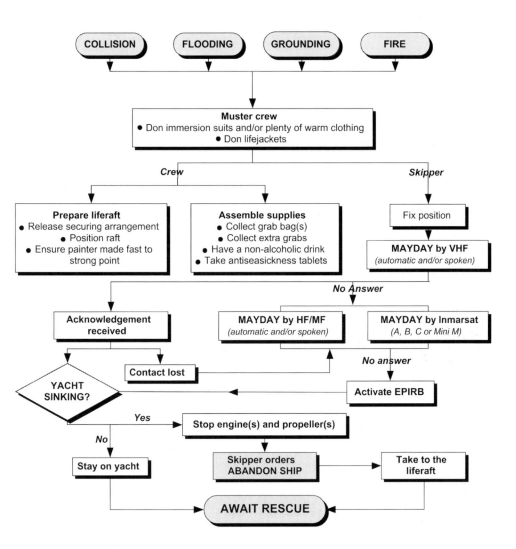

Note: Nothing in the flowchart is intended to preclude the use of any and all available means of distress alerting.

Entering the water

If there is no time, or for some other reason it is impossible to bring the liferaft alongside the yacht, crew will have to enter the water. In the event of a rapid sinking when every second counts, everyone should bear in mind the very real threats of hypothermia and drowning. If it is necessary to enter the water, choose a suitable place to leave the yacht bearing in mind: ✧ drift of the yacht ✧ position of any survival craft in the water ✧ lack of any survival craft ✧ the sea state ✧ other hazards, eg burning oil.

The windward side or as close to a survival craft as possible are generally the best choices. Exiting on the leeward side risks being trapped, as a yacht stopped and drifting will make more leeway than a swimmer. If there is no survival craft in the water, the stern or bow may be the best choice to get clear of the yacht with more certainty.

Jumping overboard

Do not jump into the water unless it is essential. Use any method available to lower people over the side, such as a ladder, a rope or even a hose. Sudden immersion into cold water, for those unaccustomed to it, produces a dramatic increase in heart rate, blood pressure and breathing rate. Although these responses decline after a few minutes' immersion, they can still incapacitate or even kill, especially in older people suffering from high blood pressure or heart problems.

 Tip: Enter the water slowly to make the temperature change in your body more gradual.

If jumping into the water is unavoidable:

◎ Never jump from a height exceeding 6m (20ft) when wearing an inflated or permanent buoyancy lifejacket.
◎ Ensure your lifejacket is securely tied.
◎ Use one hand to hold the lifejacket down, to stop it hitting your chin on entering the water.
◎ Use your other hand to block off your nose and mouth to stop the ingress of cold water.
◎ Keep your feet together with your legs slightly bent.
◎ Check below that there are no obstructions.
◎ Jump feet first, looking straight ahead. Looking down may cause tumbling forward.

In the water

Avoid remaining in the water for even one second longer than necessary, for body heat will be lost to the water faster than it can be generated. Eventually hypothermia will occur, leading to unconsciousness and death. Get into a survival craft as quickly as possible or get clear of the yacht. The danger of being struck by wreckage surfacing from a sinking yacht is greater than the suction caused by it sinking. If there is any danger of an underwater explosion, crew should grab onto anything floating and pull themselves out of the water. If that is impossible, swimming on their backs might reduce the risk of injury.

Oil

If there is surface oil burning:

◎ Paddle or swim into the headwind (against the wind).
◎ Discard the lifejacket and swim underwater as far away as possible.
◎ When forced upwards to breathe:
  – make sweeping movements with your hands to force your body clear of the surface;
  – cover your eyes, nose and mouth when surfacing;

- turn your back to the wind;
- sweep flames clear with broad arm movements;
- take deep breaths and get underwater again rapidly;
- cover your face with your hands when submerging.
◎ Swim clear of the area.

If you are in oil-covered water that is free of fire, hold your head high to keep oil out of your eyes and mouth.

Avoiding drowning and hypothermia

Once in the water, it is very important to minimise energy expenditure. If no survival craft is available, *do not swim aimlessly*. Body heat loss to the water is greatly exacerbated by exercise as the blood supply to the muscles is increased, and warmed water trapped by any clothing is forced out. By swimming or treading water, the body will cool about 35 per cent faster than when remaining still. The 'drownproofing technique', which involves putting the head into the water, will facilitate cooling 80 per cent faster than if floating still with the head out of the water. Even good swimmers quickly become exhausted in cold water, partly because it is difficult to maintain an adequate

arm and leg stroke rate while rapidly gasping for breath. It becomes all too easy to inhale water and drown.

Since swimming is difficult and dangerous, the importance of wearing a lifejacket cannot be overstated. Ideally it should be a jacket with a face visor, to give protection from wave splash and spray inhalation. Float as still as possible using the American 'HELP' position (Heat Escape Lessening Posture) to minimise heat loss to the water:

◎ Cross the arms and grip the neck of the lifejacket.
◎ Cross the ankles and draw the knees up to the chest.

Use the whistle and light attached to the lifejacket to attract attention and alert others. If possible, gather with any other survivors in the water, because a group can be more easily seen than a single person in the water, and two or more huddled together can increase survival time by 50 per cent. Use the 'huddle' position:

◎ Form a circle facing inwards.
◎ Link arms or loop them through your neighbour's lifejacket.
◎ Intertwine your legs.
◎ Place children and older people in the centre for maximum warmth.

If sea conditions are very rough it may be necessary to float with your back to the wind and sea to protect your face from wave splashes. An alternative to the 'huddle' position is the 'crocodile', when everyone joins together in a straight line so that all survivors can face in the same direction. Use the 'crocodile' to continue to maintain contact even when moving through the water – towards a liferaft, for example.

 Tip: The towing loop on the back of the lifejacket can be used to move an injured person.

If it was impossible to grab a lifejacket before going overboard, floating will be much harder. Air trapped in clothing will provide considerable flotation, but anyone without a lifejacket should:

◎ Try to grab anything that might help then float.
◎ Look for new items that may surface after the yacht sinks to help them float.
◎ Watch for the liferaft if it is fitted with a hydrostatic release.
◎ Not discard footwear; it might be valuable protection later on.
◎ Use boots to aid flotation if some air is allowed inside them so that they float on the surface.
◎ Float on their back to save energy.
◎ In cold water:
  – *not* remove any clothes;
  – keep their head out of the water.
◎ In warmer water, if nothing else is available, try using clothing to make a buoyant float, for example:
  – tie knots in the legs of trousers;
  – hold your waistband and swing to try to trap some air; repeat this when air has escaped.

Sharks

Out of several hundred species of sharks, only a handful have ever been known to attack man without provocation. It is believed that sharks are very curious and attracted by unusual noise. Therefore the highest risk of a shark encounter is when the yacht sinks. If sharks are in the water:

◆ Get out of the water if at all possible
◆ Retain all clothing, especially on the legs and feet. Historically, sharks have attacked the unclothed parts of the body first, mainly the feet.
◆ Keep as quiet as possible and only move to keep the shark in sight.
◆ Only swim using rhythmic strokes.
◆ When in a group, form a circle facing outwards.
◆ Avoid getting body fluids/substances in the water:
  – bind bleeding wounds;
  – avoid urinating – if this is unavoidable, do so in small amounts and at spaced intervals so there is time for it to disperse;
  – if you can't avoid vomiting, throw it as far away from you as possible;
  – if you are forced to defecate, throw it as far away from you as possible.
◆ If available, get into an oil patch.
◆ If an attack is imminent, splash and yell but conserve your strength to fight off the shark.
◆ If attacked by the shark, kick and strike it, going for the gills and eyes.

Boarding a liferaft from the water

Once the liferaft is reached, cling onto it, or it could drift away. Putting an arm through the grablines is better than hanging on with your hands, which can become numb quickly in cold conditions.

Boarding a survival craft unaided from the water is a difficult operation. Make maximum use of foot- and handholds, bearing in mind that, when cold, the thigh muscles are the strongest, and can be used to exert most leverage. It may help to push under the water and use extra buoyancy of the lifejacket to help you 'bob up' higher. The same technique can be used by those in the survival craft to assist in bringing a person on board. This can be done by two people in the liferaft, turning the survivor so that their back is against the liferaft, then gripping them under the arms and on top of the shoulders, and 'dunking' them several times before lifting them in.

Righting a capsized liferaft

Sometimes a liferaft may inflate in the inverted position, or be capsized by the winds and waves when the liferaft is empty. If at all possible, try to right a capsized raft without entering the water to reduce the risk of hypothermia. There are dangers in righting the raft close to the wreckage because of all the potential hazards around. It may be necessary to tow the liferaft into clear water, if circumstances permit, before attempting to right it. One person can easily right even a very large capsized liferaft from the water. To do this:

193

◎ Position the raft with the gas bottle at the downwind side.
◎ Climb onto the raft from a position close to the gas bottle.
◎ Stand on the gas bottle, grip the righting strap firmly, then stand upright.
◎ Check that the raft is tilted into the wind.
◎ Lean back and allow the liferaft to come over.
◎ As the liferaft falls backwards, exit on the back in a right-hand direction.
◎ If the raft lands on top, simply backstroke out from underneath using the righting strap if necessary to find the way out from under the raft.

WARNING: Swimmers should not attempt to clear the underside of the liferaft by a forward movement. This will bring them up against the gas bottle and the buoyancy of the lifejacket could trap them. Beware of the stability pockets because they may contain lead weights.

A fully manned liferaft is unlikely to capsize, provided that the drogue is streamed at an early stage and that the occupants sit with their backs against the sides of the liferaft. If a capsize does occur, remember that the raft will float high in the water and that air will be trapped inside it.

Tip: If a liferaft capsizes, DO NOT PANIC. Evacuate the liferaft in an orderly manner and carry out the capsize drill as detailed above.

12 Survival in the Liferaft

Successfully boarding the liferaft is not, in itself, sufficient to ensure survival, especially in rough seas and cold weather. Understanding this, the IMO, in Resolution A.657 (16), issued guidance on survival instructions to be provided in survival craft to SOLAS standards. These recommendations were endorsed by the MCA and the USCG and are included here and marked with an asterisk (*). The instructions concerning immediate action upon entering the liferaft are shown in the box below. They can be photocopied onto waterproof material, and packed in the liferaft, attached in a position where a person entering the raft can easily see them. Add another copy to the On Board Training Manual, so that every crew member can study them before or during a voyage. Lastly, include a third copy in the top of the grab bag – just in case! Use this chapter for crew practice sessions – prior training will make a real 'abandon ship' situation much less traumatic and give everyone a much better chance of a successful outcome.

Instructions for Immediate Action in the Liferaft

1 **CUT** painter and get clear of ship.

2 **LOOK** for and pick up other survivors.

3 Ensure sea anchor **STREAMED** when clear of ship.

4 **CLOSE** up entrances.

5 **READ** survival instructions.

Photocopy these instructions.

Immediate action in the liferaft

Once everyone has been embarked into the raft, the Skipper or senior crew member must take charge and ensure that the immediate action list is followed. Experience has shown that certain vital actions must be taken as soon as possible. These actions have priority over all others and can be memorised by the five 'key' words: ◇ **Cut** ◇ **Look** ◇ **Streamed** ◇ **Close** ◇ **Read:**

CUT the painter and get clear of the ship*

Crew take to the liferaft because the yacht is sinking, and they certainly do not want their new home to be damaged as the old one disappears underwater. There is less risk that crew will be pulled under and more that the raft may be swamped by a wave or cut by the wreckage. Sever the last tie from the mother ship; a safety knife to cut the painter is stowed near each liferaft entrance. The knife is designed to prevent accidental damage to the raft. Cut the painter as far from the raft as possible; it may be useful as a piece of rope in the future, as a towline, or to join liferafts together. Using the oars or paddles, manoeuvre the liferaft clear of the yacht's side, and away from any floating obstructions that may damage the raft. If the sea anchor streamed automatically, it may be necessary to pull it in first, and it may be more practical to use it to help move the raft.

Tip: Throw the sea anchor in the direction you want to go, and then heave on the hawser, thus pulling the raft towards the sea anchor.

LOOK for and pick up other survivors*

Once the raft is clear of the sides of the yacht, check for any more survivors in the water. Take a quick head count, establish who, if anyone, might be missing and instigate an immediate search. Look for lights on lifejackets, and listen for whistles or shouts from anyone in the water. Getting people out of the water quickly and into a warm and protected environment is the priority in reducing the risk of hypothermia.

With conscious swimmers, use the rescue quoit, for the less distance survivors have to swim, the less energy they use and the warmer they will stay. Maintaining a hold on the end of the line, throw the quoit with its buoyant line to the person in the water. Once the survivor has caught hold of the ring, ensure they have a tight grip before pulling them in and, if possible, make them put their arm through the quoit. Immersion in cold water can numb the extremities to the point of uselessness and holding a quoit may become impossible. In that case, or with an unconscious survivor, it may be necessary to put someone in the water to help. Do not let the rescuer into the water without his lifejacket and the quoit, to help them return to the liferaft. A rescuer must not underestimate the strength of a panic-stricken person in the water. Always approach a survivor in trouble from behind, grasp the loop at the top of the back of the lifejacket, and use it to tow them. Those in the liferaft should pull in the rescuer and the survivor using the rescue quoit line.

Assist all survivors to board the liferaft. An unconscious or weak victim can be brought aboard by turning him so that his back is against the liferaft, then gripping him under the arms and on top of the shoulders, and 'dunking' him several times before lifting him in.

Tip: Lift an exhausted survivor aboard in the horizontal position, as this reduces the chance of a sudden drop in blood pressure on removal from the water.

Ensure that the sea anchor is STREAMED when clear of the ship*

Stream the sea anchor or drogue as soon as possible. This will reduce the rate of drift away from survivors who may still be in the water. It will also stabilise the raft and stop it from moving an excessive distance from the distress position of the parent yacht, and possibly away from the area of maximum search.

The sea anchor line is permanently attached to a point to one side of one of the raft entrances. Once the line is tight, the entrance will be kept across the weather, the liferaft will be steadied and less likely to capsize, since any capsizing moment is resisted by the downward pull of the line. Adjust the sea anchor so that when the raft is on a wave crest, the drogue is in the wave trough. Check the securing lines from time to time to ensure they are not chafing or wearing away at the fabric of the raft; if necessary, wrap the rope with cloth.

CLOSE the raft entrance*

In cold weather, close the liferaft entrances. If the liferaft is fitted with internal pressure relief valves from the main buoyancy tubes, do not close the entrances until the valves have stopped venting, or there may be a build-up of poisonous CO_2 gas inside the raft. If the raft has doorway tapes, always use slipknots to tie them, or occupants could become trapped inside the raft in the unlikely event of capsizing – cold fingers cannot undo knots easily. The body heat of the occupants will rapidly warm the interior of a closed liferaft. As mentioned many times already, hypothermia is a major threat to the safe survival of shipwreck victims, and early action to avoid this is essential.

READ survival instructions*

All survival instructions in the grab bag and liferaft emergency pack should be read as soon as possible after boarding the raft, together with any operating manuals or instructions printed on equipment. They all provide a useful aide-mémoire and serve as a checklist for future actions to best aid survival. Make sure that everyone reads every bit of information too, so they can have as much independent guidance as possible to surviving.

Secondary action in the liferaft

Once the initial actions, essential for combating exposure and saving lives, have been performed, these secondary actions should be taken as soon as possible. The following instructions and information are not necessarily in the order in which they will need to be taken. This will depend on the particular circumstances of the situation at the time.

Identify the person in charge of the liferaft*

The Skipper or senior crew member will normally be in charge, but in his absence a leader will have to be appointed or elected as soon as possible. Everyone should then obey his or her orders at once. Leadership and appropriate action by the person in charge are particularly important in the first three or so hours after taking to the raft. This is the time when, typically, confusion and social fragmentation begins. Survivors slowly begin to realise what has happened and start to appreciate the extent of danger, injury and possible death that now surrounds them. During this time crew will look to their leader for assurance and evidence that he has the matter under control.

It is all too easy for the Skipper or owner of the yacht to become deeply depressed following the abandoning of their ship. The effect of the whole experience is compounded by a sense of failure, even when unfounded. A good Skipper will always feel responsible for the safety of his crew, and putting his people in the precarious security of a liferaft is enough to cause some degree of mental stress in the most sane person. Being in command of the liferaft and actively striving for the survival of the crew is important to aid the mental health of the Skipper. However, if the Skipper is disabled, physically or psychologically, then someone else, with a strong will to survive, must take over as Skipper of the liferaft for the good of everyone aboard.

Post a lookout*
With the liferaft closed it is essential to post a lookout as soon as possible. He must:

◎ Look for survivors in the water, if everyone from the original crew still has not been accounted for.
◎ Watch for lights of other survival craft, rescue vessels or aircraft.
◎ Scan the water for useful debris.

Open the equipment pack*
Take special care when opening the liferaft equipment pack if it is hermatically sealed in plastic, rather than packed in a re-sealable bag, or a valuable container will have been lost. This is the moment of truth. This is when one finds out if the torch or flashlight batteries are functioning, or if they have corroded away because the liferaft was out of date. This is also the time to take stock of what is inside the grab bag and of any other items that crew managed to grab from the 'Last Minute Grabs List' before abandoning ship. If there is an extensive survival kit on board, look just far enough to find the search and rescue items and anything else needed immediately, consulting the list in the grab bag. Deal with the essential items first; there will be time later to do a full inventory if necessary.

Issue antiseasickness medication and seasickness bags*
If there was no time to take antiseasickness tablets while on the yacht, take some now – as soon as you can. Keep taking these pills for the first 48 hours, whether you feel sick or not. Almost all people who have spent time in a liferaft, even the most experienced sailors, have reported suffering from seasickness in survival craft. This then results in loss of body fluid and subsequent incapacitation. The pills may make the survivors suffer from a dry mouth, but the urge to drink at this stage must be resisted to conserve rations. People who are affected by seasickness and who need to vomit should put their head down between their knees and try and keep warm.

 Tip: The use of seasickness disposable bags will reduce the smell of vomit, and so slow down the chance of a chain reaction if one person is being sick.

Dry the liferaft floor, and inflate it if appropriate*

Inevitably, the liferaft will be wet and, in rough conditions, it is likely to keep getting wet. Bale out as much water as possible and sponge out the rest, reserving at least one sponge if possible. Keep the separate sponges to mop up any condensation as it forms, because this can supplement the water supplies.

In cold conditions, inflate the floor of the raft, if fitted, with the hand pump. If the raft has not got an insulated floor, try to find something to sit on, such as the cockpit cushions – or, if the sea is calm, consider removing your lifejacket and sitting on top of that.

Administer first aid if appropriate*

Check the physical condition of everyone aboard and administer first aid if necessary, remembering the ABCs:

> **A** is for Airway – Is it clear?
> **B** is for Breathing – Is he?
> **C** for Circulation – Is the heart beating? Is there bleeding?

Manoeuvre towards other liferafts*

If there is more than one liferaft it is important to link them all together as two or more liferafts are much easier for searchers to see than just one. Ensure that the lines connecting the rafts are attached to strong points, such as the painter attachment patch. Once the liferafts are joined, distribute the survivors, as appropriate, between the rafts. In warm weather, spread everyone out to give them room to keep cool; in cold weather, group together for mutual warmth. Compare equipment and supplies and share it between the rafts.

If any tenders with motors are available, these should be used to collect all survival craft together and to carry out searches for other survivors in the water. When gathered together, liferafts should be made fast to each other. About 15m (49ft) distance is generally sufficient to ensure craft are on a wave crest together. This will stop rafts snatching or pulling unduly on the lines and avoid damaging the attachment points or rafts even overturning one another. If possible, keep any tenders to windward, and any other craft streamed astern of them.

Tip: Sea anchors from rescue boat tenders have superior holding power and can also be used to spread oil to flatten the seas.

Arrange watches and duties*

The Skipper should:

- Take a roll call to establish the likelihood of other survivors being found, the number available for watch, any injuries, and the expertise available on board.
- If numbers allow, arrange watches in pairs for about one hour, depending on weather conditions, with an outside lookout and an inside watch.
- Ensure that everyone knows how to keep a lookout and perform all his or her other duties. It is vitally important that they know how and when to use all the signalling equipment.

◎ See that everyone has something to do and is involved when not resting, even if it is only in bailing and keeping the bottom of the raft dry.
◎ Take charge of water and food.
◎ If possible, record the circumstances leading up to abandoning the yacht and attempt to account for as many crew as possible.
◎ Thereafter keep a log of events with times, duties organised, rations issued, first aid given, and the condition of the survivors.

The outside lookout should be:

◎ Suitably dressed and protected from the elements with a hat to give shade or warmth, sunglasses to guard against glare, and a swimming mask in rough conditions.
◎ Well secured to the craft by his harness or a rope.
◎ Responsible for keeping a lookout for other survivors, ships, aircraft and land.
◎ Watchful for all dangers.
◎ Collecting any useful debris.
◎ Alerting everyone to the possibility of rain that can be collected for drinking.
◎ Checking for abrasion of the liferaft and any attached lines.

The inside watch should:

◎ Look after anyone with injuries.
◎ Be in charge of the safety and security of all the survival equipment.
◎ Ensure the signal equipment – particularly the pyrotechnics – are ready to hand.
◎ Take responsibility for maintaining the liferaft, including bailing, ventilation and repairs.
◎ Organise the collection of rainwater.
◎ Supervise the liferaft management while the Skipper rests.

Check the liferaft for its correct operation and any damage*

It is important to constantly check the liferaft for damage or leaks and repair them as appropriate. A liferaft is constructed to withstand exposure for 30 days afloat in all sea conditions without deterioration, but this does not mean without *maintenance*. It is very easy to accidentally puncture a raft with a knife or fishing hook, for example. As early on as possible, check that no one is wearing anything sharp or rough that could damage the raft and that any high-heeled shoes are removed. In some cases, the friction from the composite soles of shoes has caused damaged to raft fabrics. Take great care when using anything sharp, especially in rough seas, and do not leave any equipment lying around.

Do not allow anyone to sit on the tubes. For the best trim, get everyone to spread out evenly around the raft, sitting on the floor with their backs to tubes, using the handholds provided as necessary. Regularly check the raft for abrasion from anything attached outside – such as the sea anchor, containers of water and other rafts.

To prevent holes getting worse, plug and repair them as soon as possible following the instructions provided with the kit in the emergency pack. Many permanent repair patches cannot be applied over damaged areas until the raft material is completely dry and clean. This will be a problem in most liferafts. Plugs are included with some rafts for large holes, including those outside; add a hose clamp from the grab bag or use string to secure them. A special repair clamp is your best friend when mending the liferaft – some liferafts include them. If they are not in the liferaft, they should be in the grab bag. Follow the instructions that came with them for a quick, permanent repair.

If carbon dioxide has entered the liferaft from the inflation cylinder, or any tube leak, keep the entrance open until the gas has disappeared.

Check the functioning of the canopy light and, if possible, conserve power during daylight hours*

A light on the top of the raft is a valuable aid to location at night. If the liferaft has one fitted, check that it is functioning and, if possible, switch it off during the daylight hours as it only has a life of between 12 and 24 hours. If the liferaft has no light or the fitted one has failed, hopefully it will be possible to externally attach the strobe light packed in the grab bag.

Adjust the canopy openings to give protection from weather, or to ventilate the liferaft as appropriate*

The sea anchor is designed not only to reduce drift and increase stability, but also to align the entrances out of the wind and spray. This is good in cold weather, but in warm conditions it is better to attach the line near one entrance, as this will allow it to lie into the wind, giving maximum ventilation with the accesses open. Even in cold weather, some ventilation is important and it may be necessary to leave a small opening to provide everyone with plenty of oxygen.

Prepare and use detection equipment, including radio equipment*

The various methods of attracting attention once help is close at hand are discussed below. It is important that all in the raft know and understand where they are stowed, which ones are to be employed in which circumstances, and how to use them.

EPIRB

If the EPIRB is not already on, switch it on now. Once it is activated, do not switch it off until directed to do so by the rescuing authorities. Do *not*, under any circumstance, turn the unit off and on, perhaps in the hope of preserving the batteries, as this will only confuse the rescuing authorities and may make the final homing using the 121.5 MHz signal impossible. Any civil aircraft over-flying the area, though far too high to see a liferaft or notice a flare, may be receiving the 121.5 MHz signal (they are required to listen out on this frequency) and notifying an MCC or Aeronautical RCC.

Most EPIRBs come with a very thin piece of nylon or polypropylene line attached. This line is supposed to be tied externally to the liferaft and the EPIRB then allowed to float clear of any obstructions outside the raft. While this may be acceptable in good weather, it is doubtful if anyone would trust the most precious of lifesaving radio equipment to this very thin line, or to a hastily tied knot – especially in rough weather. Most people might prefer to keep their EPIRB near at hand, inside their raft, until rescue is close by. A 406 MHz EPIRB must be oriented with the antenna vertical; Inmarsat E EPIRBs are less fussy – and they are all designed to float. Beacons are not intended to sit upright on a flat surface inside the raft, therefore the EPIRB must either be held or some other method of attaching it vertically must be devised. There is a second probem with keeping an EPIRB functioning inside the raft: most units are fitted with a powerful strobe light to help rescuers pinpoint survivors at night. Flashing strobe lights are very effective and can be seen up to five miles in ideal conditions, and further away with night vision equipment. Regrettably, that same flashing light will drive raft occupants crazy if they have to live with it inside the raft. A piece of duct tape from the grab bag is ideal for covering the light until it is needed to guide the rescuers.

If the liferaft has some kind of metal foil or metallic lining to aid insulation, this can affect radio signals. In this case, put the EPIRB outside the liferaft.

 Tip: Make sure the EPIRB is tied on very securely and check regularly to ensure that no abrasion is occurring to the raft or the lines used to attach the beacon.

SART

A Search and Rescue Transponder (SART) is included in some liferaft packs, or may be in the grab bag. It is designed to show a series of dashes on the radar of any vessel in range (generally about 10 miles for a ship, but 30 miles or so for an aircraft) and identifies the position of the liferaft relative to the rescue craft. Some SARTs come with poles to enable them to be held up as high as possible to maximise their range. The MOB marker buoy from the yacht makes a good rod to suspend the unit. In the absence of anything else, try to attach the SART as high as possible inside the raft. A SART is designed to operate for 96 hours in stand-by mode and in excess of 8 hours in operational mode. This should be sufficient time for someone to reach the raft except in very remote areas, so turn it on immediately if it has not automatically activated. A bonus of using a SART is that when the radar of a vessel close at hand interrogates it, the unit sounds an alarm. This is a great morale booster, as well as ensuring that everyone is alerted to the likelihood of rescuers arriving – so the Skipper can prepare other methods of signalling the raft's whereabouts.

Radar reflector

If carrying a radar reflector this should be deployed, like a SART, as high as possible in such a position as to best reflect the radar signal generated by rescue craft.

 Tip: SART and radar reflectors conflict with each other, so you should not deploy both at the same time.

Portable UHF radio

Once everyone is in the liferaft, send a MAYDAY as soon as possible – especially if contact had previously been made with potential rescuers. Keep sending distress signals at regular intervals, even if a reply is not received. Conserving the batteries will become a priority, especially if there is only one battery unit attached to the VHF. It may be necessary to send hourly signals only or reserve the VHF until help is close by. If the grab bag contains a plentiful supply of alkaline batteries that fit the handheld VHF, it can be kept on constantly to send frequent MAYDAYs.

Pyrotechnics

Flares should not be used unless it is certain that help is nearby and then only when a ship is as close as she is likely to get or, in the case of an aircraft in daytime, when it is actually sighted. Take great care, pyrotechnics are dangerous; they can easy hole a liferaft, give a nasty burn, and have even killed people.

Signalling light
Like pyrotechnics, this is best used once help is close by, as it must be aimed in the direction of the rescuers to be effective. A strobe light attached to the liferaft will be useful for all-round vision and has the benefit of not needing any supervision, but its range is more limited.

Signalling mirror
While pyrotechnics may be limited in number and must be conserved, because once set off they are exhausted, a signal mirror will go on and on. During the daytime the look-out can catch the sunlight on the mirror and reflect it around the horizon; with practice, 270° can be covered with one mirror. In normal sunlight the flash can easily be seen for 10 miles, and in the right atmospheric conditions it will be visible for 50 miles. The record rescue from a mirror is just over 100 miles. Do not try to use the signalling mirror for Morse code, as the liferaft is unlikely to be stable enough.

Kite
If the grab bag includes a parafoil rescue kit, fly it during the daytime. Tie on the radar reflector if the wind is suitable, as the higher it can be suspended the better. It may be possible to use the kite at night to lift up a strobe light.

Gather up any useful floating objects*
All useful debris should be collected. The most important items are those that can be used for signalling, such as EPIRBs or SARTs. Consider retrieving anything floating nearby if it may have value later, as an aid to survival. Heavy articles with sharp edges should not be taken aboard as they could damage the raft.

Protect against heat, cold and wet conditions*
Heat
It is essential in hot weather to keep as cool as possible to minimise dehydration. Do not inflate the floor of the raft, so as to benefit from any cooling effect of the sea. Try to get as much air through the raft while at the same time protecting the occupants from the direct sun. The drogue should be attached at the liferaft entrance to allow the raft to lie into the wind and permit any breeze to cool the inside. Regularly wetting the liferaft canopy will cool the raft. Do not be tempted to swim – there may be sharks lurking in the shade under the raft or crew may simply be too weak to re-board the raft. Keep as still as possible and stay in any shade to reduce perspiration. It can help to wet clothes with sea water, but damp clothes can increase the susceptibility to skin sores or saltwater boils. Make sure everyone has protection against the sun, including sun-screen, especially the lookout.

 Tip: Do not wet clothes too late in the day or they may still be damp by dusk – even in the tropics it can be cool at night.

Cold and wet
In cold climates it is vitally important to try to keep as warm and dry as possible. Once everyone is aboard the liferaft, wet clothing should be taken off and wrung out as much as possible before being put back on. Adjust the openings for the minimum ventilation. Once any sea water in the bottom of the raft has been removed, distribute any dry

clothing. If people are chilled or shivering, get them to huddle together, but be careful not to upset the trim of the raft. The closer survivors get to each other the warmer they get, and keeping warm is vitally important. Especially if there is no insulated floor, try to sit on something to protect against the cold water. While it is recommended that everyone wears their lifejacket at all times, in calm seas a permanent buoyancy preserver can provide valuable insulation if sat upon.

Everyone should use a TPA (thermal protective aid); if there are a limited number of these bags, allocate them to the coldest crew first. A TPA bag works by covering a survivor from head to toe; it will help warm them by reflecting back 90 per cent of the body heat. The bag is impermeable up to the zip, which means that even in a partly water-filled liferaft the feet will remain dry. One TPA can sometimes accommodate two people at once, which can be very useful as a warmer person can bundle up with a cold individual.

When everyone is warm, open up the top layer of clothing, so body warmth acts like a radiator to keep the whole raft cosy. Make sure everyone stretches their limbs, particularly wriggling their toes and fingers, to maintain blood circulation and avoid injuries from the cold.

 Tip: In very cold conditions, the lookout watch will need to be rotated at more frequent intervals.

Decide on food and water rations*

Do not issue any water or food for the first 24 hours – except to conscious, injured people, those who have lost a lot of body fluid, or young children. Collect any rainwater and start making water with a handheld watermaker immediately. Use this water and any brought aboard from the yacht first as the water in a liferaft pack will keep indefinitely. Water is a vital aid to digestion; crew should not eat anything unless they can also have a drink. *Do not* drink urine; it can kill, and contains waste products that have already been disposed of by the body. The general rule is *not* to drink sea water either.

Assuming there is some fresh water, it is best to have some food and water at set times each day and give everyone something to look forward to. Divide rations and distribute them three times a day at sunrise, midday and sunset. Cut foil water pouches with scissors; attempting to tear them open risks the loss of precious water. It is important for morale that rations are seen to be issued fairly. A minimum daily water ration should be 0.5 litre (1 pint) (1 litre (2 pints) in the tropics), the amount the human body needs to survive, except for the injured. It should be swilled round the mouth to relieve dryness before being swallowed slowly. Food rations should be distributed fairly and made to last as long as possible. The human body can survive weeks without food, but only days without water.

 Tip: Only eat anything caught, such as fish and anything else containing fats and proteins, if at least 1 litre (2 pints) of water can be drunk per person per day.

Take measures to maintain morale*

Morale and the will to survive are very important, and morale will almost certainly be at its lowest about three hours after abandoning the yacht. Seasickness, anxiety, extreme cold and the absence of either food or water all contrive to lower morale. As mentioned above, ensure that ration issues are fair and on time, and keep people's minds focused on eventual rescue and what each person will do when it becomes apparent that searchers are looking for the raft. Never permit talk of defeat or death to become a topic of conversation in the liferaft. Competitions, songs and jokes are all important to keep everyone cheerful. This is where items in the grab bag such as a pack of cards or a radio to listen to commercial broadcasts can be invaluable. Case histories have shown again and again that people with a strong will to survive can overcome seemingly impossible difficulties.

Make sanitary arrangements to keep the liferaft habitable*

All survivors should, within two hours of boarding the raft, try to urinate so as to avoid later problems caused by urine retention, which is very painful and distressing; whenever possible, survivors should also attempt a bowel movement within the first 24 hours. In calm seas, rig a safety line to allow occupants to defecate and urinate over the side. When it is rough, receptacles such as bailers or buckets should be used and, as soon as possible, emptied and cleaned. Use the special sickness bags from the liferaft pack or any plastic bag to contain vomit and throw the waste over the side.

 Tip: If sharks are around, be careful about disposing *anything* over the side of the liferaft.

Maintain the liferaft, including the topping up of buoyancy tubes and canopy supports*

It is important to your survival that the liferaft is kept in good condition. Rafts may be designed for a minimum of 30 days' use, but only with care. In hot weather gas expands, and this may be heard escaping from relief valves. Do not be alarmed, but ensure there is adequate ventilation to avoid a build-up of carbon dioxide. When the temperature falls, especially at night, the raft may become soft and the buoyancy tubes and canopy supports should be topped up using the pump. A properly inflated liferaft is less likely to wear. Unless the valves are being used, keep them blocked with the plug provided. Remove the plugs at frequent intervals, especially in tropical waters to allow excess pressure to escape.

Other regular maintenance jobs include:

◎ Keeping all loose gear inside the raft neatly stowed and secured with lanyards against rough weather and for emergency use, especially signalling equipment.
◎ Checking for wear and abrasion both inside and out.
◎ Bailing and sponging out any sea water.
◎ Collecting condensation to add to drinking water.

Make proper use of available survival equipment*

All crew must read all the survival information as soon as possible after boarding the liferaft. This must include the directions for the use of all items of equipment, especially those with potential to damage the raft or affect the survival of everyone, such as the pyrotechnics and the watermaker, if available. Everyone must understand the particular importance of all SAR equipment for his or her ultimate rescue. Care must be taken to preserve every item of equipment in perfect condition inside the liferaft, by returning it to the stowage position, or fastening it to the liferaft by means of a lanyard.

Prepare yourself for the arrival of rescue units, being taken in tow, rescue by helicopter, and landing and beaching*

Everyone aboard the liferaft must be ready for any eventuality that will end his or her time on the raft. It is vitally important that a lookout remains on duty at all times to instantly alert the rest of the crew about the possible arrival of any SAR units, or the sighting of land. Rescue can arrive by air as well as by sea, and though they may be searching for a liferaft, they still need help to find it in a large ocean – especially in rough weather. Proper use of any or all of the signalling equipment will help to attract attention.

 Tip: Remember, no one is a survivor until they have been rescued.

Rescue – the goal

While survival is necessary, rescue is the goal of everyone aboard a survival craft. The chances of rescue depend on whether ships and aircraft are searching deliberately.

It is very tempting once an aircraft or ship has been sighted to expect immediate rescue. This may not happen, though, as a vessel capable of recovering people from a liferaft might not be immediately available or there may be a higher priority. So it is important to maintain survival routines right up until the moment of rescue. Do not despair if the raft is not immediately sighted or if a crew member mistakes a star or the rising moon for a ship. It is vital for everyone's mental health that all in the liferaft remain optimistic.

Attracting the attention of SAR units

The first indication that help is at hand may be a message over the VHF, the activation of the SART, sighting a craft, or hearing an aircraft. If it is known that rescue craft are in the vicinity, it is important to use every means of attracting attention – so the following should be borne in mind:

◎ The EPIRB should be attached outside the liferaft if it has a strobe light fitted, especially at night.
◎ Flares should not be used unless it is certain that help is nearby.
◎ A regularly flashing light is more likely to be sighted than simply shining a torch in the direction of rescuers.
◎ A mirror is a very useful way of attracting attention; the movement of the survival craft will provide sufficient flashing effect. Be careful not to blind the pilot of an aircraft.
◎ Portable VHF can be used by SAR units fitted with VHF direction finding equipment to locate the liferaft.
◎ Use a whistle in restricted visibility – this is when people are making a special effort to listen for any noise.

Rescue by SAR aircraft

Fixed-wing aircraft have a much greater range than helicopters and may be the first to find survivors. Unless survivors can alert overhead aircraft to their presence, the air-crew may consider their search to be a failure and move on to another area. Therefore it is vital to give them every possible assistance to see the raft. Fixed-wing aircraft, though, can provide more help than just verification that a vessel needs help.

Droppable SAR apparatus

It is important to understand what sort of survival equipment may be dropped from aircraft, as there are many stories of people, in distress and urgent need of basic sup-plies, who have failed to realise what exactly they have just received from the skies.

The British Royal Air Force SAR Nimrod MR2 fixed-wing aircraft will drop SAR apparatus known as ASRA (Air Sea Rescue Apparatus (previously called Lindholme Gear)). This consists of three rigid cylindrical canisters joined together by 550m (1,804ft) of orange-coloured buoyant ropes. The centre and longest container holds a 10-person MS10 liferaft, which is designed to inflate automatically on striking the water. The two canisters on either end are identical and each contains the following stores: ✧ reverse osmosis manual watermaker x 1 ✧ water carriers x 3 ✧ small first aid kit x 1 ✧ signal mirror x 1 ✧ ground air codes, for use on dry land x 1 ✧ survival hoods x 5 ✧ head cover scarves x 5 ✧ survival flip card x 1 ✧ survival rations x 6 ✧ drinking water pouches containing 250 ml (1 cup) x 5 ✧ day/night distress flares x 3 ✧ whistle x 1 ✧ miniflares (8) and firing mechanism x 2 ✧ pocket knife x 1.

The aircraft may also drop, if conditions dictate, what is known as a dinghy pair. This is two canisters joined by 365m (1,197ft) of orange buoyant rope, each containing an MS10 liferaft, which automatically inflate when they enter the water. The MS10 liferaft does not have a self-deploying sea anchor, so the ASRA and Dinghy Pair are always dropped upwind of survivors, enabling them to drift downwind towards them. Once aboard, the crew must manually deploy the sea anchor. All outer containers should be

207

discarded by sinking once emptied and the contents secured, especially if the sea is rough. Do not unpack the inner containers until or unless the contents are required.

Helicopter

The ultimate in quick-fix rescues are those undertaken by helicopters. The main type of helicopter used for SAR in the UK is the Sea King. These helicopters have an automatic hover control system and can effect rescues both at night and in fog where there are no visual hover references. It is important to understand that this form of rescue is itself fraught with potential danger, particularly in rough weather, and survivors must prepare for the arrival of helicopters. Follow the procedures discussed for helicopter evacuation discussed in chapter 10.

Rescue by ship

As soon as it becomes obvious that a ship is going to rescue survivors from a raft, it is important to clear away any lines, including the sea anchor, and other gear that could cause entanglement. Everyone, including injured crew, should don lifejackets if they have been removed, unless they are likely to cause a substantial deterioration in the condition of the injured person.

A ship will probably approach so as to put the raft on its lee side, and then it will drift down onto it. If the ship comes alongside the liferaft, special care must be taken anywhere abaft the beam, to prevent the raft being sucked into the propeller. It may be safer for the rescue ship to put a rescue craft or lifeboat into the water to assist. Boarding the ship may be facilitated by winching up the liferaft, or ropes, ladders or scrambling nets may be lowered over the side for survivors to climb aboard the ship on their own.

 Tip: Remember that after any period in a liferaft, survivors are likely to be weakened, so it is very important to take extra care with any attempt to board a ship.

Towing

If the rescue craft is small or the conditions for transferring the survivors onto the rescue vessel prohibit it, towing the liferaft to a place of safety may be the only answer. If the painter or drogue lines are in good condition, either may be used as a towline. If the rescue vessel supplies a line, it should be secured to the liferaft painter patch or bridle.

Pull in the sea anchor before towing commences, and once towing has started everyone should remain as still as possible to keep the liferaft balanced. It is important to monitor the towline throughout the tow and to ensure that the towline does not chafe or damage the liferaft in any way. If possible, establish a simple communication system with the towing vessel.

Tip: Keep a knife to hand in case the towline needs to be cut in an emergency.

Definitions and Explanations

AIS – *Automatic Identification System.* A VHF-based identification transmitter and receiver placed aboard shipping which will become compulsory in the near future.

AMSA – *Australia Maritime Safety Authority.* Agency responsible for implementing marine safety and pollution prevention measures in and around Australia

AMVER – *Automated Mutal-Assistance VEssel Rescue System.* A voluntary global ship reporting system, which provides SAR authorities with accurate information on the positions and characteristics of commercial vessels near a reported distress. This enables the rescue co-ordinators to divert the best-suited ship or ships to the distress vessel.

ARPA – *Automatic Radar Plotting Aid.* Also known as Autotrack by some radar manufacturers, a system that automatically plots targets and then displays information about them on the screen.

AusSAR – *AUStralian Search and Rescue.* National search and rescue organisation, a division of AMSA.

BSS – *Boat Safety Scheme.* A body jointed created by the Environment Agency and British Waterways to promote safety on British inland waterways.

BWS – *Beaufort Wind Scale.* A code, routinely used in weather analysis and forecasts. It is a measurement of wind force, on a scale of 0 to 12, based upon sea state appearance.

COLREGs – *International REGulations for preventing COLlisions at Sea.* (Also known as the Rules of the Road.) A set of very precisely worded rules, issued by the IMO, enforced worldwide, applicable to any craft capable of being used on water.

COSPAS – *COsmicheskaya Sistyema Poiska Ava riynich Sudov* translates as Space System for the Search of Vessels in Distress, is the Russian part of the jointly operated COSPAS/SARSAT.

COSPAS/SARSAT – *COsmicheskaya Sistyema Poiska Ava riynich Sudov/Search and Rescue Satellite-Aided Tracking.* An international, humanitarian search and rescue system established by USA, Canada, France and Russia in the 1970s and now consisting of 25 nations with 28 LUTs and 15 RCCs worldwide. Uses satellites in geostationary and low earth polar orbits to detect signals transmitted by distress beacons transmitting on 121.5, 243 and 406 MHz frequencies.

CPR – *Cardio Pulmonary Resuscitation.* Heart compressions performed in an emergency when the heart stops pumping.

DGPS – *Differential Global Positioning System.* GPS supplemented by additional signals transmitted by terrestrial monitoring stations to improve the positional accuracy of the order of ±10 metres.

DSC – *Digital Selective Calling.* Reliable digital radio tone alerting system to enable semi-automatic radio watch keeping. It is part of a maritime radio acting as a 'front end', or a radio pager, to provide a means of sending a distress alert or calling either a ship or shore station. Further information and, in the case of a distress alert, a conventional distress message is then passed by voice.

ECDIS – *Electronic Chart Display and Information System.* A navigation information system which with adequate back-up arrangements can be accepted as complying with the up-to-date chart required by SOLAS regulations. These can be categorised as RCDS or ECS display and information systems.

ECS – *Electronic Chart System.* A computerised navigational tool used to supplement a complete up to date folio of paper charts.

ELT – *Emergency Locator Transmitter.* The name used by aircraft pilots for their radio distress beacons, mounted permanently in the aircraft.

ENC – *Electronic Navigational Charts.* Officially approved vector nautical charts when displayed on ECDS equipment they are equivalent to paper charts.

EPIRB – *Emergency Position-Indicating Radio Beacon.* A portable, secondary distress signalling device. A waterproof transmitter that can be thrown overboard in a distress situation. Once operating, a satellite can obtain a position fix on the beacon and send details, through an earth station, to an appropriate rescue co-ordination station.

GALILEO – A European Union and European Space Agency worldwide satellite radio navigation system complementary to the current GPS system, due in 2008.

GEOSAR – *GEOstationary Satellite Search And Rescue.* High altitude stationary satellites consisting of GOES and other geostationary satellites with 406 MHz repeaters aboard and part of the COSPAS/SARSAT search and rescue system.

GLONASS – *GLObal NAvigation Satellite System.* A GNSS operated by the Russian Federation similar in concept to GPS but stated to be accurate to 20 metres without additional signal transmissions.

GMDSS – *Global Maritime Distress Safety System.* A global communications service to ensure that ships, wherever they are in the world, can communicate with an RCC on shore. Based upon automated systems, both satellite and terrestrial, to provide distress alerting and promulgation of maritime safety information without the need for the vessel to carry a specialist radio operator.

GMT – *Greenwich Mean Time.* This is the reference point for world time, based on time at Greenwich, England, one of the places through which the longitude 0° passes.

GNSS – *Global Navigation Satellite System.* A satellite system that provides vessels fitted with suitable receivers with a means of obtaining continuous worldwide position, time and speed information using either GPS or GLONASS.

GOES – *Geostationary Operational Environmental Satellite.* Part of the NOAA weather satellite system.

GPS – *Global Positioning System.* Worldwide system providing very accurate continuous position information in all weather conditions, using 24 satellites, (3 of which are spare). Developed and controlled by the US Military, it is freely available for civilian use.

HF – *High Frequency.* Long range radio band for transmission and reception. Marine stations use the band between 4 and 27.5 MHz.

HRU – *Hydrostatic Release Unit.* A device that is designed to automatically release life-saving equipment from a sinking vessel.

IMO – *International Maritime Organisation.* Part of the United Nations responsible for the regulation of maritime affairs.

INMARSAT – *International Mobile Satellite Telecommunications Company.* A multi-national organisation providing maritime weather and safety information plus general satellite communication capability worldwide, using one of four geostationary, high orbit, satellites.

ISAF – *International Sailing Federation*. Governing body for the sport of sailing.

ISM – *International Safety Management*. IMO regulations in force on much of today's commercial shipping and an increasing number of yachts designed to improve safety at sea at all levels.

ITU – *International Telegraphic Union*. An international organisation within the United Nations System where governments and the private sector co-ordinate global telecom networks and services.

LEOSAR – *Low Earth Orbit Search And Rescue*. Currently consisting of seven satellites; three are in near-polar obit at 1000km altitude, four are in sun-synchronous near-polar orbit at 850km altitude. Each satellite makes a complete polar orbit in about 100 minutes. Part of the COSPAS/SARSAT search and rescue system.

LES – *Land Earth Stations*. Also called Coast Earth Stations (CES) and part of the Inmarsat system. Located at the specified fixed point on land, they act in a similar fashion to the LUT, to provide a link between the satellites and the telephone network.

LOF – *Lloyds Open Form*. No Pay No Cure standardised salvage agreement developed in the early 20th century, the latest version of which is LOF 2000.

LUT – *Local User Terminal*. It is a small fully automated and unmanned satellite ground receiving station. It receives alert data from COSPAS and SARSAT satellites, derives the position of the beacons, retrieves and checks coded information and forwards the result to a MCC.

MAIB – *Marine Accident Investigation Board*. UK body responsible for investigating accidents involving UK vessels and any vessel in UK waters.

MARPOL – *MARine POLlution*. Internationally agreed guidelines and regulations issued by the IMO governing the disposal of waste materials at sea and in the marine environment.

MCA – *Maritime and Coastguard Agency*. An Executive Agency of the Department of the Environment, Transport and the Regions, responsible for implementing and enforcing marine safety and pollution prevention as well as responding to maritime emergencies 24 hours a day. MCA is similar to the USCG, but without a military background.

MCC – *Mission Control Centre*. A ground system element of the COSPAS/SARSAT system, which receives distress information from the LUTs or other MCCs and passes it on to affiliated SAR points of contact or forwards it to other MCCs. Located in the USA at a NOAA office outside Washington DC and in the UK it is at RAF Kinloss in Scotland.

MEDIVAC – *MEDIcal eVACuation* of a person for medical reasons.

MEDICO – MEDICal *Advice*. Exchange of medical information and recommended treatment for sick or injured persons where treatment cannot be administered directly by prescribing medical personnel.

MF – *Medium Frequency*. Medium range radio band for transmission and reception. Marine stations use the band between 1.6 and 4 MHz.

MGN – Marine Guidance Notes.

MHz – *MegaHertz*. The radio frequency of one million cycles per second.

MMSI – *Mobile Marine Service Identity*. A unique nine-digit number, used with DSC that identifies a particular ship or shore station. The first three digits identify the nationality of a ship, the rest are the individual station identifier.

MOB – *Man Over Board*. Any person, male or female, falling over the side of a vessel. Also called COB, Crew Over Board.

MSN – Merchant Shipping Notice.

NAVAREA – *Radio NAVigational Warning AREA*. The world is divided into 16 sea areas each of which issues long-range, coastal and local weather and navigation information primarily received by Navtex and Inmarsat C.

NAVTEX – *NAVigational Information TEXt messaging system*. A narrow-band direct-printing telegraph system and a component of GMDSS. It displays or prints weather data, navigational information and other distress and safety messages via the MF radio band to a small receiver aboard a vessel. Signals are received at distances of up to 300 miles from a number of worldwide transmitters.

NIMA – *National Imagery and Mapping Agency*. Government body dealing with geospatial intelligence in all forms and from whatever source, in support of national security. Their Marine Safety Information Division provides all nautical publications such as Lists of Lights, Radio Aids and Fog Signals, chart corrections and navigational warnings.

NOAA – *National Oceanic and Atmospheric Administration*. A branch of the US Department of Commerce, it is the parent organisation of the National Weather Service (NWS). NOAA Weather Radio provides continuous 24-hour a day VHF broadcasts of weather observations and forecasts.

ORC – *Offshore Racing Council*. Governing organisation of many national and international sailing races.

PFD – *Personal Flotation Device*. US generic name for Type I, II, III and IV wearable lifejackets and Type IV throwable devices including lifrings, horseshoe buoys and buoyant cushions.

PLB – *Personal Locator Beacon*. The name used originally by aircraft pilots for their radio distress beacons which are portable and carried on the person. Now also used to describe any portable EPIRB.

RADAR – *Radio Aid to Direction finding And Ranging*. British conception from 1935, invented by Sir Robert Watson Watt. The radar beam sweeps through 360° and displays a picture of the reflected or echoed signals on a screen.

RCC – *Rescue Co-ordination Centre*. The authority that co-ordinates the search and rescue (SAR) services within a SAR region and is responsible for promoting efficient organisation of the SAR services. In the US this is the Coast Guard or the Civil Air Patrol, in the UK it is HM Coastguard via the Maritime Rescue Co-ordination Centre in Falmouth and in Australia this is AusSAR in Canberra.

RCDS – *Raster Chart Display System*. A computerised navigational tool used to display RNC data. No performance standards currently exist for RCDS but this may be subject to change when further investigated by the IMO.

RIB – *Rigid Inflatable Boat*. A small craft comprising hard bottom and inflatable tube sides.

RNC – *Raster Navigational Chart*. Official raster nautical charts. British Admiralty ARCS format charts and US NOAA format charts are examples. Currently when displayed on ECDIS or RCDS equipment they are not equivalent to paper charts.

RT – *Radio Telephone*. Two-way voice communication device, using all bands of frequencies from UHF for short distances to HF for long range.

SAR – *Search And Rescue* International, generic term given to authorities involved in marine response to distress and emergency situations.

SARSAT – *Search and Rescue Satellite-Aided Tracking* is an American-Canadian-French joint effort started in the early 1970s and became part of COSPAS/SARSAT in 1979.

SART – *Search And Rescue Transponder*. A secondary distress signalling device in the form of a battery operated beacon that produces a distinctive echo on any 3cm radar display that is within range of about five miles. It is used as a homing aid for SAR helicopters and rescue craft rather than providing an initial alert in a distress situation.

SI – *Statutory Instrument*.

SMS – *Safety Management System*. Structured and documented system designed to implement policies appertaining to the ISM safety regulations laid down by the IMO.

SOLAS – *Safety Of Life At Sea*. Code of practice issued by the IMO to regularise safety equipment and classification aboard all vessels at sea.

SRR – *Search and Rescue Region*. An SRR is an area of defined dimensions associated with an RCC within which SAR services are provided. The purpose of having an SRR is to clearly define who has primary responsibility for co-ordinating responses to distress situations in every area of the world and to enable rapid distribution of distress alerts to the proper RCC.

SSB – *Single Side Band*. Mode of emission of radio signal, which optimises range and signal strength at the expense of sound quality. It is therefore ideal for Morse code or voice but not for music radio transmissions.

STCW – *Standards of Training Certification for Watchkeeping for Seafarers*. An IMO convention that was substantially reviewed by a diplomatic conference in July 1995 to become known as STCW95.

TORS – *Telex Over Radio System*. Radio ability to use single side band telex text messages to automated shore stations for onward forwarding to terrestrial telex terminals.

TPA – *Thermal Protective Aid*. It is a specially designed bag with zip entry, covering from head to toe, to keep a survivor warm and dry by preserving body heat. Seams are heat sealed, which helps keep the bag impermeable to water and oil up to the zip.

TRS – *Tropical Revolving Storm*. A severe meteorological depression occurring in low latitudes.

UHF – *Ultra High Frequency*. Very short-range radio communication band used by SMSll handheld radio sets often employed for communication amongst crew aboard large yachts and ships.

USCG – *United States Coast Guard*. The marine law enforcement and regulatory agency of the US government.

UTC – *Universal Time Co-ordinated*. The modern mnemonic, which has replaced GMT.

VDS – *Visual Distress Signals*. Any non-radio distress signal including pyrotechnics, heliograph, flags etc.

VHF – *Very High Frequency*. Short-range (line of sight) radio band for transmission and reception. The marine stations use the band between 156 and 174 MHz.

VTS – *Vessel Traffic Services*. A reporting system for vessels using designated waterways, sometimes voluntary sometimes mandatory, designed to improve safety and efficiency of shipping movements in congested waterways and to protect the environment.

WGS84 – *World Geodetic System*. For differentiating and correcting chart-derived positions with those obtained from satellite devises.

Z – *Zulu*. Interchangeable time designation symbol to indicate the GMT or UTC standard time.

Appendix 1: A Code of practice issued by the Cruising Association

The aim of this simple Code for cruising yachtsmen and women is to encourage common-sense safety measures and other practices so that all who share the sea may do so in safety without being a nuisance or a danger to others. Furthermore, it is hoped that observance of this Code may help to reduce the number of calls made by yachtsmen to the rescue services of the RNLI. The Code is not concerned with etiquette; it is concerned with the practice of good seamanship which brings with it safe cruising.

Part A: Preparing for a cruise

Consider the following for you and your crew:

A1 Do you and your crew have adequate training and experience for the proposed cruise, even if the weather becomes worse than anticipated?

A2 Do you have a Certificate of Competence for this level of experience?

A3 Do you have a Ships Radio Licence and somebody on board with a Radio Operator's Licence?

A4 Does anyone on board have experience or qualifications in first aid and resuscitation?

A5 If you become incapacitated at any time during the cruise, can your crew deal with any situation which may occur?

Consider the following for your boat:

A6 How long is it since your boat, its engine and steering were professionally surveyed?

A7 How long is it since your liferaft, lifejackets and safety harnesses were properly serviced?

A8 Is your boat fully insured for the area to be cruised, is the third party insurance adequate, and are you, your crew and passengers fully covered for all injuries?

A9 Is the vessel's name or number prominently displayed for identification purposes and is its registration still valid?

A10 Is the vessel registered with the Coastguard under the CC66 Scheme and are the details still up to date? Is the 'agent' (nominated by you on the form as a contact for emergency purposes) likely to be available and able to play his part?

Part B: Before you start

B1 Consider especially the presence, condition and serviceability of the following items immediately before starting. They have all been found to be regular causes of difficulty and distress:

◎ Seacocks, cockpit drains, bilge pumps and adjoining plumbing.
◎ Fuel and lubricants sufficient for the intended voyage plus a reserve.
◎ Diesel, oil and water-cooling filters, tools and access.
◎ Gas and liquid fuel pipes, cocks and joints.

◎ Rigging, lifelines, jackstays, reefing gear and other heavy weather equipment.
◎ Batteries fully charged with electrolyte, checked and properly secured.

B2 Consider especially how you will cope with a man overboard situation, and how your crew will cope if it is you who goes overboard:

◎ Lifejackets with marker lights and harnesses for each person on board.
◎ Lifebelts with markers and lights, accessible each side of vessel to helmsman.
◎ Simple danbuoy with marker flag and light.
◎ Inflatable liferaft or inflatable dinghy (actually inflated or with automatic inflation).
◎ Specialised recovery or lifting equipment.

B3 Can a second person on board navigate the vessel properly and operate communication radio? Do all your crew have an adequate understanding of fire and emergency procedures?

B4 Are your medical first aid supplies up to date and sufficiently comprehensive?

B5 Are your engine and fuel system spares and tools sufficiently complete?

B6 Do you have efficient and adequate means of signalling distress by day and night and by several different means – GMDSS, radio, EPIRB, flares?

B7 Can you adequately indicate the presence of your vessel under all conditions:

◎ White flares; powerful torch; fog horn, bell, whistle; navigation lights.
◎ Radar reflector properly mounted and of adequate size?

B8 Do you have an adequate number of fire extinguishers to the correct modern specification, and a fire blanket, immediately accessible wherever fire could break out, eg galley and engine areas? Can you get direct access to firefighting equipment from all sleeping berths and hatches?

B9 Do you have at least two anchors of full size for the boat with plenty of chain and warp?

B10 Do you have material and equipment for repairing sails, tapered plugs for broken seacocks, spare batteries for GPS and torches, etc?

B11 Have you checked your compass deviation for all directions? Do you have a second compass?

B12 Are your charts sufficiently comprehensive, corrected up to date, and do they cover adjacent areas where you may have to seek refuge? Do you have current pilot books and tidal data?

B13 Have you informed somebody ashore of your plans? Is this the person named on your CG66?

Part C: At sea

Know and observe the International Regulations for Preventing Collisions at Sea (the COLREGs). Have a copy of the Regulations readily available. Your attention is drawn particularly to the following:

◎ Keep a good lookout all round at all times and instruct your crew to do similarly.
◎ Have a hand-bearing compass readily available to check for changing bearings of vessels on closing courses.

◎ When altering course to clear, make alteration large and visible to other vessels.
◎ When altering course to clear another vessel, make the alteration in good time.
◎ Use navigation lights, anchor ball, anchor light and motorsailing cone according to the rules.
◎ Have white flares handy, and do not hesitate to use them if a dangerous situation appears to be developing.

C2 Ensure you and all your crew members are aware of distress and urgency procedures, including GMDSS procedures.

C3 Maintain a listening watch on VHF channel 16 and VHF VTS channels in areas where this is required. Observe correct VHF procedures and channel allocations. Do not use the VHF unnecessarily for conversation between vessels.

C4 Keep a regular and proper plot of the ship's position both on your chart and in your log book. Do not rely on electronic systems.

C5 Note weather forecasts and plot barometer readings regularly. Amend your passage plan if necessary.

C6 Consider at all times the strength of your crew:

◎ Organise watches and ensure that everyone has proper rest.
◎ See that safety harnesses are worn in heavy weather, at night, and especially on lone watch.
◎ Take proper rest yourself, but ensure that the crew on watch understand when you must be called.
◎ Treat seasickness seriously. Discover the most effective remedy for yourself and crew and use in good time.

C7 Ensure that at all times everything is properly stowed for sea. This is particularly important for heavy items such as anchors, fuel containers, batteries and gas bottles.

C8 Keep a good lookout for fishing gear – small flags or floats (possibly being dragged just below the surface in strong tides) within about five miles of the coast, particularly around rocky headlands.

C9 Check harbour entry requirements and signals in good time and observe them meticulously.

Part D: In harbour

D1 Observe local harbour regulations, bye-laws and signals.

D2 If you are berthing alongside another vessel, run out your own lines ashore or to piles / buoy, and use springs and adequate fenders. Advise expected time of departure. Cross the foredeck of any neighbouring vessel when going ashore.

D3 If you pick up someone else's mooring, do not overload it, or leave your vessel unattended without permission.

D4 Anchor clear of other vessels, moorings, oyster and mussel beds, allowing for other vessels swinging as well as yourself, and judging how both yourself and others are likely to lie when the tide changes. Check against dragging before going ashore. Moor with two anchors if necessary.

D5 If you leave your vessel for a period away from your home port, tell some responsible local person how to get in touch with you.

D6 When using the dinghy, always carry oars and properly secured rowlocks; guard against overloading, especially at night. Wear lifejackets in adverse conditions and at night. Carry a torch at night. Remember that dinghies are required to show a light at night, and that if two boats are running outboards, neither may be able to hear the other.

Part E: Protect the environment

Everyone putting to sea has a legal and moral responsibility to protect the natural environment both for the welfare of animals, birds and plants and for the greater comfort of themselves and other seafarers. Take a responsible attitude and in particular:

E1 Do not cause pollution: observe the prohibition on dumping refuse at sea – 'Over the Side is Over'. Retain all waste on board especially bottles, cans and other indestructible materials.

E2 Dispose of rubbish ashore responsibly. All yacht berthing now has adequate disposal arrangements.

E3 Do not discharge oily bilge into the sea.

E4 Keep down noise, especially at night, from radio, charging plant and unwrapped halyards.

E5 Proceed cautiously at slow speed in harbour and near shorelines, observing your wash and its effects.

Part F: Customs

It is important not to prejudice the good relationship that exists between yachtsmen and HM Customs. Notice 8 of HM Customs and Excise gives all details concerning pleasure craft using UK ports. This Notice is available from any Customs office and most yacht clubs. Carrying and observing Notice 8 is obligatory. The Cruising Association has a joint agreement with HM Customs to assist in combating the drugs trade. Note in particular:

F1 You are required to advise local Customs when entering or leaving any UK port from or to overseas if you have anyone on board with a non-UK passport.

F2 Different rules apply to passages that cross frontiers between UK ports, EU countries, EEA countries, countries party to the Schengen agreement and any two countries outside Europe. It is your responsibility to be aware of these rules before departure.

F3 Different rules may apply to foreign-registered vessels, who should also consult their own Customs Authorities.

F4 Carry international code flag 'Q' and use it where required. Where a Customs inspection is required, do not permit any crew member to go ashore until the inspection is complete.

F5 Report suspicious activity to HM Customs immediately on arrival at a port or via secure communications.

Appendix 2: Passage Plan and Checklists

Passage Planning Checklist

Individual passage plans

	FROM	TOWARDS	DISTANCE	ETD	ETA
1					
2					
3					
4					
5					

Charts required (paper/electronic)

ALL AVAILABLE ☐   ALL CORRECTED ☐

Navigational publications

ADMIRALTY SAILING DIRECTIONS VOLS	ADMIRALTY LIST OF LIGHTS VOLS
COMMERCIAL PILOTS/GUIDE BOOKS	
TIDE TABLES AND ATLAS	NAUTICAL ALMANACS
OTHER	

Crew list

NAME	USEFULNESS	TEL	NOTES

CREW GENERAL FAMILIARISATION ☐   WATCHKEEPER'S FAMILIARISATION ☐

NOMINATED CHEF	MENU PLANNED ☐	PROVISIONS ABOARD ☐

Safety documents

CG66/MSF6000 LOGGED AND/OR CHECKED ☐	VOYAGE DETAILS PLAN ☐
NOMINATED SHORESIDE CONTACT	TEL

Documents required for foreign cruise

For Yacht:	CERTIFICATE OF REGISTRATION ☐	CUSTOMS CLEARANCE ☐	VALID INSURANCE ☐
For Crew:	ICC ☐ VALID PASSPORTS ☐	VACCINATIONS ☐	VISAS ☐

Weather forecasts

START MONITORING ON (DATE/TIME)	SOURCE
START MONITORING ON (DATE/TIME)	SOURCE
START MONITORING ON (DATE/TIME)	SOURCE

Watch system

TIME	ON WATCH	BELOW

Extra items to put on board

Notes

Individual Passage Plan (No _____)

FROM	TOWARDS	DISTANCE (M)	ETD	ETA

CHARTS REQUIRED: _____

CHARTS READY ☐   CUSTOMS ☐   MARINA PAID ☐   SHORE CONTACT ☐   LATEST WEATHER ☐

Departure port information

Destination and alternate port information

PORT				
PILOT BOOK				
ACCESS				
TIDES				
DANGERS				
SHELTER				
FUEL				

Tidal data: SPRINGS / BETWEEN / NEAPS

DEPARTURE PORT:

DATE	HW (Time/Ht)	LW (Time/Ht)

ARRIVAL PORT:

DATE	HW (Time/Ht)	LW (Time/Ht)

FAVOURABLE TIDAL STREAM

DATE	FROM	TO

ADVERSE TIDAL STREAM

DATE	FROM	TO

Route Plan   ASSUMED SPEED _____   WAYPOINTS ENTERED ☐

WAYPOINT	LATITUDE	LONGITUDE	COURSE	DISTANCE	TIME	NOTES

Dangers On Route   TRAFFIC SEPARATION SCHEME ☐   PROHIBITED AREAS ☐   OTHER _____

DANGER	MARKED BY	CLEARING BEARINGS

LAT/LONG	AID	CHARACTERISTICS

VOYAGE DETAILS PLAN

Details of Vessel

NAME OF VESSEL: ....

REGISTERED OWNER: ....

WHERE NAME DISPLAYED: ....

OFFICIAL NO: .... SAIL OR FISHING NO: ....

Description of Vessel

TYPE: MOTOR ☐ SAIL ☐   RIG: SCHOONER ☐ KETCH ☐ SLOOP ☐ OTHER.........................

MAKE: .... LENGTH OF VESSEL: ....METRES/FEET

COLOUR OF SAILS: .... COLOUR OF TOPSIDES: ....

COLOUR OF HULL ABOVE WATERLINE: .... COLOUR OF HULL BELOW WATERLINE: ....

ANY SPECIAL IDENTIFYING FEATURES: ....

....

ENGINE TYPE: .... NO OF ENGINES: ....

HP: .... FUEL CAPACITY: ....

DINGHY: MAKE AND MODEL .... DINGHY: COLOUR ....

Captain of Vessel

NAME: .... AGE: ....

ADDRESS: ....

....

....

TELEPHONE: .... MOBILE: ....

NAUTICAL QUALIFICATIONS: ....

ANY ADDITIONAL INFORMATION: ....

....

....

Lifesaving Equipment

NUMBER OF LIFEJACKETS: .... COLOUR OF LIFEJACKETS: ....

LIFERAFT MAKE AND MODEL: .... LIFERAFT COLOUR: ....

LIFERAFT EMERGENCY PACK: .... GRAB BAG ☐   CONTENTS LIST ATTACHED ☐

FLARES CARRIED: ....

121.5 MHZ EPIRB ☐   406 MHZ EPIRB ☐   INMARSAT E EPIRB ☐   SART ☐

Radio and Navigation Equipment

FIXED VHF ☐   PORTABLE VHF ☐   SHORT-WAVE ☐   DSC DISTRESS ALERT ☐

RADIO CALLSIGN: .... MMSI NO: ....

SATELLITE SYSTEM: INMARSAT ☐   IRRIDIUM ☐   MODEL: ....

SATELLITE TELEPHONE NO: ....

RADAR ☐   GPS ☐   ECHO SOUNDER ☐

Planned trip

DATE AND TIME OF DEPARTURE: ....

DEPARTURE FROM: ....

DEPARTURE TO: ....

EXPECTED DATE AND TIME OF ARRIVAL: ....

Number of crew/passengers aboard

NUMBER OF PERSONS ABOARD: ....

NAME: ....

AGE: ....

ADDRESS: ....

SPECIAL MEDICAL CONCERNS: ....

NAME: ....

AGE: ....

ADDRESS: ....

SPECIAL MEDICAL CONCERNS: ....

NAME: ....

AGE: ....

ADDRESS: ....

SPECIAL MEDICAL CONCERNS: ....

NAME: ....

AGE: ....

ADDRESS: ....

SPECIAL MEDICAL CONCERNS: ....

NAME: ....

AGE: ....

ADDRESS: ....

SPECIAL MEDICAL CONCERNS: ....

ADDITIONAL INFORMATION: ....

....

What to do if vessel is overdue

IF NO CONTACT MADE BY:

CALL THE COASTGUARD OR LOCAL AUTHORITY ON:

NOTES: This passage plan has been left with you and only with you, as I know you can be relied upon to contact the number(s) above if necessary. If for any reason our departure is delayed I promise to phone you immediately so our expected arrival date can be changed. I also promise to phone you as soon as possible should there be any other change of plan and immediately upon our arrival at each stop.

If you need to contact us while we are under way:

....

....

CHECKLIST PRIOR TO DEPARTURE

Tick the boxes below when each item is completed and/or has been tested and checked:

Crew

- ☐ Crew aboard and all persons not sailing ashore
- ☐ Crew dressed for sea with lifejackets and harnesses
- ☐ Crew passports, certifications of competency, etc logged with captain
- ☐ General familiarisation given to all crew sailing
- ☐ Personal needs, eg prescription drugs, eye glasses

Documentation and notification

- ☐ Charts for the intended voyage corrected up to date and courses laid off
- ☐ Harbour/marina dues paid
- ☐ Nautical publications, sailing directions to hand and corrected up to date
- ☐ Nearby yachts and harbourmaster advised of departure
- ☐ Passage plan for the intended voyage
- ☐ Shoreside contact updated with any change of plan
- ☐ Weather forecast and tide state
- ☐ Yacht's papers, insurance documents, certifications

Below decks

- ☐ Accommodation secured for sea
- ☐ All watertight doors shut
- ☐ All hatches, windows and portholes closed and dogged
- ☐ Bilges clear
- ☐ Deadlights fitted to all portholes
- ☐ Gas cylinder(s) adequate for voyage
- ☐ Provisions stowed, passage food ready

Engine

- ☐ Battery level and state of charge noted
- ☐ Bilge pumps
- ☐ Bowthrusters
- ☐ Bridge and engine controls, including revolution indicators
- ☐ Drive belts, hoses and hose clamps
- ☐ Gauges
- ☐ Generator(s)
- ☐ Lubricating oil and engine coolant
- ☐ Power to entire vessel and battery charging switched to sea
- ☐ Ventilation, powered and natural
- ☐ Water, gas and fuel topped up (or sufficient for voyage, plus a third)

Navigation and watchkeeping

- ☐ Ancillary bridge equipment – binoculars, handbearing compass, etc
- ☐ Barometer
- ☐ Clocks corrected and synchronised
- ☐ Deck power
- ☐ Echo sounder and lead line

☐ Electronic navigational position fixing aids including GPS and chart plotter
☐ Gyrocompass
☐ Magnetic compass, noting variation and deviation
☐ Navigation lights/shapes, including emergency navigation lights
☐ Portable VHF radios
☐ Radar and associated plotting aids
☐ Screen washers and wipers
☐ Speed/distance recorder
☐ Steering gear, including manual, autopilot, emergency

On deck
☐ All deck equipment secured
☐ All ropes and lines clear of sides
☐ All shore power, telephone and TV cables disconnected
☐ Anchor ready for immediate use
☐ Dinghy raised and secured
☐ Ensign and burgee hoisted
☐ Gangway and/or boarding ladder stowed
☐ Spare fenders and mooring line

Safety equipment
☐ Emergency steering gear
☐ EPIRB
☐ Fire extinguishers secured
☐ First aid kit
☐ Flashlights/torches
☐ Fog horn and whistles
☐ GMDSS radio equipment
☐ Grab bag
☐ Lifelines
☐ Liferaft
☐ MOB equipment
☐ NAVTEX receiver
☐ SART
☐ Signalling lamps
☐ Visual distress signals

After departure
Tick the boxes below when the following have been completed
☐ Anchor secured for sea passage when clear of fairway
☐ Mooring lines and fenders stowed

Appendix 3: Safety equipment checklist

ITEM			WHERE STOWED	TEST/ REPLACE DATE
LIFERAFT		CAPACITY:		
GRAB BAG				
DISTRESS FLARES	TYPE	NUMBER		
	Red parachute			
	Red handheld			
	Orange smoke buoyant			
	Orange smoke handheld			
	White handheld			
EPIRB				
PLB				
PORTABLE VHF				
LIFEJACKETS				
SAFETY HARNESSES				
IMMERSION SUITS				
LIFEBUOYS				
DANBUOYS				
BUOYANT LINE	LENGTH:			
FIRE EXTINGUISHERS	TYPE AND CAPACITY			
E/R FIREFIGHTING SYSTEM				
FIRE BLANKET				
BILGE PUMPS				
TOWING WARP	TYPE:	LENGTH:		
EMERGENCY TILLER				
FIRST AID KIT CONTENTS:				

Appendix 4: Medical stores for vessels categories A, B and C

(Recommended quantity for 10 workers or crew of lifeboat or liferaft)

Ref No	Treatment	Specific use of drug	Possible trade name	Generic name	A	B	C
			1 Cardiovascular medicines				
1a	Cardiovascular analeptics	Severe allergy, anaphylactic shock, allergic airway obstruction	Adrenaline (epinephrine) or EpiPen®	Adrenaline injection 1mg in 1ml	10*	5*	–
				Adrenaline 0.3mg	5	5	–
1b	Anti-angina treament and prevention	Suspected heart attack or heart pain	Nitrolingual pumpspray	Glyceryl trinitrate spray 400mcg/metered 200 dose	1	1	1
			Transiderm-Nitro	Transdermal patches 5mg x 2	2	2	–
1c1	Diuretics	Diuretic swelling and breathlessness due to heart failure	Lasix	Frusemide/Furosemide tablets 40mg	28*	28*	–
1c2			Lasix	Frusemide injection 10mg in 1ml	2		–
1d1	Anti-haemorrhagics	To prevent bleeding in newborn baby	Konakion neonatal	Phytomenadione (Vitamin K) paediatric injection	1*	1*	–
1d2	Anti-haemorrhagics	Bleeding after miscarriage and immediately after delivery of baby	Syntometrine	Ergometrine oxytocin injection	2*	1*	–
1e	Anti-hypertensive	Hypertension (high BP) and angina	Tenormin	Atenolol 50mg tablets	28	–	–
			2 Gastrointestinal medicines				
2a1	Gastric and duodenal disorders	Anti-acid drug for heartburn, dyspepsia, stomach and duodenal ulcers	Tagamet	Cimetidine 400mg	60	–	–
2a2	Proprietary antacid	Heartburn, dyspepsia, etc	Gaviscon/Rennies etc	Aluminium hydroxide tablets	As reqd	As reqd	–
2b1		Sickness due to ear problems (vertigo) and drugs (morphine)	Buccastem	Prochlorperazine maleate 3 mg buccal tabs	50*	50*	–
2b2	Anti-emetic	Anti-sickness and anti-histamine for severe motion sickness and severe allergic reactions	Phenergan	Promethazine hydrochloride injection	10*	–	–
2b3		Over-the-counter motion sickness drugs	Kwells	Hyoscine hydrobromide 0.3mg tabs	60	60	60
			Stugeron	or Cinnarizine 15mg			
2c	Lubricant laxative	Constipation	Glycerol Suppositories	Glycerol suppository 4mg	12	–	–
2d	Anti-diarrhoeal	Diarrhoea	Imodium	Loperamide 2mg capsules	30	30	30
2e1	*Intestinal antiseptics use 7b, 7a2, 7e*			Trimethoprim 200mg tablets	use 7b	use 7b	–
2e2				Ciprofloxacin 500mg tablets	use 7a2	use 7a2	–
2e3				Metronidazole 400mg tablets	use 7e	use 7e	–
2f	Haemorrhoid preparation		Anusol Plus	Proprietary preparation	As reqd	As reqd	–
			3 Analgesic and anti-spasmodic medicines				
3a1	Analgesics, anti-pyretics and anti-inflammatory	Simple painkiller for mild to moderate pain	Panadol	Paracetamol 500mg tablets	100	50	50
3a2		Anti-inflammatory painkiller – headaches, limb pain	Brufen	Ibuprofen 400mg tablets	100	50	50
3a3		Anti-inflammatory painkiller for most pain, especially bone, joint and muscle	Voltarol	Diclofenanc sodium 50mg suppositories	10	–	–

Ref No	Treatment	Specific use of drug	Possible trade name	Generic name	A	B	C
3b1	Powerful analgesics	Strong painkiller for moderate to severe pain	Codeine Phospate	Codeine phospate 30mg tablets	28	28	–
3b2		Very strong painkiller for all severe pain	Morphine or Nubain	Morphine sulphate 10mg/1ml injection	10	10	–-
3b2				Nalbuphine 10mg/1ml injection – morphine alternative			
3c	Spasmolytics	Anti-spasmodic for abdominal cramps and colic	Buscopan	Hyoscine butylbromide 10mg tablets	56	56	–
4 Nervous system							
4a1	Anxiolytics	Anti-anxiety, sedation medication, also muscle spasm in injury and low back pain	Diazemuls	Diazemuls 5mg/2ml injection	5*	–	–
4a2	Anxiolytics		Diazepam	Diazepam 5mg tablets	28*	–	–
4b1	Neuroleptics	Sedates and controls symptoms in acute psychosis, especially violent or disturbed patients	Largactil	Chlorpromazine hydrochloride 25mg injection	5*	–	–
4b2	Neuroleptics			Chlorpromazine hydrochloride 25mg tablets	28*	28*	–
4c	Seasickness use 2b3			Hyoscine hydrobromide 0.3mg tabs or cinnarizine 15mg	use 2b3	use 2b3	use 2b3
4d	Anti-epileptics	To control fits	Diazepam rectubes	Diazepam rectal dispenser 10mg/2.5ml	5	5	–
5 Anti-allergics and anti-anaphylactics							
5a	Antihistamine	Over-the-counter anti-allergy for itching rashes and hayfever-like symptoms	Benadryl One a Day	Cetririzine 10mg tablets	30*	30*	–
5b1	Injectable gluccorticoids	Anti-allergy steroid for serious allergies and collapse	Solu-Cortef	Hydrocortisone 100mg injection	3	1	–
5b2	Oral glucocorticoids	Anti-allergy steroid also for acute asthma	Prednisolone	Prednisolone 5mg tablets	28	28	–
6 Respiratory system							
6a1	Bronchospasm preparation	Asthma and allergic wheezing	Ventolin	Salbutamol 100mcg per dose inhaler with volmatic	1	1	–
6a2	Bronchospasm preparation	Anti-asthma steroid ususally used with salbutamol	Becotide	Beclomethasone 100mcg per dose inhaler	1	1	–
6b	Anti-tussives			Proprietary cough mixture	As reqd	As reqd	–
6c	Colds and sinusitis			Proprietary cold remedy or use 3a1 (paracetamol)	As reqd	As reqd	–
7 Anti-infection							
7a1		Serious infections such as cellulitis and meningitis	Crystapen	Benzylpenicillin 600mg injection plus water	10	2	–
7a2		Broad spectrum	Ciproxin	Ciprofloxacin 500mg tablets	20	10	–
7a3	Antibiotics	Broad spectrum, protection for major wounds, use for penicillin-allergic patients	Zinacef	Cefuroxime 750mg injection plus water	20	–	–
7a4		Broad spectrum, use for penicillin-allergic patients	Erythrocin	Erythromycin 250mg tablets	28	28	–
7a5		Sexually transmitted diseases and sinusitis	Vibramycin	Doxycycline 100mg capsules	8	–	–
7b/7c	Anti-bacterial/urinary antiseptics	Antibiotic for urinary tract infection and bronchitis	Trimethoprim	Trimethoprim 200mg tablets	14	14	–
7d	Anti-parasitic	Gut infestations, eg threadworm	Vermox	Mebendazole 100mg tablets	6*	6*	–
7e1	Intestinal anti-infectives	Antibiotic and anti-protazoal – trichomonas, amoebic and acute dental infections	Flagyl	Metronidazole suppositories 1g	10	–	–
7e2				Metronidazole 400mg tablets	21	21	–
7f1	Anti-tetanus vaccine	Protection against tetanus infection for unprotected and as booster	Diftavax	Tetanus vaccine 0.5ml ampoule or adsorbed diphtheria (low dose) and tetanus vaccine (preferred)	5*	1*	–
7f2	Anti-tetanus immunoglobulins	Protection against tetanus in high-risk wounds	Tetabulin	Tetanus immunoglobulin	1*	–	–

Ref No	Treatment	Specific use of drug	Possible trade name	Generic name	A	B	C
8 Compounds promoting rehydration, caloric intake and plasma expansion							
8	Oral rehydration salts – WHO generic formula	Dyhydration from vomiting, diarrhoea or illness	Dioralyte	Sodium chloride & dextrose sachets	1 box	1 box	–
9 Medicines for external use – skin medicines							
9a1	Antiseptic solutions	Cleaning skin wounds and disinfection		100ml solution or pre-impregnated wipes	1	1	1
9a2	Antibiotic ointment	Superficial bacterial infection of skin	Cicatrin	Neomycin/Bacitracin cream 15mg tube	1	1	1
9a3a	Anti-inflammatory and analgesic ointment	Anti-inflammatory weak steroid cream – rashes, bites	Hydrocortisone cream	Hydrocortisone 1% cream 15g	2	–	–
9a3b	Anti-inflammatory and analgesic ointment	Over-the-counter anti-inflammatory painkiller	Ibuleve	Proprietary NSAID gel/ointment	As reqd	As reqd	As reqd
9a4a	Anti-mycotic skin cream	Anti-fungal to treat athletes foot, ringworm, etc	Whitfields Ointment	Benzoic ointment BP 50mg	3	1	–
9a4b	Anti-mycotic skin cream	Anti-fungal to treat athletes foot, ringworm, etc	Daktarin	Miconazole nitrate 2% cream 30g	2	1	–
9a4c	Anti-mycotic skin cream	Vaginal or vulval thrush	Canesten	Clotrimazole 500mg pessary (if women aboard)	2	1	–
9a5a	Burns preparations	Anti-bacterial for protection against infection in burns	Flamazine Cream	Silver sulphadiazine cream	–	1	–
9a5b	Burns preparations			Proprietary antiseptic cream	–	–	1
9a6a	Miscellaneous	Lice and scabies	Lyclear	Permethrin 1% cream rinse	2*	2*	–
9a6b	Miscellaneous	Moisturising ointment for dry skin conditions	Zinc Ointment BP	Zinc oxide 15% 25g	1*	–	–
9a6c	Miscellaneous	Cleansing and deodorising oozing wounds or rashes	Permitabs	Potassium permanganate crystals 10g container or tabs	1*	–	–
9b Eye medicines							
9b1	Antibiotic ointment	Broad spectrum for eye infection, eg conjunctivitis	Chloromycetin	Chloramphenicol 1% 4g tube	4	1	–
9b2	Antibiotic drops	Broad spectrum to prevent and treat eye infections		Neomycin sulphate 0.5% eyedrops in single dose form	20*	20*	–
9b3	Anti-inflammatory drops	Inflamed irritated eyes		Dexamethasone sodium phosphate 0.1% in single dose	20*	20*	–
9b4	Anaesthetic drops	Acute pain and to allow removal of foreign bodies		Amethocaine hydrochloride 0.5% in single dose form	20*	20*	–
9b5	Hypotonic myotic drops	Glaucoma (raised pressure in eye)		Pilocarpine nitrate 2% in single dose form	20*	20*	–
9b6	Diagnostic drops	To detect foreign bodies, scratches and lesions		Fluorescein sodium 1% in single dose form	20*	20*	–
9c Ear/nose medicine							
9c1	Antibiotic/anti-inflammatory solution	Broad spectrum for outer ear infection	Ostosporin	Hydrocortisone, neomycin sulphate, polymyxin B sulphate	1*	1*	–
9c2	Decongestant solution	Nasal decongestant	Ephedrine	0.5% Ephedrine hydrochloride 10ml bottle	1*	1*	–
9d Oral and throat infection medicines							
9d1	Antibiotic or antiseptic mouthwash	Sore throat, mouth sores, etc	Corsodyl	Chlorhexidine gluconate 0.2% mouthwash 300ml	1	1	–
9e Local anaesthetic							
9e1	Local anaesthetics by injection	Numb small wounds for treatment		Lignocaine/lidocaine hydrochloride injection 5ml amps	5	5	–
9e2	Local anaesthetic gel	Urethral catheterisation	Instillagel	Lignocaine/lidocaine gel + chlorhexidine syringe	1	–	–
9e3a	Dental anaesthetics and antiseptics	Mouth sores	Bonjela	Proprietary gel	1	1	–
9e3b	Dental anaesthetics and antiseptics	Natural oil for toothache		Oil of cloves 10ml	1*	1*	–

Appendix 5: Radio medical advice form

IN CASE OF ILLNESS

Routine particulars about yacht_____

CALL SIGN / MMSI / INMARSAT NO_____

DATE _____ TIME _____ GMT

POSITION _____ COURSE _____ SPEED _____

LAST PORT OF CALL_____

DESTINATION _____ DISTANCE _____ hours/days

NEAREST PORT _____ DISTANCE _____ hours/days

ALTERNATIVE PORT _____ DISTANCE _____ hours/days

LOCAL WEATHER (IF RELEVANT) _____

Routine particulars about patient

NAME (optional) _____

ETHNIC ORIGIN _____ SEX _____ AGE _____

Particulars of illness

WHEN FIRST BEGAN? _____ HOW?(suddenly, slowly etc) _____

WHAT THE PATIENT COMPLAINED OF FIRST _____

ALL COMPLAINTS AND SYMPTOMS _____

COURSE OF ILLNESS TO DATE _____

PAST ILLNESSES/INJURIES/OPERATIONS_____

FAMILY HISTORY (if relevant) _____

SOCIAL AND OCCUPATIONAL HISTORY (if relevant) _____

ALL MEDICINES TAKEN BEFORE ILLNESS _____

ANY KNOWN ALLERGIES _____

ALCOHOL/RECREATIONAL DRUG USE _____

Results of examination of patient

TEMPERATURE _____ PULSE _____ RESPIRATION _____ B/P_____

GENERAL APPEARANCE OF PATIENT _____

APPEARANCE OF AFFECTED PARTS _____

DETAIL OF EXAMINATION OF AFFECTED PARTS (swelling, tenderness, etc) _____

TESTS AND RESULTS _____

Diagnosis

PROBABLE ILLNESS _____

OTHER POSSIBILITIES _____

Treatment

DETAILS OF ALL DRUGS ADMINISTERED SINCE ILLNESS BEGAN _____

PATIENT'S RESPONSE TO TREATMENT _____

Problems

CURRENT WORRIES _____

ADVICE NEEDED _____

OTHER COMMENTS _____

Radio doctor comments

_____

_____

_____

IN CASE OF INJURY

Routine particulars about yacht_____

CALL SIGN / MMSI / INMARSAT NO_____

DATE _____ TIME _____ GMT

POSITION _____ COURSE _____ SPEED _____

LAST PORT OF CALL_____

DESTINATION _____ DISTANCE _____ hours/days

NEAREST PORT _____ DISTANCE _____ hours/days

ALTERNATIVE PORT _____ DISTANCE _____ hours/days

LOCAL WEATHER (IF RELEVANT) _____

Routine particulars about patient

NAME (optional) _____

ETHNIC ORIGIN _____ SEX _____ AGE _____

Particulars of injury

HOW INJURY AROSE_____ WHEN _____

UNCONSCIOUSNESS AT TIME? _____ DETAILS _____

ALL COMPLAINTS AND SYMPTOMS _____

PAST ILLNESSES/INJURIES/OPERATIONS_____

ALL MEDICINES TAKEN BEFORE ILLNESS _____

ANY KNOWN ALLERGIES _____

ALCOHOL/RECREATIONAL DRUG USE _____

Results of examination of patient

TEMPERATURE _____ PULSE _____ RESPIRATION _____ B/P _____

GENERAL CONDITION OF PATIENT _____

INJURIES IN ORDER OF SERIOUSNESS_____

ANY BLOOD LOSS (details) _____

TESTS AND RESULTS _____

Treament

FIRST AID _____

FURTHER TREATMENT _____

DETAILS OF ALL DRUGS ADMINISTERED SINCE ILLNESS BEGAN _____

_____

PATIENT'S RESPONSE TO TREATMENT _____

Problems

CURRENT WORRIES _____

ADVICE NEEDED _____

OTHER COMMENTS _____

Radio doctor Comments

_____

_____

_____

Index